Place-based Economic Development and the New EU Cohesion Policy

The new EU Cohesion Policy is one of the largest integrated development policies in the Western world, and one of the largest of such programmes anywhere in the world. The reforms to the EU Cohesion Policy contain many different elements, each of which interlink in order to provide a cohesive overall framework. Some of the key elements in the reforms, however, relate to the conditionalities employed and their effects on policy governance and the control mechanism, the smart specialization approach to policy prioritization and resource allocation, the underlying place-based logic of the policy, and the overall results orientation and evaluation emphasis of the policy. In each of the areas of the EU Cohesion Policy reforms, many different scholars from the fields of regional studies, regional science and economic geography have played important roles in shaping the new policy, and the chapters here highlight these increasing interactions between the policy and academic spheres of debate. The collection of essays in this book each deal with specific aspects of these critical elements of the Cohesion Policy reforms. In particular, they examine some of the strengths and weaknesses of these individual elements and allow for a better understanding of the origins and backgrounds of many of the ideas underpinning these reforms. This book was previously published as a special issue of *Regional Studies*.

Philip McCann holds *The University of Groningen Endowed Chair of Economic Geography* in the Faculty of Spatial Sciences at the University of Groningen, The Netherlands, and is also the *Tagliaferri Research Fellow* in the Department of Land Economy at the University of Cambridge 2015–2018. He is one of the world's most highly cited and widely published economic geographers and spatial economists of his generation.

Attila Varga is Professor and Director of the Regional Innovation and Entrepreneurship Research Centre at the University of Pécs, Hungary. He is an internationally renowned researcher of the field of regional innovation and economic development. He publishes widely and serves on the editorial boards of various international journals.

Regions and Cities

Series Editor in Chief
Susan M. Christopherson, *Cornell University, USA*

Editors
Maryann Feldman, *University of Georgia, USA*
Gernot Grabher, *HafenCity University Hamburg, Germany*
Ron Martin, *University of Cambridge, UK*
Martin Perry, *Massey University, New Zealand*
Kieran P. Donaghy, *Cornell University, USA*

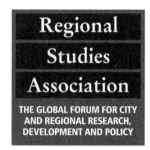

In today's globalised, knowledge-driven and networked world, regions and cities have assumed heightened significance as the interconnected nodes of economic, social and cultural production, and as sites of new modes of economic and territorial governance and policy experimentation. This book series brings together incisive and critically engaged international and interdisciplinary research on this resurgence of regions and cities, and should be of interest to geographers, economists, sociologists, political scientists and cultural scholars, as well as to policy-makers involved in regional and urban development.

For more information on the Regional Studies Association visit www.regionalstudies.org

There is a **30% discount** available to RSA members on books in the ***Regions and Cities*** series, and other subject related Taylor and Francis books and e-books including Routledge titles. To order just e-mail alex.robinson@tandf.co.uk, or phone on +44 (0) 20 7017 6924 and declare your RSA membership. You can also visit www.routledge.com and use the discount code: **RSA0901**

Place-based Economic Development and the New EU Cohesion Policy

Edited by
Philip McCann and Attila Varga

Routledge
Taylor & Francis Group

LONDON AND NEW YORK

First published 2017 by Routledge

2 Park Square, Milton Park, Abingdon, Oxfordshire OX14 4RN
52 Vanderbilt Avenue, New York, NY 10017

Routledge is an imprint of the Taylor & Francis Group, an informa business

First issued in paperback 2018

British Library Cataloguing in Publication Data
A catalogue record for this book is available from the British Library

ISBN13: 978-1-138-68609-0 (hbk)
ISBN13: 978-0-367-19139-9 (pbk)

Typeset in Bembo
by RefineCatch Limited, Bungay, Suffolk

Publisher's Note
The publisher accepts responsibility for any inconsistencies that may have
arisen during the conversion of this book from journal articles to book chapters,
namely the possible inclusion of journal terminology.

Disclaimer
Every effort has been made to contact copyright holders for their permission to
reprint material in this book. The publishers would be grateful to hear from any
copyright holder who is not here acknowledged and will undertake to rectify
any errors or omissions in future editions of this book.

Contents

Citation Information

The chapters in this book were originally published in *Regional Studies* volume 49, issue 8 (August 2015). When citing this material, please use the original page numbering for each article, as follows:

Chapter 1
Editorial: The Reforms to the Regional and Urban Policy of the European Union: EU Cohesion Policy
Philip McCann and Attila Varga
Regional Studies, volume 49, issue 8 (August 2015) pp. 1255–1257

Chapter 2
Conditionalities and the Performance of European Structural Funds: A Principal–Agent Analysis of Control Mechanisms in European Union Cohesion Policy
John Bachtler and Martin Ferry
Regional Studies, volume 49, issue 8 (August 2015) pp. 1258–1273

Chapter 3
Quality of Government and the Returns of Investment: Examining the Impact of Cohesion Expenditure in European Regions
Andrés Rodríguez-Pose and Enrique Garcilazo
Regional Studies, volume 49, issue 8 (August 2015) pp. 1274–1290

Chapter 4
Smart Specialization, Regional Growth and Applications to European Union Cohesion Policy
Philip McCann and Raquel Ortega-Argilés
Regional Studies, volume 49, issue 8 (August 2015) pp. 1291–1302

Chapter 5
When Spatial Equilibrium Fails: Is Place-Based Policy Second Best?
Mark D. Partridge, Dan S. Rickman, M. Rose Olfert and Ying Tan
Regional Studies, volume 49, issue 8 (August 2015) pp. 1303–1325

Chapter 6
The Potential Application of Qualitative Evaluation Methods in European Regional Development: Reflections on the Use of Performance Story Reporting in Australian Natural Resource Management
Frank Vanclay
Regional Studies, volume 49, issue 8 (August 2015) pp. 1326–1339

Chapter 7
RHOMOLO: A Dynamic General Equilibrium Modelling Approach to the Evaluation of the European Union's R&D Policies
Andries Brandsma and D'Artis Kancs
Regional Studies, volume 49, issue 8 (August 2015) pp. 1326–1339

For any permission-related enquiries please visit:
http://www.tandfonline.com/page/help/permissions

Notes on Contributors

John Bachtler is Professor in the European Policies Research Centre, School of Government & Public Policy, University of Strathclyde, Glasgow, UK.

Andries Brandsma is a researcher in the DG Joint Research Centre, European Commission, IPTS, Seville, Spain.

Martin Ferry is Senior Research Fellow in the European Policies Research Centre, School of Government & Public Policy, University of Strathclyde, Glasgow, UK.

Enrique Garcilazo is Head of Unit for the Rural and Regional Development Programme within the Regional Development Policy Division, Directorate for Public Governance and Territorial Development, at the OECD.

D'Artis Kancs is Senior Scientist and Team Leader of the DG Joint Research Centre, European Commission, IPTS, Seville, Spain.

Philip McCann is Professor in the Department of Economic Geography, Faculty of Spatial Sciences, University of Groningen, Groningen, the Netherlands.

M. Rose Olfert is Emeritus Professor in the Graduate School of Public Policy, University of Saskatchewan, Saskatoon, Canada.

Raquel Ortega-Argilés is the Rosalind Franklin Research Fellow in the Department of Global Economics and Management, Faculty of Economics and Business, University of Groningen, Groningen, the Netherlands.

Mark D. Partridge is Professor in the Department of Agricultural, Environmental, and Development Economics, The Ohio State University, Columbus, USA.

Dan S. Rickman is Professor in the Department of Economics and Legal Studies in Business, Oklahoma State University, Stillwater, USA.

Andrés Rodríguez-Pose is Professor in the Department of Geography and Environment, London School of Economics, London, UK.

Ying Tan is a PhD candidate and graduate teaching assistant in the Spears School of Business, Oklahoma State University, Stillwater, USA.

Frank Vanclay is Professor and Head of the Department of Cultural Geography, Faculty of Spatial Sciences, University of Groningen, Groningen, the Netherlands.

Attila Varga is Professor and Director of the Regional Innovation and Entrepreneurship Research Centre at the University of Pécs, Pécs, Hungary.

Introduction: The Reforms to the Regional and Urban Policy of the European Union: EU Cohesion Policy

PHILIP MCCANN† and ATTILA VARGA‡

†*Faculty of Spatial Sciences, University of Groningen, Groningen, the Netherlands.*

‡*Department of Economics and Regional Studies, Faculty of Business and Economics, University of Pécs, Pécs, Hungary*

Regional and urban policy within the European Union (EU) operates on different levels. There is a wide range of policies enacted within individual countries which are purely domestic in nature. Although obviously important, these policies are not the concern or focus of this special issue. At the same time, however, there is a very large portfolio of regional and urban development programmes and their associated specific policy actions and interventions which are undertaken by member states of the EU in conjunction with EU funding. These various policies and programmes operate under the banner and remit of EU Cohesion Policy, which is one of, if not the, largest integrated development policy in the Western world, and one of the largest of such programmes anywhere in the world. There are many different aspects to EU Cohesion Policy and over recent years both the underlying logic and the legal and governance architecture underpinning the policy and the programmes have been reshaped and reoriented to different degrees. There are many different elements in these policy reforms each of which has both an analytical and a pragmatic logic to it. Understanding how the reforms have taken place requires a range of different issues to be considered (MCCANN, 2015). Some aspects of the policy reforms relate to a rethinking and a reconsideration of the general case for, and the role of, development policy at the regional and urban levels. Such a rethinking, however, does not take place in a vacuum, but in the specific context of the EU. The EU spans an economic area characterized by enormous disparities in incomes and the level of development, which are almost equivalent to the range of incomes spanned by the whole of the Organisation for Economic Co-operation and Development (OECD) group of economies. At the same time, the EU is also a highly heterogeneous space in terms of institutional and governance issues, in terms of both the different national and regional modes, architecture and systems of governance as well as in terms of the quality of governance. As such, any policy that spans this highly complex economic and institutional arena needs, on the one hand, to be sufficiently flexible in order to adapt to the local context. On the other hand, it needs to maintain a solid core in terms of its logic, objectives and management systems so as to ensure that the policy is used for correct purposes and is targeted at the intended recipients.

As just mentioned, the reforms to EU Cohesion Policy contain many different elements each of which interlink in order to provide a cohesive overall framework, and the details of the various parts of these reforms, their analytical bases and their historical evolution in the broader context of EU budget debates are discussed elsewhere (MCCANN, 2015; BACHTLER *et al.*, 2013). Some of the key elements in the reforms, however, relate to the conditionalities employed and their effects on policy governance and the control mechanism, the smart specialization approach to policy prioritization and resource allocation, the underlying place-based logic of the policy, and the overall results orientation and evaluation emphasis of the policy. In each of the areas of the EU Cohesion Policy reforms many different scholars from the fields of regional studies, regional science and economic geography have played important roles in shaping the new policy, and the papers here highlight these increasing interactions between the policy and academic spheres of debate.

The papers in this special issue of *Regional Studies* each deal with specific aspects of these critical elements of the Cohesion Policy reforms. In particular, they examine some of the strengths and weaknesses of these individual elements and this allows for a better understanding of the origins and backgrounds of many of the ideas underpinning the policy reforms.

In the first paper by JOHN BACHTLER and MARTIN FERRY (2013, in this issue), entitled 'Conditionalities and the performance of European Structural Funds: a principal–agent analysis of control mechanisms in European Union Cohesion Policy', the authors discuss the ways in which the EU has sought to use control mechanisms in order to influence the use of Structural Funds by member states. BACHTLER and FERRY use a principal-agent type of framework to unpick the political economy of these mechanisms in the case of the absorption of funds, the outcomes of the interventions and the targeting of expenditure during the period 2000–13. What is revealed by the paper are different levels of effectiveness for these different controls depending on the political economy of the negotiations and the possible tensions between the various conditionalities. On the basis of these observations, the paper then discusses the limits of top-down control mechanisms and points to key areas of attention for future programming periods.

These institutional-type issues are taken up again but from a different perspective by ANDRES RODRIGUEZ-POSE and ENRIQUE GARCILAZO (2015, in this issue) in their paper entitled 'Quality of government and the returns of investment: examining the impact of Cohesion expenditure in European Regions'. Using data from the recent European quality of regional and local government surveys, they analyse the relationships between the quality of government and the effectiveness of Structural Fund investment at the regional level. The institutional and governance issues are central to the recently published Sixth Cohesion Report (EUROPEAN UNION, 2014) which highlights the importance of 'softer' forms of government investment and business support, including the building up of institutional capabilities and governance capacity aimed at improving policy design and requisite knowledge transfer between all the key development policy actors and targeted recipients.

The paper entitled 'Smart specialization, regional growth and applications to European Union Cohesion Policy', by PHILIP MCCANN and RAQUEL ORTEGA-ARGILÉS (2013, in this issue) examines the evolution of thinking and the ideas underpinning the smart specialization approach, an approach which is now widely used as a key policy prioritization framework in EU Cohesion Policy. As explained in the paper, the ideas underpinning this approach were initially aspatial and motivated by concerns over Europe's weaker performance in adopting and adapting new technologies and innovation. The originators of the concept, however, increasingly came to see the issues as being particularly pertinent to EU regions and regional policy. Yet, translating the original non-spatial concept to the regional context in a way that is practical and workable for regional and urban policy requires a consideration of parallel ideas that had also been emerging in economic geography. As the paper makes clear, there is a great deal of convergence between the non-spatial and spatial literatures and recasting the original concept in the language of economic geography unravels the approach which does indeed have a strong analytical basis.

The paper by MARK PARTRIDGE, DAN RICKMAN, ROSE OLFERT and YING TAN (2013, in this issue),

entitled 'When spatial equilibrium fails: is place-based policy second best?', reviews the empirical evidence for the United States, which in terms of interregional migration is one of the most geographically mobile societies in the world, to consider the extent to which the spatial equilibrium hypothesis holds. They find at best weak support for the spatial equilibrium hypothesis and argue that this leaves a possible role for place-based policy. However, the informational requirements and political economy considerations associated with place-based policies are significant, and they therefore discuss the issues that must be addressed in order for place-based policies to be effective.

The paper by FRANK VANCLAY (2013, in this issue), entitled 'The potential application of qualitative evaluation methods in European regional development: reflections on the use of performance story reporting in Australian natural resource management', discusses the important roles that qualitative techniques can play in enhancing and shaping policy evaluation. Countries such as Australia and Canada have been at the forefront of embedding evaluation approaches into policy systems and, in particular, qualitative story-telling techniques have provided evaluation approaches with much-needed depth and flexibility in understanding what aspects of policies and their delivery systems do or do not work and why this is the case. Many of these types of ideas are currently being taken up in the European arena and the experience of adopting these evaluation techniques as part of a broader portfolio of quantitative and qualitative evaluation techniques also encourages self-reflection and learning on the part of the policy-makers, a critical part of capacity building.

The final paper entitled 'RHOMOLO: a dynamic general equilibrium modelling approach to the evaluation of the EU's regional policies', by ANDRIES BRANDSMA and D'ARTIS KANCS (2015, in this issue), discusses the new spatial general equilibrium interregional economic model RHOMOLO built by the EU in order to assess quantitatively policies such as Cohesion Policy. The RHOMOLO model is the combined result of the work of dozens of scholars and specialists over many years and allows for the incorporation of spatial economic features such as agglomeration and spillovers into the framework. This implies that the model is also much better suited to investigating the effect, for example, of either transport infrastructure investments or innovation capacity investments than previous generations of models.

Obviously not all the key aspects of the policy context, policy logic, policy reforms and expected policy outcomes can be addressed in a single special issue. However, these six papers provide important insights into some of the key elements of the policy reforms and also a few of the key challenges ahead for the implementation of the policy in the coming years.

Disclosure statement – No potential conflict of interest was reported by the guest editors.

REFERENCES

BACHTLER J. and FERRY M. (2013) Conditionalities and the performance of European Structural Funds: a principal-agent analysis of control mechanisms in European Union Cohesion Policy, *Regional Studies*. doi:10.1080/00343404.2013.821572

BACHTLER J., MENDEZ C. and WISHLADE F. (2013) *EU Cohesion Policy and European Integration: The Dynamics of EU Budget and regional Policy Reform*. Ashgate, Aldershot.

BRANDSMA A. and KANCS D'A. (2015) RHOMOLO: a dynamic general equilibrium modelling approach to the evaluation of the EU's regional policies, *Regional Studies*. doi:10.1080/00343404.2015.1034665

EUROPEAN UNION (2014) *Investment for Jobs and Growth – Promoting Development and Good Governance in EU Regions and Cities: Sixth Report on Economic, Social and Territorial Cohesion*. Publications Office, Brussels.

MCCANN P. (2015) *The Regional and Urban Policy of the European Union: Cohesion, Results – Orientation and Smart Specialisation*. Edward Elgar, Cheltenham.

MCCANN P. and ORTEGA-ARGILÉS R. (2013) Smart specialization, regional growth and applications to European Union Cohesion Policy, *Regional Studies*. doi:10.1080/00343404.2013.799769

PARTRIDGE M., RICKMAN D., OLFERT R. and TAN Y. (2013) When spatial equilibrium fails: is place-based policy second best, *Regional Studies*. doi:10.1080/00343404.2013.837999

RODRIGUEZ-POSE A. and GARCILAZO E. (2015) Quality of government and the returns of investment: examining the impact of Cohesion expenditure in European Regions, *Regional Studies*. doi:10.1080/00343404.2015.1007933

VANCLAY F. (2013) The potential application of qualitative evaluation methods in European regional development: reflections on the use of performance story reporting in Australian natural resource management, *Regional Studies*. doi:10.1080/00343404.2013.837998

Conditionalities and the Performance of European Structural Funds: A Principal–Agent Analysis of Control Mechanisms in European Union Cohesion Policy

JOHN BACHTLER and MARTIN FERRY

European Policies Research Centre, School of Government & Public Policy, University of Strathclyde, Glasgow UK.

BACHTLER J. and FERRY M. Conditionalities and the performance of European Structural Funds: a principal–agent analysis of control mechanisms in European Union cohesion policy, *Regional Studies*. In the context of debates on the performance of European Union cohesion policy, this paper considers how the European Union has used control mechanisms to influence the use of Structural Funds by member states. Using the principal–agent model, this paper examines empirically three case studies of conditionalities applied to the absorption of funding (decommitment rule), outcomes of interventions (performance reserve) and targeting of expenditure (earmarking) in European Union programmes over the 2000–2013 period. The findings reveal different levels of effectiveness of the three conditionalities, attributable to the differential scope for trade-offs during the regulatory negotiations, external pressure and principal self-interest. The paper discusses an effectiveness threshold for introducing controls, the tensions between multiple conditionalities and the limitations of top-down control mechanisms in influencing agent behaviour.

BACHTLER J. and FERRY M. 制约性与欧洲结构基金的绩效：欧盟凝聚政策中调控机制的委託–代理分析，区域研究。在欧盟凝聚政策绩效的辩论脉络中，本文考量欧盟如何运用调控机制，影响成员国对结构基金的使用。本文运用委托–代理模型，经验性地检视欧盟在2000年至2013年间的计画中，运用于吸收资金（解承诺规则）、干预结果（绩效储备）与支出目标（专款专用）的三个制约性案例研究。研究发现显示出上述三个制约性在不同层级的效能，并可归因于在管制协商、外部压力与委托自利中不同范围的权衡。本文探讨引入调控的绩效门槛、多重制约性之间的冲突，以及由上而下的调控机制影响代理行为的局限性。

BACHTLER J. et FERRY M. Les conditionnalités et la performance des fonds structurels européens: une analyse principal–agent des mécanismes de contrôle dans la politique de cohésion de l'Union européenne, *Regional Studies*. Dans le cadre des débats sur la performance de la politique de cohésion de l'Union européenne, ce présent article considère comment l'Union européenne a employé des mécanismes de contrôle pour influencer l'utilisation des fonds structurels par les pays membres. À partir du modèle principal–agent l'article examine empiriquement trois études de cas des conditionnalités appliquées à l'absorption de fonds (dégagement d'office), aux résultats des interventions (la réserve de performance) et au ciblage des dépenses (l'affectation) des programmes européens entre l'an 2000 jusqu'à 2013. Les résultats laissent voir des niveaux d'efficacité différents pour les trois conditionnalités, ce qui est imputable à la portée différentielle des compromis faits pendant les négociations sur les règlements, à la pression venant de l'extérieur et à l'intérêt personnel du principal. L'article discute d'un seuil d'efficacité pour mettre en oeuvre des contrôles, des tensions qui existent entre les conditionnalités multiples et des limites des mécanismes de contrôle de type descendant pour influencer le comportement des agents.

BACHTLER J. und FERRY M. Konditionalitäten und die Leistung von europäischen Strukturfonds: eine Prinzipal-Agent-Analyse der Kontrollmechanismen in der Kohäsionspolitik der Europäischen Union, *Regional Studies*. In diesem Beitrag wird im Kontext der Debatten über die Leistungsfähigkeit der Kohäsionspolitik der Europäischen Union untersucht, mit welchen Kontrollmechanismen die EU Einfluss auf die Nutzung von Strukturfonds durch die Mitgliedstaaten nimmt. Anhand eines Prinzipal-Agent-Modells untersuchen wir auf empirische Weise drei Fallstudien von Konditionalitäten für die Absorption der Finanzmittel

(Aufhebungsregel), für die Ergebnisse der Maßnahmen (leistungsgebundene Reserve) und für die Zielgerichtetheit der Ausgaben („earmarking") in EU-Programmen des Zeitraums von 2000 bis 2013. Die Ergebnisse verdeutlichen für die drei Konditionalitäten verschiedene Stufen der Wirksamkeit, was auf den unterschiedlichen Spielraum für Kompromisse während der rechtlichen Verhandlungen, den Druck von außen und das Eigeninteresse des Auftraggebers zurückzuführen ist. Wir erörtern einen Schwellenwert der Wirksamkeit bei der Festlegung von Kontrollen, die Spannungen zwischen verschiedenen Konditionalitäten und die Grenzen von Top-down-Kontrollmechanismen bei der Beeinflussung des Verhaltens von Agenten.

BACHTLER J. y FERRY M. Condicionalidades y el rendimiento de los Fondos Estructurales de la Unión Europea: un análisis principal–agente de los mecanismos de control en la política de cohesión de la Unión Europea, *Regional Studies*. En el contexto de los debates sobre el rendimiento de la política de cohesión de la Unión Europea, en este artículo analizamos los mecanismos de control que la Unión Europea usa para influir en el modo en que los Estados miembros utilizan los Fondos Estructurales. Mediante el modelo principal–agente, examinamos empíricamente tres estudios de casos de condicionalidades aplicadas a la absorción de fondos (norma de liberación), los resultados de intervenciones (reserva de eficacia) y la orientación específica de los gastos (asignación de fondos) en los programas de la Unión Europea para el periodo entre 2000 y 2013. Los resultados indican diferentes niveles de eficacia de las tres condicionalidades, lo que se debe al alcance diferencial para concesiones durante las negociaciones reglamentarias, la presión externa y el interés propio del principal. Debatimos un umbral de eficacia para introducir controles, las tensiones entre las diferentes condicionalidades y las limitaciones de los mecanismos de control verticalistas a la hora de influir en el comportamiento de los agentes.

INTRODUCTION

Over the past two decades, the performance of European Union (EU) cohesion policy has come under increasing scrutiny, focusing on the impact of Structural and Cohesion Funds and the accountability of member states for their spending decisions. This is evident in the introduction of control mechanisms termed 'conditionalities' in the regulatory framework for Structural and Cohesion Funds for the 2014–2020 period as part of a new performance framework (EUROPEAN COMMISSION, 2011a). These require member states to have specific legal, institutional and policy frameworks in place before their multi-annual development programmes are approved by the European Commission (*ex-ante* conditionalities), and they make the disbursement of funding dependent on member states complying with economic governance policies, relating to budgetary discipline (macro-economic conditionality). These provisions are supplemented by other measures to improve policy performance through a greater focus on results and new reporting and monitoring frameworks.

Conditionalities have been part of cohesion policy since the reform of Structural Funds in 1988. Spending under cohesion policy requires compliance with EU public procurement law, state aid rules, environmental regulations and the additionality principle. The approval of funding programmes is conditional on the elaboration of a strategy in line with EU guidelines, quantified targets, a financing plan, specific implementation arrangements and a list of major projects. Payments to member states are subject to increasingly strict financial management, audit and control obligations. However, there are systemic weaknesses in the design and application of these control mechanisms. Development strategies often lack a rationale for interventions and do not have the necessary institutional prerequisites for effective use of the funds (BACHTLER and GORZELAK, 2007; BARCA, 2009). Further, the progress of development programmes cannot be meaningfully assessed because of the lack of meaningful and timely information on programme performance (APPLICA *et al.*, 2010).

The case of cohesion policy is a classic example of a problem facing all multilevel governance systems: how to ensure that policy outcomes are achieved in line with the original objectives when there are asymmetries in the information, capacity and resources of actors at different levels, and potentially differences in priorities and values (KASSIM and MENON, 2003; ELGIE, 2002; BAUER, 2006). Operating public policy in a multilevel governance system requires shared understanding and commitment to policy goals, trust and resource interdependence. However, performance and accountability are difficult to manage in systems such as cohesion policy where authority is diffused vertically between levels of government and horizontally between government and non-state actors (BOVENS, 2007).

In the context of policy and academic debates on the performance of cohesion policy, this paper examines how the EU has used conditionalities to influence member state use of Structural Funds. Specifically, it tests whether the proposition of BLOM-HANSEN (2005) – that EU control mechanisms are weak – applies to cohesion policy. Using the principal–agent model, and drawing on a review of academic and policy literatures on the application of conditionalities in different jurisdictions, the paper develops an analytical framework for assessing the effectiveness of control mechanisms in cohesion policy. This is applied empirically to three case studies of conditionalities established by the EU to influence the pace of spending (decommitment rule), the outcomes of Structural Funds programmes (performance reserve), and the targeting of funding (earmarking) over the 2000–2013 period. The paper concludes with a discussion of the implications for research on control mechanisms in principal–agent frameworks and the policy lessons for cohesion policy.

CONCEPTUALIZING THE USE OF CONTROL MECHANISMS

Principal–agent analysis and conditionalities

The implementation of cohesion policy has been studied extensively using the concept of multilevel governance. However, while providing insights into the relations and interactions between levels of government, the concept is less useful for exploring top-down control, performance and accountability. A more promising framework used in recent research on control and performance management in cohesion policy is the principal–agent model (BLOM-HANSEN, 2005; BAUER, 2006).

Originally developed as a theoretical construct in the field of organizational economics, the principal–agent framework is used to analyse contractual relationships between two parties, where one party (the agent) is authorized to act on behalf of the other (the principal). The so-called 'principal's problem' arises because a principal cannot assume that an agent will always act in the principal's best interests, particularly when activities that are useful to the principal are costly to the agent, and where elements of what the agent does are costly for the principal to observe. There is also an information asymmetry: an agent has the advantage of greater knowledge and specialized abilities, enabling it to use the principal's resources to pursue goals that benefit the agent. The combination of conflicts of interest, asymmetric information and potential for moral hazard require the contractual relationship between the principal and agent to incorporate oversight, incentive or punitive mechanisms to ensure that the agent acts in the principal's best interest (MOE, 1984; SHEPSLE and BONCHEK, 1997).

Applying the principal–agent framework to public policy, THATCHER and STONE SWEET (2002, p. 4) identified four rationales for principals to delegate functions to agencies: to resolve commitment problems; to overcome information asymmetries in technical areas of governance; to enhance the efficiency of rule-making; and to avoid taking blame for unpopular policies. However, as studies of the relationships between public policy institutions have shown – for example, between the US Congress and executive agencies (WEINGAST and MORAN, 1983; MOE, 1987) or between international financial institutions and donors/recipients (GROSSMAN and HART, 1983; MILNER, 2004) – the analysis of delegation is complex. The interconnectedness of contemporary public policy administration means that actions under a given policy heading are likely to involve multiple principals (THATCHER and STONE SWEET, 2002). Also, multiple agencies may be involved; indeed, most public agencies are likely to be performing several tasks. The profusion of institutional forms make it more difficult to exert control (WORSHAM, 2003; GOLDEN, 2000). In some contexts, as in the EU, the enforcement environment is constrained by a 'dual principal–agent' model where a principal is simultaneously an agent acting in the name of its broader constituency (TALLBERG, 2003; ANCYGIER, 2011).

Given that the delegation of administrative authority by a principal carries the risk of agency slack, such as slippage or shirking (DAMRO, 2007; DA CONCEIÇÃO-HELDT, 2013), the contractual relationship is often subject to 'conditionalities' in the form of prerequisites or commitments related to policy implementation or performance (KILLICK, 1997; KIEWIET and McCUBBINS, 1991). Conditionalities may be related to actions (policies, strategies, instruments), processes (governance systems, administrative capacity) or outcomes (outputs, results of interventions) (BUITER, 2007). They may involve setting predefined qualification criteria (*ex-ante* conditionality) or assessing implementation performance (*ex-post* conditionality). A distinction can also be drawn between 'negative conditionality', which involves sanctions for failing to comply with conditions, and 'positive conditionality' that rewards good performance by offering incentives for compliance (RICH, 2004).

The influence of conditionalities, particularly those related to improved governance, is disputed. While some argue that conditionality is a key factor for a principal to incentivize better performance (MUUKA, 1998; WOOD and LOCKWOOD, 1999), others regard it as ineffective, on the grounds that changes in performance are rarely related to conditionality (KILLICK, 1997). Conditionalities can have negative consequences for the perceived legitimacy and fairness of policies (KAPUR and WEBB, 2000) and problems of implementation involving goal conflict and lack of ownership (DRAZEN, 2002). Even where there is agreement on broad development objectives, the design of specific policies and programmes is complex, a variety of policy prescriptions is available and the eventual impact of different approaches is uncertain. In these circumstances, the selection of appropriate conditionalities is not straightforward: who can legitimately claim to 'know best'? This is a weakness of the principal–agent approach, which has often insufficiently heeded 'the ideological concern for democratic legitimacy' (POLLACK, 1997, p. 107).

There are also practical constraints on the use of conditionalities: the relationship between inputs, outputs, and impacts must be known and measurable, the indicators associated with incentives must capture performance under the control of the agent, the agent must be able to influence the indicators over the timescale being measured, and negative indirect effects need to be avoided. As VAN THIEL and LEEUW (2002) have observed, there is a 'performance paradox': weak correlation between performance indicators and performance itself can create dysfunctional effects – ossification, short-termism, lack of innovation or risk aversion.

Research conducted on the delegation of authority to agents and the use of conditionalities in international development programmes and EU policy-making (for example, EGAN, 1998; SCHUKNECHT, 2004; SCHIMMELFENNIG and SEDELMEIER, 2004; SEDELMEIER, 2008; SIPPEL and NEUHOFF, 2009) suggests that the relevance and influence of conditionalities is related to several factors. First, there is the issue of *customization* (sometimes discussed as 'ownership') – the degree to which the programme, plans or strategies, and specifically the setting of conditionalities, are agreed between the principal and the agent. The imposition of conditionalities reduces their effectiveness through inappropriate design and negative effects on compliance, such as agents finding ways to circumvent the conditionality and causing it to fail (DRAZEN, 2002; BUITER, 2007). KOEBERLE *et al* (2005) argue that conditionalities need to be limited to policy and institutional actions under the control of the implementing agency.

Second, the influence of conditionalities depends on their *credibility*, specifically that compliance will be consistently rewarded and non-compliance sanctioned. Conditionalities are weakened where the principals fail to enforce sanctions (SCHIMMELFENNIG and SEDELMEIER, 2004; KILBY, 2009). However, political constraints, difficulties in measuring or agreeing fulfilment of a conditionality, and the 'Samaritan dilemma' (the difficulties a donor experiences in implementing sanctions because it wants and is expected to help) may prevent enforcement (DREHER, 2002; KOEBERLE, 2003; SVENSSON, 2003).

Third, a layering of multiple conditionalities (*ex-ante*, *ex-post*, process or outcome related) produces complexity and inconsistency in fulfilment. Research indicates the importance of *criticality*, that is, that conditions are limited in number and restricted to those necessary to ensure that funding is used for its stated purpose (WORLD BANK, 2005).

Fourth, both principals and agents need *predictability*. Effective conditionality frameworks are associated with continuity and predictable frameworks for compliance over the lifetime of a policy or programme (LEANDRO *et al.*, 1999). Disjointed requirements and instability create uncertainties that weaken the fulfilment of conditionalities (COLLIER *et al.*, 1997).

Lastly, the *transparency* of reporting and monitoring of compliance has been found to affect the status of conditionality frameworks. A common feature of multilevel governance contracts between principals and agents is the use of indicator systems to monitor performance and overcome information asymmetries across administrative tiers (ORGANISATION FOR ECONOMIC CO-OPERATION AND DEVELOPMENT (OECD), 2009). Deficiencies in monitoring and evaluation have affected the ability of principals to respond to the non-fulfilment of conditionalities (KILLICK, 1997; MARCHESI and SABANI, 2007).

Applying the principal–agent framework to analysis of conditionalities in cohesion policy

Much of the recent research on principal–agent relations in EU policy-making has focused on how the Commission has sought to circumvent or weaken control by member states in foreign or trade policies (for example, DELREUX and KERREMANS, 2010; DÜR and ELSIG, 2011; DA CONCEIÇÃO-HELDT, 2013). Cohesion policy is distinctive in being formulated and implemented through a hierarchy of principal–agent relationships starting with the Council and extending downwards via the Commission, member state managing authorities, subnational implementing bodies to local project managers (BLOM-HANSEN, 2005). At the policy implementation stage, the Commission is acting as the principal with the member states as agents; for the Commission, the 'principal's problem' is how to ensure that – once the budget allocations to individual countries and implementation regulations have been determined – the member states fulfil cohesion policy goals and comply with regulatory requirements. Although the allocation of EU resources is subject to a range of conditionalities, these leave scope for 'agency drift', leading BLOM-HANSEN (2005) to conclude that member states were 'in full control of the implementation process' (p. 637); soft Commission control mechanisms meant that 'the EU, as a principal, appears weak' (p. 644).

The problem of Commission control has been particularly acute since 1999 when, as part of the negotiations on reforming cohesion policy for the 2000–2006 period, the Commission was forced to devolve greater implementation responsibility to the member states (BACHTLER, 1998). The Commission sought to compensate for the loss of influence over operational decisions at programme level with higher-level incentive and control systems (EUROPEAN COMMISSION, 1997; HALL and ROSENSTOCK, 1998). This led to the introduction of two new, quantitative conditionalities, with incentivizing and sanctioning effects: the decommitment rule, which stipulated that the Commission could withdraw funding from member states if the finance committed to an EU-funded project was not spent within two years; and the performance reserve, which allowed additional funding to be allocated to the 'best-performing' programmes. Both were introduced in the regulations for the 2000–2006 period and maintained in 2007–2013 (on a voluntary basis in the case of the reserve). A further, partly qualitative conditionality – in the form of 'earmarking' expenditure – was introduced for the 2007–2013 period to influence the sectoral composition of spending in line with the EU's 'Lisbon Agenda'.

The following empirical analysis examines whether and to what extent these conditionalities have strengthened EU-level control mechanisms and what their operation reveals about the principal–agent relationship between the Commission and member states. Assessing the three case studies in turn, the first question is whether the decommitment rule, performance rule and earmarking were effective in meeting their objectives; and secondly whether effectiveness can be related to the design and implementation of the three conditionalities. The analysis uses quantitative measures (principally related to expenditure) to establish how the allocation of funding changed. It also uses an implementation index (Table 1) to assess the compliance of the conditionalities with the key factors identified in the above literature review – customization, credibility, criticality, predictability, transparency – and seeks to establish the influence of these factors using a scale of 'high', 'moderate' and 'low' compliance.

The case study research draws on several sources at the EU level: European Commission data on cohesion policy spending and outcomes from DG Budget and DG Regio; and EU-level assessments of conditionalities in the *ex-post* evaluations of cohesion policy in the 2000–2006 period (commissioned by DG Regio) and independently by the European Court of Auditors (ECA), notably its annual reports as part of the EU's annual budget discharge procedure. The research also uses information on the application of conditionalities by national and regional authorities, derived from secondary sources (particularly member state responses to EU consultations), and interviews conducted each year over the 2000–2013 period with Structural Funds managing authorities in fifteen member states as part of a longitudinal research programme (IQ-Net) on the management and implementation of Structural Funds conducted by the authors together with colleagues (for example, BACHTLER et al., 2000; RAINES and TAYLOR, 2002; TAYLOR et al., 2004).

ASSESSMENT OF CONTROL MECHANISMS IN COHESION POLICY

Conditionality on spending: the decommitment rule

The first case concerns the most basic requirement of a policy intervention: allocating the available funds. A

conditionality on spending was introduced in the 1999 Structural Funds regulations for the 2000–2006 period in the form of the 'decommitment rule' – generally known as 'n+2'. Under the rule, any funding committed (awarded) to a project needs to be paid out within two years or else is lost to the programme (COUNCIL OF THE EUROPEAN UNION, 1999).

The decommitment rule was introduced to speed up the implementation of Community-funded programmes. During the 1990s there was growing concern at the EU level about the poor financial performance of some EU regional development programmes: funds would be committed to a project but it might take several years before the project was carried out and the money was actually spent. In 1998, for example, the Commission was still making payments of €555 million for projects approved in the 1989–1993 period. For 1994–1999, evaluation found that 38% of projects were more than twelve months late, with figures of 50% and 71% for Spain and Italy, respectively (ECOTEC, 2003).

The n+2 rule was introduced in the 1999 regulatory framework for the 2000–2006 period (COUNCIL OF THE EUROPEAN UNION, 1999). It was maintained in the regulations for 2007–2013, albeit with flexibility for poorer countries, whereby the EU-10, Greece and Portugal had to make payments within three years rather than two (n+3), and there was scope for exceptions in cases such as *force majeure* interrupting the implementation of a programme (COUNCIL OF THE EUROPEAN UNION, 2006). The decommitment rule was also amended in 2010 as a response to the economic crisis, reducing the n+2 risk for various member states.

Interview research found that the member state authorities responsible for programme management responded to the introduction of n+2 by upgrading monitoring systems to ensure a clearer picture of programme expenditure and progress at the measure level. They sought to identify possible bottlenecks in spending and to avoid decommitment by reallocating resources between projects or measures. The rule also led to the introduction of risk-assessment procedures to evaluate the likelihood of project failure, the creation of expenditure profiles for larger projects and closer tracking of actual expenditure at project level (TAYLOR et al., 2001). More emphasis was placed on publicity and communication with project managers to ensure that the rule was widely understood among beneficiaries and to identify problems at an early stage (TAYLOR and RAINES, 2003). From the first year of its application, two years into the 2000–2006 programme period, the Commission asserted that virtually all programmes under each of the funds were achieving a 'satisfactory' rate of implementation (EUROPEAN COMMISSION, 2003a).

Figures for overall spending in 2000–2006 indicate that the decommitment rule was effective in improving absorption. Evaluation studies found that n+2

Table 1. Framework for assessing the implementation of conditionalities

Factors	Research questions	Assessment criteria	Level of compliance		
			High	Moderate	Low
Customization	Is the conditionality negotiated with the agent? Is it customized to individual agents?	Role of the agent in the design of conditionalities. Customization of implementation to local conditions	Design of conditionality is negotiated with the agent. Implementation is customized to local circumstances	Design is negotiated with the agent or implementation is customized	Design of conditionality is not negotiated with the agent. Implementation is not customized
Credibility	Is the conditionality enforced in practice?	Partial or non-fulfilment of conditionality has consequences such as interruption of funding	Fulfilment is monitored and assessed. Sanctions are applied consistently	Incomplete or inconsistent monitoring and assessment. Sanctions are applied inconsistently	No monitoring or assessment. Little or no sanction
Criticality	Are conditions limited in number and restricted to those necessary to ensure that funding is used for its stated purposes?	Number of conditions. Clarity of purpose. Binding versus non-binding conditions	Clear, measurable objectives. Binding commitments on both principal and agents	Objectives only partly measurable. Mix of binding and non-binding commitments	Poorly specified, difficult-to-measure objectives. Non-binding or voluntary commitments
Predictability	Are the implementation and outcome predictable over the medium/long-term?	Changes to the conditionality during the funding period	Highly predictable outcome. Little or no change to conditionality during the funding period	Partly predictable with some uncertainties. Some change during the funding period	Significant unpredictability. Substantial change during the funding period
Transparency	Is the implementation and outcome of the conditionality transparent to all stakeholders?	Publication and open access to information on the implementation and outcome of the conditionality	Full information collected on design and use. Open access to information	Partial information collected. Access with some restrictions	Little or no information collected. Limited or no access

encouraged greater discipline in project planning and promoted timely programme implementation (CENTRE FOR INDUSTRIAL STUDIES (CSIL), 2010). Analysis of the budgetary implementation of Structural and Cohesion Funds by DG Budget showed that, at the end of 2008 (two years after the end of the 2000–2006 period), cumulative payments had reached 89.9% for the EU-15 and 93.1% for the EU-10 (EUROPEAN COMMISSION, 2010). Seventeen of the twenty-five member states had cumulative payment levels between 90% and 95% (Table 2), a level of absorption significantly higher than at the equivalent point after the 1994–1999 period. At EU level, the cumulative level of decommitment was only 2.8% for the EU-15 and 1.6% for the EU-10, but with substantial amounts decommitted in the Netherlands (11.1%), Luxembourg (10.8%) and Denmark (6.1%).

However, information from national and regional sources indicates several problems with n+2, notably its rigidity. The pace and profile of programme spending varied greatly across the EU, with absorption affected by factors such as project planning timescales and the investment climate (BACHTLER and TAYLOR, 2003).

The decommitment rule also had unintended effects. In particular, studies found that n+2 was influencing managing authorities and implementing bodies to focus on the pace of spending rather than the quality of interventions (POLVERARI *et al.*, 2007; CSIL, 2010). There is evidence from Austria, Finland, France, Germany and the UK that innovative, experimental or otherwise risky projects were less likely to be approved than 'safer' projects guaranteed to use allocated funding in line with plans (ACT CONSULTANTS, 2005; DAVIES *et al.*, 2004). An EU-wide consultation found widespread dissatisfaction with the inability to adapt the design and implementation of decommitment rule to specific regional and national contexts (EUROPEAN COMMISSION, 2011b).

Successive annual reports by the ECA drew attention to the risk of n+2 encouraging member states to submit claims to the Commission as soon as payments were made to final beneficiaries rather than when expenditure was actually incurred. There was also evidence of ineligible projects being submitted, without proper verification by member state authorities (ECA, 2003, 2006, 2010). Some member states reduced the decommitment

Table 2. Cumulative payments and decommitments at the end of 2008 as a percentage of initial national allocations for the 2000–2006 period (2004–2006 for EU-10)

	Payments	Decommitments		Payments	Decommitments
Austria	94.5	0.2	Cyprus	83.7	0.0
Belgium	88.7	1.4	Czech Republic	90.7	0.0
Denmark	81.1	6.1	Estonia	95.0	0.0
Finland	94.7	0.0	Hungary	94.0	0.0
France	89.6	0.5	Latvia	95.0	0.0
Germany	93.8	0.6	Lithuania	95.0	0.0
Greece	90.9	0.1	Malta	95.0	0.0
Ireland	93.9	0.7	Poland	93.1	0.0
Italy	85.0	0.3	Slovenia	90.8	0.1
Luxembourg	73.8	10.8	Slovak Republic	92.5	0.7
Netherlands	75.0	11.1			
Portugal	92.3	0.5	EU-15	89.9	0.6
Spain	90.2	0.1	EU-10	93.1	0.1
Sweden	93.1	0.6			
United Kingdom	89.9	0.5			

Note: Some funding for 2000–2006 still needed to be executed in 2009.
Source: EUROPEAN COMMISSION (2010).

risk by allocating funds to aid schemes or financial instruments which counted as 'spending' even though funds had not been paid out to beneficiaries (BACHTLER and MENDEZ, 2010). The management of decommitment led to pressure on administrative resources at national and Commission levels: according to the ECA (2004), over half of payments were submitted between September and December, one-quarter in December alone.

Drawing the evidence together, the decommitment rule was effective in achieving the goal of improving financial absorption, which was significantly faster in 2000–2006 than in previous periods (EUROPEAN COMMISSION, 2011a). In terms of the implementation index (Table 3), the credibility of the conditionality was high: the rule was applied rigidly and consistently to all programmes in the 2000–2006 period, in line with the regulations. Criticality, predictability and transparency were also high. The rule was relatively simple to understand; it was maintained unchanged during 2000–2006; and data on decommitment were published. However, the conditionality scores poorly in terms of customization, with no adaptation to local circumstances (until the 2007–2013 period). As a result, the rule had unintended consequences for the management of spending. Member states used various devices to inflate their spending in making claims to the Commission, and the focus on the pace of expenditure adversely affected the quality of projects supported.

Conditionality on outcomes: the performance reserve

The performance reserve was introduced in the 1999 regulations to ensure better programme management in 2000–2006 by keeping back a proportion of the budgetary resources allocated to programmes to reward the most successful programmes on the basis of financial and

Table 3. Assessment of the implementation of the decommitment rule

Factors	Rating	Summary assessment
Customization	Low	High level of top-down control. No customization in 2000–2006. Some flexibility introduced in 2007–2013
Credibility	High	High level of enforcement; decommitment was automatic if funds were not spent in time
Criticality	High	Clear and straightforward for stakeholders to understand. No changes to conditions during the period
Predictability	High	High level of consistency over the programme period
Transparency	High	Implementation was transparent. Data on decommitted funding were published

physical performance. It originated in concerns about the impact of the assistance being provided (EUROPEAN COMMISSION, 1997; BACHTLER, 1998). The ECA (1998), for example, noted that it was not always possible to determine which were the most efficient measures and that the 'added value' of spending was not being maximized.

The Commission's initial proposal was for 10% of Structural Funds allocations to be kept as a reserve, to be allocated to programmes at a later stage (DG XVI, 1998). This would be based on a Community-wide competition between programmes, with the better performing programmes receiving an additional allocation of 10–20%. This was not acceptable to member states (AALBU and BACHTLER, 1998), and subsequent negotiations led to a much-reduced reserve (of 4%) being agreed, with the competition limited to programmes *within* member states (COUNCIL OF THE EUROPEAN UNION, 1999). Early in the 2000–2006 period, the negotiation of the 1999 reforms was reopened by member states concerned about the perceived complexity and bureaucracy of Structural Funds administration, leading to reduced indicator requirements, simplified procedures and greater transparency for the reserve (EUROPEAN COMMISSION, 2003b).

Operationalization of the performance reserve involved each member state selecting indicators for performance assessment, drawing on an indicative list proposed by the Commission (DG REGIO, 1999). During 2003, the member states, together with the Commission, assessed the performance of each of the operational programmes by measuring the mid-term results in relation to their initial targets. A programme was considered to have fulfilled the assessment criteria if it met 75% of its targets. Member states drew up a list of the programmes, or parts of programmes, that were considered to be 'successful', and these were allocated the reserve by the Commission. Programmes could receive more than 4% if they were part of an objective that included unsuccessful programmes or parts of programmes (Tables 4 and 5).

The regulations gave discretion to member states to implement the performance reserve according to their own institutional and policy priorities. While most countries based the allocation of the reserve on a competition between programmes, the federal EU countries implemented the reserve more restrictively, on the basis of a competition between the priorities/measures *within* individual programmes. There were also differences in how member states met their obligations under the regulations. A Commission assessment distinguished

between countries such as Belgium, Finland, Italy and Sweden that were using the performance reserve as a 'real management (tool) and incentive for innovation', and other member states such as France, Greece, Ireland, the Netherlands, Portugal, Spain and the UK, which were judged to be applying the instrument correctly, but not going beyond the regulations (EUROPEAN COMMISSION, 2000). Of particular note was the approach taken by Italy and Portugal, which supplemented the EU reserve with a national variant, thereby increasing the leverage effect.

For the most part, allocations between programmes were close to 4%, indicating that the gains or losses from the reserve were marginal. The exceptions were in Belgium (Wallonia), Greece, Italy and the UK (England) where the reserve was used to allocate an additional 5–9% of funding to some programmes. The reallocations within programmes were larger: in many countries, between 50% and 100% of the reserve was allocated to a single priority.

Notwithstanding the variation in its application, the Commission saw the performance reserve as an incentive for good management practice (EUROPEAN COMMISSION, 2004). It argued that the requirement to meet targets and deadlines influenced member states to ensure that resources were spent, evaluations were produced on time, better monitoring systems were put in place, financial control systems were implemented and project selection was more transparent.

There is only partial support for the Commission's argument from evidence on the application of the

Table 4. *Allocation of the performance reserve in Objective 1 regions, 2000–2006*

	Commitment (€, millions)[a]	Reserve (€, millions)[b]	Allocation range (%)	Competition
Competition between programmes				
Finland	948	41	4.32	Between two programmes
France	3948	171	3.2–5.1	Between six of eight programmes
Greece	21 389	945	4.00–9.33	Between fourteen of twenty-five programmes
Ireland	3061	134	100	To one programme out of six
Italy	21 638	996	2.3–7.2	Between thirteen programmes; between priorities for one phasing-out programme
Portugal	19 177	855	3.66–5.01	Between sixteen of nineteen programmes
Spain	39 548	1717	4.41	Between twenty of twenty-three programme
Sweden	748	32	4.25–4.30	Between two programmes
UK – England	3003	130	4.18–5.15	Between three programmes
Competition between priorities				
Austria	271	12	8–36	Between all priorities of one programme
Belgium	645	28	7–35	Between all priorities of one programme
Germany	20 602	899	2.3–100	Between priorities of nine programmes
Netherlands	126	6	18–46	Between three of four priorities of one programme
UK – Northern Ireland	890	39	13–65	Between three of five priorities of one programme
UK – Scotland	306	13	17–64	Between three of four priorities of one programme
UK – Wales	1853	81	7–34	Between five of six priorities of one programme

Notes: [a] 1999 prices.
[b] Current prices.
Source: EUROPEAN COMMISSION (2004).

Table 5. Allocation of the performance reserve in Objective 2 regions, 2000–2006

	Commitment (€, millions)[a]	Reserve (€, millions)[b]	Allocation range (%)	Competition
Competition between programmes				
Belgium – Flanders	186	8	4.09–4.20	Between all four programmes
Belgium – Wallonia	217	9	2.19–5.05	Between all priorities of two programmes
Finland	507	23	4.41–4.58	Between all three programmes
France	6262	273	2.0–6.5	Between twenty-two of twenty-three programmes
Italy	2608	113	4.32–4.35	Between all fourteen programmes
Netherlands	823	36	4.20–4.58	Between all four programmes
Spain	2748	119	4.31–4.34	Between all seven programmes
Sweden	423	17	3.99–4.05	Between all four programmes
UK – England	3774	170.9	4.02–5.96	Between all nine programmes
UK – Scotland	807	35	4.35–4.39	Between all three programmes
Competition between priorities				
Austria	703	31	5–100	Between priorities of eight programmes
Belgium – Brussels	44	2	25–75	Between all priorities of one programme
Denmark	189	8	20–75	Between three of four priorities of one programme
Germany	3626	159	6–100	Between priorities of eleven programmes
Luxembourg	41	3	100	To one of four priorities of the one programme
UK – Wales	121	5	28–92	Between two of three priorities of one programme
UK – Gibraltar	83	0.36		Between priorities of the one programme

Notes: [a]1999 prices.

[b]Current prices.

Source: EUROPEAN COMMISSION (2004).

performance reserve on the ground. A survey of managing authorities in fifteen member states found some evidence for an incentivizing effect (POLVERARI *et al.*, 2004). Specifically, in Italy, studies concluded that the combination of the EU and national performance reserves strengthened the exposure of regional and local administrations to public scrutiny, and it encouraged them to take responsibility for objectives and targets, contributing to the long-term goal of improving the effectiveness of public investments (ANSELMO and RAIMONDO, 2003; CASAVOLA and TAGLE, 2003; OECD, 2009).

The evidence from other countries is less positive. In Austria, policy-makers asserted that it was impossible to control the implementation of programmes using objective quantitative indicators or to use the performance reserve as a credible incentive for raising effectiveness (BUNDESKANZLERAMT (BKA), 2003). Managing authorities in other countries agreed that meaningful comparison was not feasible and indeed was likely to generate conflict between and within programmes (POLVERARI *et al.*, 2004). Further, the ECA found at least one case, from the Netherlands, where new commitments of €24 million were allocated from the performance reserve to a programme that had lost €79 million through the decommitment rule, partly negating the effects of both conditionalities (ECA, 2006).

Against the implementation criteria set out above, the performance reserve is given a relatively poor assessment (Table 6). The degree of customization gave member states the flexibility to determine how the reserve would be applied (at programme or sub-

programme level), but the form and timing of its application was imposed on programmes, and it was often regarded as an administrative exercise rather than as a spur to better performance. Similarly, its credibility was mixed: the implementation processes were put in place and the allocation of funding at the mid-point of the 2000–2006 programmes was enforced, but there were often no serious consequences for weak performance at programme level in many member states. The reserve has mixed ratings against other criteria: predictability was problematic as the conditions for implementing reserve were amended during the programme period; the decision-making on the allocation of the reserve to individual programmes was partly opaque; and the complexity of the scheme made it difficult to communicate to implementing bodies and beneficiaries. Operationally, it was not evident that changes in achievement could be influenced by the expenditure choices of programme managers. Arguably one of the most important outcomes was the demonstration effect of the EU performance reserve that led some countries – Italy and Portugal – to develop their own supplementary national variants in 2000–2006 and for it to be used on a voluntary basis by Italy and Poland in 2007–2013.

Conditionality on the targeting of spending: earmarking

The third and most recent conditionality was applied in the 2007–2013 period and sought to prioritize the allocation of funding. Member states were obliged to dedicate a large proportion of their programme allocations to supporting the EU's Lisbon Agenda objectives of

Table 6. Assessment of the implementation of the performance reserve

Factors	Rating	Summary assessment
Customization	Partial	High level of customization by country, albeit within a single regulatory framework, but low 'ownership' at the programme level in many cases
Credibility	Partial	All member states had to implement the reserve, but with limited sanctions for many programmes
Criticality	Low	Implementation involved a range of country-specific indicators based on Commission guidance
Predictability	Low	The regulatory framework was reviewed almost immediately and only finalized two years after programmes had started
Transparency	Partial	The process and outcomes were published by the Commission, but the decision-making was subjective and decided through internal Commission–member state consultations

increased competitiveness and job creation. The conditionality known as 'earmarking' originated in the negotiations on the 2007–2013 Multiannual Financial Framework. It was proposed by the Commission in October 2005 to achieve a compromise agreement on the EU budget by convincing the net contributor countries that cohesion policy spending in 2007–2013 would target EU priorities of growth and jobs (BACHTLER *et al.*, 2013).

The operationalization of the earmarking condition required 60% of expenditure under Convergence programmes and 75% under Regional Competitiveness & Employment (RCE) programmes to be allocated to certain categories of investment: innovation; the knowledge economy; information and communication technology; employment; human capital; entrepreneurship; small and medium-sized enterprise support; and access to risk capital (COUNCIL OF THE EUROPEAN UNION, 2006). The application of the conditionality to individual programmes was agreed between the Commission and member state authorities as part of the programming process during 2006–2007.

Data for the allocation of funding by expenditure categories at the start of the 2007–2013 period have been used by the Commission to suggest a high level of compliance with the earmarking requirement (EUROPEAN COMMISSION, 2007a). Across the EU-15, 76% of funding in Convergence programmes and 81% in RCE programmes were allocated to so-called earmarked categories of investment, in both cases considerably exceeding the EU targets (Table 7). In the EU-12, where earmarking was voluntary, the proportions of funding allocated to Lisbon priorities were 59% and 56% for Convergence and RCE programmes, respectively.

The caveat to the figures in Table 7 is that the Commission's definition of what constituted 'Lisbon-relevant expenditure' was widened considerably in the regulatory negotiations with the member states. At the insistence of Germany, a generic category of European Regional Development Fund expenditure ('other investment in firms') was added to the list (TAYLOR, 2006). Three extra categories of European Social Fund expenditure were also added. Other member states insisted on a flexibility clause in the regulations, allowing them to include additional categories of expenditure as part of their Lisbon quota, a provision utilized by five countries – Cyprus, France, Greece, Portugal and Spain – to include environmental, cultural, social and broadband infrastructure. Many of these categories were inconsistent with the spirit of the Lisbon agenda (for example, childcare infrastructure and waste water treatment), inflating the amount of funding counted as Lisbon expenditure (MENDEZ *et al.*, 2010). Lastly, the agreed regulations referred to earmarking percentages as 'targets', giving member states the latitude to allocate less to Lisbon expenditure categories than the recommended levels – for example, the RCE programmes in Greece (54%) and Spain (71%).

Examining the effect of the earmarking requirement on the strategic investment planning of member states, there is evidence that the conditionality influenced the allocation of resources. Specifically, it encouraged managing authorities to focus their development strategies for 2007–2013 on a limited number of priorities; in doing so they used the EU earmarking regulation to resist pressure from other government departments to disperse resources across a wider range of policy fields (BACHTLER and MENDEZ, 2010). This is most apparent in the EU-12 where domestic funding for research and development (R&D) and innovation policy had been historically low (TECHNOPOLIS, 2006; NORDREGIO, 2009). According to Commission figures, the relative share of funding planned for R&D and innovation in 2007–2013 was three times the proportion allocated in 2000–2006 (EUROPEAN COMMISSION, 2007b). Planned spending on earmarked categories of expenditure rose substantially in Poland, Slovenia, Slovakia, Latvia, Cyprus and the Czech Republic – although these countries were not formally bound by the condition and had major investment needs in basic infrastructure support (NORDREGIO, 2009; BAUN and MAREK, 2009). However, the direct influence was much less in the EU-15, where cross-national research indicates that *domestic* policy objectives and priorities determined the strategic investment decisions in the 2007–2013 programmes (for example, Denmark, Finland, Ireland, the Netherlands, Sweden and the UK), particularly where cohesion policy allocations were relatively low and/or had fallen substantially (POLVERARI *et al.*, 2006; see also TÖDTLING-SCHÖN-HOFER and WIMMER, 2008; MENDEZ, 2011).

Assessing the implementation of earmarking (Table 8), there was only partial customization of the

Table 7. Lisbon earmarking – share of 2007–2013 programme funding allocated to Lisbon investment categories

	Convergence	Regional competitiveness and employment		Convergence	Regional competitiveness and employment
Austria	87	91	Bulgaria	54	
Belgium	77	83	Cyprus		51
Denmark		90	Czech Republic	58	80
Finland		86	Estonia	47	
France	56	80	Hungary	54	49
Germany	74	84	Lithuania	53	
Greece	70	54	Latvia	57	
Ireland		80	Malta	49	
Italy	69	81	Poland	66	
Luxembourg		87	Romania	53	
Netherlands		80	Slovenia	66	
Portugal	88	80	Slovak Republic	58	72
Spain	80	71			
Sweden		87			
United Kingdom	81	88			
EU-15	76	81	EU-12	59	56

Source: European Commission data accompanying the Strategic Report 2012 (available at: http://ec.europa.eu/regional_policy/how/policy/strategic_report_en.cfm#sr2013).

conditionality. Although introduced with fixed percentages of expenditure in the regulations, it was varied by type of programme and was voluntary for the EU-12. Member states were able to negotiate additional categories of expenditure to be included within their targets, and expenditure thresholds were calculated as an average across all programmes in a member state, that is, individual programmes could have higher or lower earmarking percentages. Nevertheless, the programme-level 'ownership' of the conditionality is questionable: when it was first mooted by the Commission, in October 2005, strategic planning for 2007–2013 was already well advanced in many regions, and there is evidence that earmarking was perceived as a 'top-down' condition in which the aims and objectives of the Lisbon Agenda were not adequately understood by lower levels of government (LEONARDI and NANETTI, 2011).

With respect to the other assessment factors, earmarking has partial credibility. Member states have been expected to report annually on how they use cohesion policy to support Lisbon Agenda goals against a set of targets. However, earmarking is not a legally binding requirement, and there are no sanctions for missing these targets. Criticality is low: ultimately, earmarking could be extended by member states to a range of interventions, not all of which had direct links with the Lisbon Agenda. Conversely, the conditionality has been implemented with a high level of predictability and transparency. Once negotiated, the regulatory conditions have remained unchanged, and progress with spending under earmarked and non-earmarked categories of expenditure by member state has been published periodically in strategic reports (for example, EUROPEAN COMMISSION, 2013).

CONCLUSIONS

The aim of this paper has been to examine how the EU has used conditionalities to influence the use of Structural Funds by member states. The context is a growing concern with the performance of cohesion policy and the assumption in the literature that existing control mechanisms are weak and poorly understood. Using the principal–agent framework, and drawing on research on conditionalities in other fields, the article has analysed the design and implementation of three case studies of conditionality in cohesion policy. The paper extends the application of the principal–agent framework by both identifying and rating the importance of relevant implementation factors.

The decommitment rule and performance reserve were proposed as new control measures by the

Table 8. Assessment of the implementation of the earmarking requirement

Factors	Rating	Summary assessment
Customization	Partial	High level of customization at member state level (to the detriment of the condition) but low 'ownership' at regional/programme level
Credibility	Partial	Implementation and annual reporting but no sanctions
Criticality	Low	Definition of 'Lisbon expenditure' was weakened and the goals were sometimes poorly understood
Predictability	High	Consistent regulatory framework
Transparency	High	Strategic reports published progress with spending on earmarked and non-earmarked categories

European Commission to compensate for the greater flexibility for the implementation of Structural Funds demanded by member states for the 2000–2006 period. The earmarking requirement was introduced by the Commission, as part of the 2005 budget negotiations, to convince member states that cohesion policy would meet the net payer goal of shifting EU spending towards the Lisbon goals 'growth and competitiveness'. The introduction of these mechanisms supports the argument of BAUER (2006) that EU policies operating over the long-term come under increasing scrutiny as to their performance, putting pressure on the Commission to demonstrate accountability and involve itself in supervising the implementation of policy programmes.

The findings reveal different levels of effectiveness of the three conditionalities: strong in the case of the decommitment rule but weak for the performance reserve and partially effective (to date) for earmarking (Table 9). The results partly challenge the general contention of BLOM-HANSEN (2005) that:

> EU control mechanisms are weak and the goals formulated at the EU level are likely to be remoulded in the implementation process in order to suit the preferences of the implementing actors at the national level.
>
> (p. 624)

This did not apply to the decommitment rule: the inability of member states to adapt (and weaken) the regulatory objective – combined with high credibility (strict enforcement and sanctions), criticality (simple measures), predictable and transparent application – is associated with a high level of ultimate effectiveness in meeting the goal of improving financial absorption. The negative effect of weak customization did, however, come into play with unintended consequences for the quality of spending.

By contrast, there was substantial remoulding of the performance reserve and the earmarking requirement. In the case of the reserve, member states were able to determine the level of competition and the rigour with which it was pursued; they were responsible for commissioning the mid-term evaluation/review on which the allocation was based; and they could influence the Commission decision on the allocation of the

reserve. Even after the initial regulatory framework had been agreed, the member states were able to pressure the Commission to reopen the negotiations in 2001–2003 to change the ways in which the reserve would be applied. This weakened the credibility, criticality and predictability of the reserve, and limited its scope for significantly influencing the performance of programmes unless member states themselves decided that it was in their interests to implement it rigorously (as in the case of Italy).

The potential influence of earmarking was also weakened during the negotiations, principally to give member states more flexibility in what spending would count as 'earmarked expenditure'. Again, this affected the credibility and criticality of the conditionality although the targets and reporting mechanisms were retained. Thus, earmarking has influenced the allocation of spending in some member states (particularly the EU-12), although not to the extent originally envisaged. The ultimate outcome – whether earmarking influenced achievement of the goals of the Lisbon Agenda – will not be known until *ex-post* evaluations of the 2007–2013 programmes have been conducted.

The results demonstrate how the use of control mechanisms in cohesion policy is profoundly affected by the dual status of the Commission and the member states in the principal–agent relationship (TALLBERG, 2003; ANCYGIER, 2011). At the policy formation stage – the negotiation of the budget and regulations for cohesion policy – the member states (in Council), and to a lesser extent the European Parliament, are the principals and the Commission is the agent, yet in the implementation of the policy, the Commission is the principal and member state authorities are the agents. Thus, the objectives set for cohesion policy by member states and delegated to the Commission as part of the policy formation process – to change the allocation, efficiency and effectiveness of spending – potentially clash with national preferences and administrative practices in implementing Structural and Cohesion Funds programmes. All three of the conditionalities discussed in this paper are measures that presented administrative difficulties and costs for the member states as agents; the controls limited national or regional flexibility to implement the funds and they carried potential political and financial threats through the proposed sanctions.

The question is why, in the case of the decommitment rule, did the member states sanction the Commission to have powers that could be used against them? The findings of this paper indicate three explanations. The first is the role of *trade-offs* in the bargaining between the Commission and member states. As noted by DA CONCEIÇÃO-HELDT (2013) in other EU policy domains, Council decisions on the regulations for cohesion policy have a high decision threshold but agreement invariably requires compromises and trade-offs which the Commission is able to exploit. In the

Table 9. Assessment of the conditionalities

	Decommitment rule	Earmarking	Performance reserve
Effectiveness	High	Partial	Low
Factors			
Customization	Low	Partial	Partial
Credibility	High	Partial	Partial
Criticality	High	Low	Low
Predictability	High	High	Low
Transparency	High	High	Partial

case of the decommitment rule, the Commission argued successfully that giving the member states more flexibility in the financial implementation of the funds needed to be balanced with a mechanism to allow the Commission to ensure that the planned progress of programmes was maintained.

A second factor is *external pressure*. Financial absorption was the only publicly visible and politically important indicator of the performance of the policy and the effectiveness of implementation systems in the member states. It could be measured and understood using straightforward and easily comprehensible indicators (proportion of funding committed and paid out) against which the policy could be (and was) held to account by the Council, Parliament and ECA. During the late 1990s, the ECA was increasingly critical of the EU's budget surplus, in particular because of 'underutilisation of commitments' under cohesion policy – for which the Commission blamed weaknesses in national management systems, justifying the introduction of a new control.

Third, *principal self-interest* played a part. Given that most of the under-spend in the 1990s was accounted for by Italy, Greece and Spain, several richer EU member states saw the issue as a 'southern problem' and (mistakenly) assumed that the effect of the decommitment rule would not affect them; further, the 'net contributor' countries had a vested interest in unused funding being returned and were therefore prepared to support the Commission in introducing the control. Several national officials admitted that they 'were not able to fully appreciate the implications'.

These factors were much weaker or absent in the case of the performance reserve. In the late 1990s there was little public or political discussion, at national or EU levels, on performance issues. The physical outcomes of the policy were unclear with limited evaluation evidence. Thus, there was weak external pressure or principal self-interest among member states to support the Commission's original proposal for a performance reserve, and the potential for trade-off was limited. As one member state negotiator commented:

> [our] view was that it was a bit of an irrelevance, but we could not object to what was said to be a quest for better value for money.

The earmarking requirement falls between the two. There was strong external pressure to improve the 'added value' of cohesion policy and its contribution to overall EU objectives (the Lisbon Agenda). The ring-fencing of allocations for certain thematic priorities also appealed to certain self-interests of the principals: for the net contributor countries it was a way of diverting EU funding to their preferred objectives, and for the net recipient member states it was a 'price worth paying' for

securing an EU budget agreement that would provide sizeable receipts under Structural and Cohesion Funds (BACHTLER *et al.*, 2013). However, there were insufficient trade-offs in the regulatory negotiations to persuade enough member states to support the Commission's original proposal, which was weakened considerably.

Lastly, there are three important policy implications for the use of conditionalities in cohesion policy. First, there is arguably a need to consider an 'effectiveness threshold' for control mechanisms. In negotiating conditionalities between the Commission and member states, it is inevitable that member states will seek to constrain the power of the Commission and weaken control mechanisms. However, there is potentially a point beyond which the cost–benefit ratio is negative in terms of the effectiveness of the control in relation to the cost of its implementation and when consideration should be given to abandoning the conditionality. The experience with the performance reserve is a case in point.

Second, research has highlighted the negative effects of multiple conditionalities on policy effectiveness. Promoting *faster* spending through the decommitment rule has conflicted with the goal of more *effective* spending through the performance reserve and more *targeted* spending under the earmarking requirement. The criticality of a combination of controls has to be explicitly acknowledged and balanced in framing agreements between the Commission and member states.

Finally, further attention needs to be given to the implications of control mechanisms for the 'sub-agents' – implementing bodies and beneficiaries – that have the responsibility for implementing cohesion policy projects in line with regulatory requirements and whose interests are only indirectly represented (and perhaps imperfectly mediated) by those negotiating the regulatory frameworks. The evidence from cohesion policy is that top-down control mechanisms relying on arbitrary thresholds or targets (n+2, 4% reserve, 75% ring-fencing) have severe limitations in changing agent behaviour effectively on the ground. As research in other policy fields has shown, customization is fundamental to the effectiveness of conditionalities.

Acknowledgements – The authors are grateful to their European Policies Research Centre (EPRC) colleagues for their contribution to the longitudinal IQ-Net interview research on which the paper has drawn, and particularly to Carlos Mendez for helpful comments on an earlier draft of the manuscript. The authors are also grateful for valuable comments and insights on the negotiation of conditionalities provided by current and former senior officials from DG Regio and several national government authorities, as well as helpful comments made by two anonymous reviewers. The usual disclaimer applies.

REFERENCES

AALBU H. and BACHTLER J. (1998) *Options for a Technically Feasible Performance Reserve Scheme*. Working Paper Number 1998:4. Nordregio, Stockholm.

ACT CONSULTANTS (2005) *Contribution des programmes Objectif 1 et Objectif 2 au developpement des territoires prioritaires de la politique e la ville*. Report to the European Commission (DG Regio). ACT Consultants, Paris.

ANCYGIER A. (2011) Dual P-A model 'inverted' principal–agent as a new tool to explain the implementation of the European renewable energy policy. Paper presented at the 'Exchanging Ideas on Europe', University Association for Contemporary European Studies (UACES) Conference, University of Cambridge, Cambridge, UK, 5–7 September 2011.

ANSELMO I. and RAIMONDO L. (2003) The Objective 1 Italian performance reserve: a tool to enhance the effectiveness of programmes and the quality of evaluation. Paper presented at the 4th European Conference on Evaluation of the Structural Funds, Edinburgh, UK, 18-19 September 2000.

APPLICA, ISTITUTO DI RICERCA INDISCIPLINARIE EUROPA (ISMERI) and VIENNA INSTITUTE FOR INTERNATIONAL ECONOMIC STUDIES (WIIW) (2010) *Financial Implementation of Structural Funds, Ex Post Evaluation of Cohesion Policy Programmes 2000–2006 Co-Financed by ERDF (Objective 1 and 2) – Task 1: Coordination, Analysis and Synthesis*. Final Report to the European Commission (DG Regio). Applica, ISMERI and WIIW.

BACHTLER J. (1998) Reforming the Structural Funds: challenges for EU regional policy, *European Planning Studies* **6(6)**, 645–664.

BACHTLER J. and GORZELAK G. (2007) Reforming EU cohesion policy: a reappraisal of the performance of the Structural Funds, *Policy Studies* **28(4)**, 309–326.

BACHTLER J. and MENDEZ C. (2010) *Review and Assessment of Simplification Measures in Cohesion Policy 2007–2013*. European Parliament, Brussels.

BACHTLER J. and TAYLOR S. (2003) *The Added Value of the Structural Funds*. IQ-Net Thematic Paper Number 13(2). European Policies Research Centre, University of Strathclyde, Glasgow.

BACHTLER J., DOWNES R., MICHIE R., ROONEY M.-L. and TAYLOR S. (2000) *New Structural Fund Programming: Laying the Foundations*. IQ-Net Thematic Paper Number 6(2). European Policies Research Centre, University of Strathclyde, Glasgow.

BACHTLER J., MENDEZ C. and WISHLADE F. (2013) *European Integration and Cohesion Policy: The Dynamics of Budget and Policy Reform*. Ashgate, Farnham.

BARCA F. (2009) *An Agenda for a Reformed Cohesion Policy, A Place-Based Approach to Meeting European Union Challenges and Expectations*. Independent report to the European Commission (DG Regio), Brussels.

BAUER M. W. (2006) Co-managing programme implementation: conceptualizing the European Commission's role in policy execution, *Journal of European Public Policy* **13(5)**, 717–735.

BAUN M. and MAREK D. (2009) *EU Cohesion Policy After Enlargement*. Palgrave, Basingstoke.

BLOM-HANSEN J. (2005) Principals, agents, and the implementation of EU cohesion policy, *Journal of European Public Policy* **12(4)**, 624–648.

BOVENS M. (2007) Analysing and assessing accountability: a conceptual framework, *European Law Journal* **13(4)**, 447–468.

BUITER W. H. (2007) Country ownership: a term whose time has gone, *Development in Practice* **17(4/5)**, 647–652.

BUNDESKANZLERAMT (BKA) (2003) *Light Governance' for Multi-Level Policies, Austrian Contribution to the Debate on Simplification of Structural Funds Management After 2006*. Mimeo, June. Bundeskanzleramt, Vienna.

CASAVOLA P. and TAGLE L. (2003) Building capacity for evaluation: lessons from Italy. Paper presented at the 5th European Conference on Evaluation of the Structural Funds, Budapest, Hungary, 26–27 June 2003.

CENTRE FOR INDUSTRIAL STUDIES (CSIL) (2010) *Lessons from Shared Management in Cohesion, Rural Development and Fisheries Policies*. Final Report to the European Commission (DG Regio), Centre for Industrial Studies, Milan.

COLLIER P., GUILLAUMONT P., GUILLAUMONT S. and GUNNING J. W. (1997) Redesigning conditionality, *World Development* **25(9)**, 1399–1407.

COUNCIL OF THE EUROPEAN UNION (1999) Council Regulation (EC) No. 1260/1999 of 21 June 1999 laying down general provisions on the Structural Funds, *Official Journal of the European Communities* **L161(26 June)**.

COUNCIL OF THE EUROPEAN UNION (2006) Council Regulation (EC) No. 1083/2006 of 11 July 2006 laying down general provisions on the European Regional Development Fund, the European Social Fund and the Cohesion Fund and repealing Regulation (EC) No. 1260/1999, *Official Journal of the European Communities* **L210(31 July)**.

DA CONCEIÇÃO-HELDT E. (2013) Do agents 'run amok'? A comparison of agency slack in the EU and US trade policy in the Doha Round, *Journal of Comparative Policy Analysis: Research and Practice* **15(1)**, 21–36.

DAMRO C. (2007) EU delegation and agency in international trade negotiations: a cautionary comparison, *Journal of Common Market Studies* **45(4)**, 883–903.

DAVIES S., MENDEZ C. and QUIOGUE N. C. (2004) *Cohesion Policy Funding for Innovation and the Knowledge Economy*. IQ-Net Thematic Paper Number 15(2). European Policies Research Centre, University of Strathclyde, Glasgow.

DELREUX T. and KERREMANS B. (2010) How agents weaken their principals' incentives to control: the case of EU negotiations an EU member states in multilateral negotiations, *Journal of European Integration* **32(4)**, 357–374.

DG REGIO (1999) *Working Paper 4: Implementation of the Performance Reserve. The Programming Period 2000–2006: Methodological Working Documents*. European Commission, Brussels.

DG XVI (1998) *Draft Council Regulation Chapter IV: Performance Reserve*, Doc 7609/98, 13 May. Brussels.

DRAZEN A. (2002) Conditionality and ownership in IMF lending: a political economy approach, *IMF Staff Papers* **49** [Special Issue], 36–67.

DREHER A. (2002) *The Development and Implementation of IMF and World Bank Conditionality.* Hamburgisches Welt-Wirtschafts-Archiv (HWWA) Discussion Paper Number 165. HWWA, Hamburg.

DÜR A. and ELSIG M. (2011) Principals, agents, and the European Union's foreign economic policies, *Journal of European Public Policy* **18(3)**, 332–338.

ECOTEC (2003) *Ex-Post Evaluation of Objective 1 1994–1999 Final Report to the European Commission (DG for Regional Policy).* ECOTEC Research & Consulting, Birmingham.

EGAN M. (1998) Regulatory strategies, delegation and European market integration, *Journal of European Public Policy* **5(3)**, 485–506.

ELGIE R. (2002) The politics of the European Central Bank: principal–agent theory and the democratic deficit, *Journal of European Public Policy* **9(2)**, 186–200.

EUROPEAN COMMISSION (1997) *Agenda 2000 for a Stronger and Wider Union.* Communication from the Commission of the European Communities, COM(97) 2000 final, 15 July. Commission of the European Communities, Brussels.

EUROPEAN COMMISSION (2000) *Performance Reserve: Analysis of the Situation in the Member States. Objectives 1 and 2. Synthesis Report.* December. DG Regio Evaluation Unit, Commission of the European Communities, Brussels.

EUROPEAN COMMISSION (2003a) *14th Annual Report on the Implementation of the Structural Funds.* Commission of the European Communities, COM(2003) 0646 final. Commission of the European Communities, Brussels.

EUROPEAN COMMISSION (2003b) *Communication from the Commission on the Simplification, Clarification, Coordination and Flexible Management of Structural Policies 2000–06.* C(2003) 1255, 25 April. Commission of the European Communities, Brussels.

EUROPEAN COMMISSION (2004) *A Report on the Performance Reserve and Mid-Term Evaluation.* Report by DG Regio to the Committee on the Development and Conversion of the Regions, 27 July. Commission of the European Communities, Brussels.

EUROPEAN COMMISSION (2007a) *Member States and Regions Delivering the Lisbon Strategy for Growth and Jobs Through EU Cohesion Policy, 2007–2013.* Communication from the Commission, COM(2007) 798, 11 December. Commission of the European Communities, Brussels.

EUROPEAN COMMISSION (2007b) *Regions Delivering Innovation Through Cohesion Policy.* Commission Staff Working Document, SEC(2007) 1547, 14 November. Commission of the European Communities. Brussels.

EUROPEAN COMMISSION (2010) *Analysis of the Budgetary Implementation of the Structural and Cohesion Funds in 2009.* Directorate-General for the Budget, Commission of the European Communities, Brussels.

EUROPEAN COMMISSION (2011a) *Impact Assessment of Funds Covered by the Common Strategic Framework.* Commission Staff Working Paper, SEC(2011) 1141 final, 6 October. Commission of the European Communities. Brussels.

EUROPEAN COMMISSION (2011b) *Results of the Public Consultation on the Conclusions of the Fifth Report on Economic, Social and Territorial Cohesion.* Commission Staff Working Paper, SEC(2011) 590 final, 13 May. Commission of the European Communities. Brussels.

EUROPEAN COMMISSION (2013) *Cohesion Policy: Strategic Report 2013 on Programme Implementation 2007–2013.* Report from the Commission to the European Parliament, the Council, the European Economic and Social Committee and the Committee of the Regions, COM(2013) 210 final, 18 April. Commission of the European Communities, Brussels.

EUROPEAN COURT OF AUDITORS (ECA) (1998) Opinion No. 10/98 of the European Court of Auditors on certain proposals for regulations within the Agenda 2000 framework, *Official Journal of the European Communities* **C401, Vol. 41(22 December)**.

EUROPEAN COURT OF AUDITORS (ECA) (2003) Court of Auditors – annual report concerning the financial year 2002, *Official Journal of the European Union* **C286, Vol. 46(28 November)**.

EUROPEAN COURT OF AUDITORS (ECA) (2004) Court of Auditors – annual report concerning the financial year 2003, *Official Journal of the European Union* **C293, Vol. 47(28 November)**.

EUROPEAN COURT OF AUDITORS (ECA) (2006) Court of Auditors – annual report concerning the financial year 2005, *Official Journal of the European Union* **C263, Vol. 49(31 October)**.

EUROPEAN COURT OF AUDITORS (ECA) (2010) Court of Auditors – annual report concerning the financial year 2009, *Official Journal of the European Union* **C303, Vol. 53(9 November)**.

GOLDEN M. M. (2000) *What Motivates Bureaucrats?* Columbia University Press, New York, NY.

GROSSMAN S. and HART O. (1983) An analysis of the principal–agent problem, *Econometrica* **51(1)**, 7–45.

HALL R. and ROSENSTOCK N. (1998) Agenda 2000 – the reform of EU cohesion policies, *European Planning Studies* **6(6)**, 635–644.

KAPUR D. and WEBB R. (2000) *Governance-Related Conditionalities of the International Financial Institutions.* G-24 Discussion Paper Series 6. United Nations Conference on Trade and Development (UNCTAD), New York and Geneva.

KASSIM H. and MENON A. (2003) The principal–agent approach and the study of the European Union: promise unfulfilled?, *Journal of European Public Policy* **10(1)**, 121–139.

KIEWIET D. R. and McCUBBINS M. D. (1991) *The Logic of Delegation: Congressional Parties and the Appropriations Process.* University of Chicago Press, Chicago, IL.

KILBY C. (2009) The political economy of conditionality: an empirical analysis of World Bank loan disbursements, *Journal of Development Economics* **89(1)**, 51–61.

KILLICK T. (1997) Principals, agents and the failings of conditionality, *Journal of International Development* **9(4)**, 483–495.

KOEBERLE S. G. (2003) *Should Policy-Based Lending Still Involve Conditionality?* The World Bank Research Observer Number 18:2. The World Bank, Washington, DC.

KOEBERLE S. G., BEDOYA H., SILARSZKY P. and VERHEYEN G. (Eds) (2005) *Conditionality Revisited: Concepts, Experiences and Lessons.* The World Bank. Washington, DC.

LEANDRO J. E., SCHAFER H. and FRONTINI G. (1999) Towards a more effective conditionality: an operational framework, *World Development* **27(2)**, 285–299.

Leonardi R. and Nanetti R. (2011) The cohesion-isation of the Lisbon Strategy through the implementation of Europe 2020. Paper presented at the Regional Studies Association European Conference 2012, 'Network Regions and Cities in Times of Fragmentation: Developing Smart, Sustainable and Inclusive Places', Delft University of Technology, Delft, The Netherlands, 13–16 May 2012.

Marchesi S. and Sabani L. (2007) IMF concern for reputation and conditional lending failure: theory and empirics, *Journal of Development Economics* **84(2)**, 640–666.

Mendez C. (2011) The Lisbonisation of EU cohesion policy: a successful case of experimentalist governance?, *European Planning Studies* **19(3)**, 519–537.

Mendez C., Kah S. and Bachtler J. (2010) *Taking Stock of Programme Progress: Implementation of the Lisbon Agenda and Lessons for Europe 2020*. IQ-Net Thematic Paper Number 27(2). European Policies Research Centre, University of Strathclyde, Glasgow.

Milner H. (2004) *Why Multilateralism? Foreign Aid and Domestic Principal–Agent Problems*. Columbia University, New York, NY.

Moe T. M. (1984) The new economics of organization, *American Journal of Political Science* **28(4)**, 739–777.

Moe T. M. (1987) An assessment of the positive theory of 'Congressional dominance', *Legislative Studies Quarterly* **12(4)**, 475–520.

Muuka G. N. (1998) In defense of World Bank and IMF conditionality in structural adjustment programs, *Journal of Business in Developing Nations* **2(2)** (available at: http://www.ewp.rpi.edu/jbdn/jbdnvol2.htm).

Nordregio (2009) *The Potential for EU Structural Funds to Contribute to the Lisbon and Göteborg Objectives*. Report to the European Commission (DG Regio), Nordregio, Stockholm.

Organisation for Economic Co-operation and Development (OECD) (2009) *Governing Regional Development Policy: The Use of Performance Indicators*. OECD, Paris.

Pollack M. A. (2007) *Principal–Agent Analysis and International Delegation: Red Herrings, Theoretical Clarifications, and Empirical Disputes*. College of Europe Working Papers, February. College of Europe, Bruges.

Polverari L., Davies S. and Michie R. (2004) *Programmes at the Turning Point: Challenges, Activities and Developments for Partner Regions*. IQ-Net Thematic Paper Number 14(1). European Policies Research Centre, University of Strathclyde, Glasgow.

Polverari L., Mendez C., Gross F. and Bachtler J. (2007) *Making Sense of European Cohesion Policy: 2007–13. On-Going Evaluation and Monitoring Arrangements*. IQ-Net Thematic Paper Number 21(2). European Policies Research Centre, University of Strathclyde, Glasgow.

Polverari L., McMaster I., Gross F., Bachtler J., Ferry M. and Yuill D. (2006) *Strategic Planning for Structural Funds in 2007–13*. IQ-Net Thematic Paper Number 18(2). European Policies Research Centre, University of Strathclyde, Glasgow.

Raines P. and Taylor S. (2002) *Mid-Term Evaluation of the 2000–06 Structural Fund Programmes*. IQ-Net Thematic Paper Number 11(2). European Policies Research Centre, University of Strathclyde, Glasgow.

Rich R. (2004) Applying conditionality to development assistance, *Agenda* **11(4)**, 321–334.

Schimmelfennig F. and Sedelmeier U. (2004) Governance by conditionality: EU rule transfer to the candidate countries of Central and Eastern Europe, *Journal of European Public Policy* **11(4)**, 661–679.

Schuknecht L. (2004) *EU Fiscal Rules: Issues and Lessons from Political Economy*. Working Paper Number 421. European Central Bank, Frankfurt.

Sedelmeier U. (2008) After conditionality: post-accession compliance with EU law in East Central Europe, *Journal of European Public Policy* **15(6)**, 806–825.

Shepsle K. A. and Bonchek M. S. (1997) *Analysing Politics: Rationality, Behavior, and Institutions*. Norton, New York, NY.

Sippel M. and Neuhoff K. (2009) A history of conditionality: lessons for international cooperation on climate policy, *Climate Policy* **9(5)**, 481–494.

Svensson J. (2003) Why conditional aid does not work and what can be done about it?, *Journal of Development Economics* **70(2)**, 381–402.

Tallberg J. (2003) The agenda-shaping powers of the EU council presidency, *Journal of European Public Policy* **10(1)**, 1–19.

Taylor S. (2006) Trouble for Commission's 'Lisbonisation' project, *European Voice* **1 June**.

Taylor S., Bachtler J., Josserand F. and Polverari L. (2004) *Achieving the Aspirations of the 2000–06 Programming Period*. IQ-Net Thematic Paper Number 14(2). European Policies Research Centre, University of Strathclyde, Glasgow.

Taylor S., Bachtler J. and Polverari L. (2001) *Information into Intelligence: Monitoring for Effective Structural Funds Programming*. IQ-Net Thematic Paper Number 8(2). European Policies Research Centre, University of Strathclyde, Glasgow.

Taylor S. and Raines P. (2003) *Getting the Message – Structural Funds Publicity and Communication*. IQ-Net Thematic Paper Number 12(2). European Policies Research Centre, University of Strathclyde, Glasgow.

Technopolis (2006) *Strategic Evaluation on Innovation and the Knowledge Based Economy for the Programming Period 2007–2013*. Synthesis Report to DG Regio, Brussels.

Thatcher M. and Stone Sweet A. (Eds) (2002) Theory and practice of delegation to non-majoritarian institutions in Europe, *West European Politics* **25(1)**, 1–22.

Tödtling-Schönhofer H. and Wimmer H. (2008) *Governance and Partnership in Regional Policy*. European Parliament, Brussels.

Van Thiel S. and Leeuw F. L. (2002) The performance paradox in the public sector, *Public Performance and Management Review* **25(3)**, 267–281.

Weingast B. R. and Moran M. J. (1983) Bureaucratic discretion or congressional control? Regulatory policymaking by the Federal Trade Commission, *Journal of Political Economy* **91(5)**, 765–800.

Wood A. and Lockwood M. (1999) *The 'Perestroika of Aid'? New Perspectives on Conditionality*. Report of the Bretton Woods Project. Washington, DC.

World Bank (2005) *Review of World Bank Conditionality: 2005 Conditionality Survey*. The World Bank, Washington, DC.

Worshan J. (2003) Multiple principals, multiple signals: a signaling approach to principal–agent relations, *Policy Studies Journal* **33(3)**, 363–376.

Quality of Government and the Returns of Investment: Examining the Impact of Cohesion Expenditure in European Regions

ANDRÉS RODRÍGUEZ-POSE† and ENRIQUE GARCILAZO‡

†*Department of Geography and Environment, London School of Economics, Houghton Street, London, UK*
‡*Regional Development Policy Division, Directorate for Public Governance and Territorial Development (OECD/GOV), Paris, France*

RODRÍGUEZ-POSE A. and GARCILAZO E. Quality of government and the returns of investment: examining the impact of cohesion expenditure in European regions, *Regional Studies*. This paper sets out to examine the relationship between the quality of local and regional governments and regional economic performance, linking government quality to the returns of European Union Structural and Cohesion Funds. Using primary data on government quality collected by the Quality of Government Institute, combined with World Bank Global Governance Indicators data, a two-way fixed effect panel regression model is conducted for a total of 169 European regions during the period 1996–2007. The results of the analysis underline the importance of government quality both as a direct determinant of economic growth as well as a moderator of the efficiency of Structural and Cohesion Funds expenditure. The analysis finds that both European Union investments targeting regions and quality of government simultaneously make a difference for regional economic growth, but that above a threshold of cohesion expenditure – calculated at more than €120 of cohesion expenditure per capita per year – government quality improvements are a far more important and realistic option for regional development than additional public investment. In many of the regions receiving the bulk of Structural Funds, further improvements in economic growth would require massive amounts of additional investment, unless the quality of government is significantly enhanced.

RODRÍGUEZ-POSE A. and GARCILAZO E. 政府素质与投资报酬：检视欧洲区域凝聚支出的影响，区域研究。本文将政府素质与欧盟结构及凝聚基金的报酬进行连结，着手检视地方及区域政府的素质和区域经济表现之间的关联性。本研究主要运用"政府机构素质"组织所搜集的政府素质数据，结合世界银行全球治理指标之数据，为欧盟 1996 年至 2007 年期间的一百六十九个全数区域，进行二元固定效果追踪迴归模型。分析结果，凸显出政府治理同时作为经济成长的直接决定因素与结构及凝聚积金支出效率的调节者之重要性。本研究分析发现，针对区域和针对政府素质的欧盟投资，皆对区域经济成长产生影响，但超过凝聚支出的一定门槛时—以超过每年人均一百二十欧元的凝聚支出为计算分野—政府素质的改善，则较增加公共支出而言，是区域发展更为重要且实际的选项。在诸多接受大量结构基金的区域中，除非政府素质显着地改善，否则便需要大量的额外投资来促进经济成长。

RODRÍGUEZ-POSE A. et GARCILAZO E. La qualité des pouvoirs publics et les rendements des investissements: un examen de l'impact des dépenses de cohésion dans les régions européennes, *Regional Studies*. Cet article cherche à examiner le rapport entre la qualité des pouvoirs publics locaux et régionaux et la performance économique régionale, établissant un lien entre les rendements des Fonds structurels et des Fonds de cohésion de l'Union européenne. Employant des données primaires sur la qualité des pouvoirs publics receuillies par le Quality of Government Institute, combinées aux données provenant des World Bank Global Governance Indicators, on construit un modèle de régression bidirectionnel des données de panel à effets fixes auprès de 169 régions européennes pendant la période allant de 1996 jusqu'à 2007. Les résultats de l'analyse soulignent l'importance de la qualité des pouvoirs publics à la fois comme facteur déterminant direct de la croissance économique ainsi qu'un facteur modérateur de l'efficacité des dépenses des Fonds structurels et des Fonds de cohésion. À partir de cette analyse, il est à constater que les investissements de l'Union européenne ciblant simultanément les régions et la qualité des pouvoirs publics influent sur la croissance économique régionale, bien que l'amélioration de la qualité des pouvoirs publics soit une option beaucoup plus importante et réaliste pour le développement régional que ne le sont les investissements publics supplémentaires, au-dessus d'un seuil des dépenses de cohésion – ce qui représente plus de €120 par tête de dépenses de cohésion par an. Dans beaucoup des régions bénéficiaires de la part du lion des Fonds structurels, des améliorations complémentaires de la croissance économique nécessiteraient l'injection de fonds supplémentaires considérables, à moins que la qualité des pouvoirs publics ne soit sensiblement accrue.

RODRÍGUEZ-POSE A. und GARCILAZO E. Regierungsqualität und die Erträge von Investitionen: Untersuchung der Auswirkung von Kohäsionsausgaben in europäischen Regionen, Regional Studies. In diesem Beitrag wird die Beziehung zwischen der Qualität von lokalen und regionalen Regierungen und der regionalen Wirtschaftsleistung untersucht, wobei die Regierungsqualität mit den Erträgen aus den Struktur- und Kohäsionsfonds der Europäischen Union verknüpft wird. Anhand der vom Institut für Regierungsqualität erfassten Primärdaten über Regierungsqualität in Kombination mit den Daten der Weltbank über globale Governance-Indikatoren wird ein wechselseitiges Festeffekt-Panelregressionsmodell für insgesamt 169 europäische Regionen im Zeitraum von 1996 bis 2007 erstellt. Die Ergebnisse der Analyse bestätigen die Wichtigkeit der Regierungsqualität sowohl als direkter Determinant des Wirtschaftswachstums als auch als Moderator für die Effizienz der Ausgaben von Struktur- und Kohäsionsfonds. Die Analyse zeigt, dass sich sowohl EU-Investitionen in Regionen als auch die Regierungsqualität gleichzeitig auf das regionale Wirtschaftswachstum auswirken, wobei aber oberhalb eines Schwellenwerts der Kohäsionsausgaben – der auf mehr als 120 € Kohäsionsausgaben pro Kopf und Jahr beziffert wird – die Verbesserungen der Regierungsqualität eine weitaus wichtigere und realistischere Option für die regionale Wirtschaftsentwicklung darstellen als zusätzliche öffentliche Investitionen. In zahlreichen Regionen, die einen Großteil der Strukturfonds erhalten, wären für weitere Verbesserungen des Wirtschaftswachstums zusätzliche Investitionen in enormer Höhe erforderlich, sofern sich die Regierungsqualität nicht erheblich verbessert.

RODRÍGUEZ-POSE A. y GARCILAZO E. Calidad del Gobierno y el beneficio de la inversión: análisis del efecto del gasto de cohesión en las regiones europeas, Regional Studies. En este artículo se estudia la relación entre la calidad de los Gobiernos locales y regionales y el crecimiento económico, vinculando la calidad del Gobierno al impacto de los fondos europeos estructurales y de cohesión. Utilizamos datos primarios de calidad de Gobierno recogidos por el Instituto de Calidad de Gobierno y combinados con datos de los Indicadores de Gobernanza Global del Banco Mundial en un modelo de regresión bivariado de datos de panel con efectos fijos para un total de 169 regiones europeas durante el periodo comprendido entre 1996 y 2007. Los resultados del análisis subrayan la importancia de la calidad de Gobierno como factor directo del crecimiento económico y como factor moderador de la eficacia del gasto en fondos estructurales y de cohesión. Nuestro análisis pone de manifiesto que tanto el gasto en desarrollo regional de la Unión Europea (EU), como la calidad de Gobierno influyen en el crecimiento económico de manera simultánea, pero que por encima de un cierto umbral – calculado en más de 120 euros de gasto en cohesión por persona y año – las mejoras en calidad de Gobierno son una opción más importante y realista para generar desarrollo regional que las inversiones públicas adicionales. En muchas de las regiones que reciben la mayoría de los fondos estructurales, ulteriores mejoras en crecimiento requerirían un aumento masivo de la inversión, a no ser que se mejore de manera significativa la calidad de Gobierno.

INTRODUCTION

There has been much debate in policy and scholarly circles investigating whether the quality of institutions, in general, and the quality of government, in particular, affect the delivery and efficiency of public investment. The growing agreement is that institutions and government quality make an important difference for economic development (AMIN, 1999; HALL and JONES, 1999; ACEMOGLU et al., 2001; RODRIK et al., 2004). Places with weak and/or inefficient institutions suffer from a variety of problems, which can range from pervasive corruption, rent-seeking, insider–outsider problems, clientelism and nepotism to principal agent or impacted information problems (RODRÍGUEZ-POSE and STORPER, 2006). Different combinations of these problems lead to imperfectly functioning markets, to a loss of efficiency and growth potential, and to institutional and government failure, affecting, in turn, the

capacity of governments to adequately design and efficiently deliver public goods and policies.

The European Union (EU) has also adopted the view that poor institutions undermine efforts to achieve greater economic and social cohesion. As stated in the EU's Fifth Cohesion Report, 'poor institutions can, in particular, hinder the effectiveness of regional development strategies' (EUROPEAN UNION, 2010, p. 65). The quality of local and regional institutions is thus perceived to mediate the potential returns of investment in regional cohesion: the weaker the institutional setting, the greater the difficulties in transforming European regional development investment into growth and development. Regions with weak institutions have been considered incapable of absorbing regional development and Cohesion Funds and of making the most of the investments taking place in their territory. Many of them have also invested Cohesion and Structural Funds in what can be considered a suboptimal manner. It comes, therefore, as no surprise that, as early as 1997 in its draft Agenda 2000, the European Commission sought to establish a ceiling of regional development expenditures, stating that in order 'to avoid major problems with regard to absorption, the level of annual aid should increase gradually, subject to the general limit of 4% of national GDP, which would apply to the Structural Funds and the Cohesion Fund together' (EUROPEAN UNION, 1997, p. 25).

Yet, despite the growing interest in institutional factors, the empirical literature on how the quality of government impinges on the potential to achieve European regional cohesion is still in its infancy. While in development economics there has been a growing body of literature linking, for example, the institutions associated with colonial origins and economic outcomes (e.g. ACEMOGLU et al., 2001), there is still relatively little evidence about whether and how government quality has shaped economic trajectories at the regional level in Europe. Early attempts by BEUGELSDIJK and EIJFFINGER (2005) – who introduce in their analysis of the effectiveness of structural policy in the EU a national corruption index – have not been properly followed. Even less is known about the mechanisms at play in the interaction between regional political institutions – beyond social capital (BEUGELSDIJK and VAN SCHAIK, 2005a, 2005b) and culture (e.g. TABELLINI, 2010) – and economic development. At the EU level there is to our knowledge no clear-cut evidence about how the quality of government of the different regions shapes the returns of European cohesion support. There is also little evidence, beyond the work of BECKER et al. (2012), that the returns of European cohesion efforts decline as cohesion investment increases and none that they diminish when regional transfers exceed a threshold of 4% of gross domestic product (GDP).

The present paper combines data on the investment undertaken by the EU in cohesion and structural policies targeting regions with data on government quality gathered by the Quality of Government Institute at the University of Gothenburg. This allows the assessment of whether different local combinations taking into account the rule of law, the control of corruption, government effectiveness, and voice and accountability affect regional growth and shape the returns of European Structural and Cohesion Fund investments across the regions of the EU during the period between 1996 and 2007. In particular, of interest is whether and how the quality of government in any given European region moderates the returns of European investments and whether these effects are larger or smaller beyond a given threshold of cohesion investment.

The results indicate that although at first sight the quality of government does not seem to affect the returns of European investment across the whole sample of regions considered, it does play a major role in determining whether European peripheral regions catch up to European standards. For those regions receiving the greatest amount of support – on average more

than €80 of cohesion expenditure per capita per year – government quality tends to be on the whole a more important determinant for growth than European regional support. The relevance of government quality increases significantly as the level of cohesion expenditure rises. In addition, the analysis using interaction terms finds that for regions receiving a considerable amount of funds and sharing a similar level of quality of government, greater cohesion expenditure has a marginal effect on economic growth. And while greater aggregate growth can be achieved by significantly increasing the cohesion budget, improving government quality is a far more realistic alternative.

INSTITUTIONS, QUALITY OF GOVERNMENT AND ECONOMIC DEVELOPMENT

Across all areas of the social sciences there is a growing scholarly consensus that institutions matter for economic development. Economic sociologists (TÖNNIES/LOOMIS, 1887/1957; WEBER/ROTH and WITTICH, 1921/1968; GRANOVETTER, 1973; COLEMAN, 1988) have for over a century stressed the importance of institutions for the effectiveness of public policy and economic development. Different types of institutions not only create the rules of the game by which economic activities are governed, but also de facto shape the incentives and disincentives driving economic interactions, making them essential determinants for the economic outcomes in any given territory. The baton laid by economic sociologists has been taken over in recent decades by a raft of other social scientists. Geographers (AMIN and THRIFT, 1994; AMIN, 1999), political scientists (PUTNAM, 1993, 2000) and economists (NORTH, 1990; ACEMOGLU et al., 2001; RODRIK et al., 2004) have of late delved into how institutions influence economic development, indicating that long-term economic outcomes are frequently the result of institutional conditions more than of alternative economic factors (RODRIK et al., 2004).

One essential form of political institution is that related to the quality of government. Government, in general, and local and regional governments, in particular, are the key organizations determining the rules of the game at the local level. The quality of local governments will therefore influence economic development and help shape the efficiency and the returns of public investments. Accountable and transparent governments, staffed by well-trained civil servants and led by trustworthy politicians who have the interests of the local community at heart, will, in all likelihood, design and implement policies and deliver public goods and services needed by its citizenry, benefitting the community as a whole. Unaccountable and poorly staffed governments and governments with inept and/or corrupt politicians at the helm will, by contrast, deliver inefficient policies or, worse still, lead to situations where rent-seeking and insider–outsider problems are pervasive.

The views that institutions matter for economic growth and that the quality of local governments affects the effectiveness and returns of public policies has been accepted at face value by the EU in the application of its regional cohesion policy. This is important because, although all member states of the EU should have adopted the so-called *Acquis Communautaire*,[1] or the accumulated legislation and court decisions of the EU, it is plainly evident that the functioning of these formal institutions varies considerably from country to country and even within countries. This is because, as underlined by VACHUDOVA (2009), especially in the case of former transition countries that have joined the EU since 2004, the requirements to improve the transparency and efficiency of state institutions have been adopted, rather than enforced. This leads to still considerable differences across the EU in the quality of formal institutions and, in particular, in informal institutions. Corruption and clientelism still represent major obstacles for an effective functioning of the rule of law in many areas of the former transition countries of Central and Eastern Europe (GUASTI and DOBOVSEK, 2011; RODRÍGUEZ-POSE and MASLAUSKAITE, 2012). Hence, across parts of Europe there are different combinations of corruption, pervasive rent-seeking, self-serving decision-makers, and a low quality of bureaucracy – all indicators of the presence of weak governmental institutions and a low quality of government – likely to hurt the effectiveness of all types of public policies and, in the case of the EU cohesion effort, undermine the assimilation of funds and affect the potential returns of EU expenditure in Structural and Cohesion Funds. Furthermore, the quality of government at the local level is key for coordinating actions across tiers of government, aligning policy objectives, enhancing the delivery of goods and services, and ensuring that local needs are represented and taken into account in the policy design across the different government layers.

From this perspective, the lower the quality of government, the lower the capacity to absorb development funds, the lower the efficiency and returns of public investments, and the lower the growth.[2] This sort of reasoning is at the heart of the 4% of GDP expenditure limit proposed in the Agenda 2000: if institutions and the quality of government of any given European region are deficient, more expenditure on development would, at best, only have a marginal impact on economic growth, unless the institutional conditions that limit the effectiveness of expenditure are improved.

MEASURING THE QUALITY OF GOVERNMENT

Linking government quality to regional economic growth is difficult and there is little empirical evidence so far that establishes such a nexus. Perhaps the main problem in this respect is that of defining and measuring the quality of government. Government quality is an elusive concept. It may mean different things to different people and it is likely to be affected by a myriad of factors. Notwithstanding this, the number of studies and indices that have looked at issues of quality of government and governance at national level has not ceased to grow (e.g. KAUFMAN *et al.*, 2009). However, sub-national regions, cities and localities remain – despite the widespread perception of wide internal variations in government quality within countries – virtually uncharted territories. Some studies have ventured more in depth into how the quality of governmental institutions affects economic performance in different parts of the country. This type of analysis has been prevalent for the case of Italy, where a large number of local *Meridionalisti* (e.g. TRIGILIA, 1992; DIAMANTI *et al.*, 1995; BODO and VIESTI, 1997) and many foreign scholars (e.g. PUTNAM, 1993) have delved for the roots of the differences in development between the North and the South of the country in the variation of the efficiency of local governments. But analyses covering sub-national entities beyond the borders of the nation-state are conspicuously absent.

This lack of comparable cross-European data on government quality across national borders for Europe has recently been addressed in a report by the Quality of Government Institute of the University of Gothenburg (CHARRON *et al.*, 2010). This study resorts to survey data of 34 000 respondents, living in 172 NUTS-1 and NUTS-2 regions (NUTS-2 is largely equivalent to the Organisation for Economic Co-operation and Development's (OECD) Territorial Level 2)[3] in 18 EU states[4] in order to measure the perception of the quality of regional and local governments across Europe. In the report, following ROTHSTEIN and TEORELL (2008), government quality is assimilated to the concept of impartial government institutions, that is 'when public officials who implement policies do not take anything about the citizen/case into consideration that is not beforehand stipulated in the policy or the law' (CHARRON *et al.*, 2010, p. 9). In order to operationalize this concept, the Quality of Government Institute resorts to decomposing the idea of government quality into four components: (1) rule of law; (2) corruption; (3) quality of the bureaucracy or bureaucratic effectiveness; and (4) democracy and the strength of electoral institutions (p. 21).

Thirty-four questions regarding these four components were included in a survey which – after the thematic and geographical aggregation of the different answers by the 34 000 respondents – resulted in the formation of a regional-level quality of government index and to the first mapping of regional government quality across regions of the EU in 2009.

The data provided by the Quality of Government Institute are only available for a single year (CHARRON *et al.*, 2010).[5] Following CHARRON *et al.* (2014), values are interpolated across a longer time period by combining the data with the World Bank's World Governance Indicators, available at the national level. The interpolated data provide a time series for the analysis. The assumption is that regional variations in government quality within countries are relatively stable; and variations at the national level are captured by the World Bank World Governance Indicators. Details on how this indicator is calculated can be found in CHARRON et al. (2014).

The combined interpolated data for 2009 are presented in Fig. 1. It displays a picture of quality of government in Europe that is strongly associated with the levels of socio-economic development and social trust of the regions of the EU, but uncorrelated to other factors, such as population and area size (CHARRON et al., 2014). It reveals the presence of an West/East and, to a much lesser extent, North/South divide in the sub-national quality of government in Europe. Regions in Denmark, Finland, Sweden and the Netherlands rank among those with the best government quality in Europe, as is the case of Scotland in the UK, Schleswig-Holstein and Thuringia in Germany, and Burgenland in Austria. Among the regions in the South, Alto Adige in Italy is also amongst the best performers. Some Spanish regions, such as Aragon, Asturias, the Basque Country, Extremadura or Galicia, also score relatively highly in the index. Friuli-Venezia Giulia, Trentino and Val d'Aosta in Italy also perform well. The worst scores are found in the South East of Europe. Bulgarian and Romanian regions have, according to the results of the survey, the worst quality of government. Some southern Italian regions, such as Calabria, Campania, Puglia and Sicily, are also in the same category (Fig. 1).

Internal contrasts are visible in a number of countries. This is more evident in countries with an overall low sub-national quality of government (Slovakia being the main exception). Italy represents the most extreme case. While some northern regions have levels of government quality similar to those of Scandinavian countries or the Netherlands, there is very little difference in the perception of the quality of government between regions in the South of the country and those of Bulgaria or Romania. In Romania some regions in the west of the country – Nord Vest and Centru – perform relatively well, whereas Bucharest ranks well below the national mean. Strong internal variation can also be observed in Belgium, Bulgaria, Portugal or Spain. In sum, the strong internal country variation observed in Fig. 1 confirms the relevance of the quality of local and regional institutions.

MODEL AND DATA

Model specification

In light of the theoretical discussion, the hypotheses are that (1) 'good governance is a necessary requirement for countries to foster economic development' (CHARRON et al., 2010, p. 19) and that (2) government quality shapes the capacity to transform investment into economic activity and development. In order to check whether this is the case, an econometric model is estimated using panel data, which aims to assess the connection between government quality and regional growth and to establish whether the returns of European economic and social cohesion expenditure are affected by the quality of the government of the regions receiving funds. Also controlled are a series of regional factors deemed to affect economic performance. In this interactive model, the growth of GDP per capita across regions in Europe between 1996 and 2007 is specified by the following equation:

$$\Delta y_i = \alpha + \beta y_i + \delta \, \text{Cohesion}_i + \phi \, \text{QGov}_i \\ + \gamma \, \text{Cohesion}^* \text{QGov}_i + \boldsymbol{\phi} \, \mathbf{X}_i + v_i \quad (1)$$

where Δy is the average annual growth of real GDP per capita of region i over the period 1996–2007; y_i is the GDP per capita in the previous period in region i; *Cohesion* is the main independent variable of interest and represents the per capita investments undertaken by the EU in region i under the structural and cohesion policy framework; *QGov* is the moderator, proxied by the composite indicator of the quality of government in any given European region, collected by the Quality of Government Institute at the University of Gothenburg; *Cohesion**QGov is the interaction term between the previous two variables; $\mathbf{X}$ denotes a vector of variables controlling for other factors assumed to influence growth, including the level of education and training of the adult population of the region, measures of infrastructure endowment, levels of employment and agglomeration effects; and finally v is the corresponding disturbance term.

The main interest lies in the coefficients δ, ϕ and γ, which intend to capture the connection between the level of investments of the EU on regional cohesion, the quality of regional and local governments, and the interaction of both terms, respectively, with economic growth.

By expanding model (1), the following specification is obtained, which is used as the empirical model:

$$\ln \left(\frac{\text{GPDpc}_{i,t}}{\text{GDPpc}_{i,t-1}} \right) = \alpha + \beta_1 \ln (\text{GDPpc}_{i,t-1}) \\ + \beta_2 (\text{CohesionExp}_{i,t-1}) \\ + \beta_3 (\text{QualGov}_{i,t-1}) \\ + \beta_4 (\text{CohesionExp} * \text{QualGov}_{i,t-1}) \\ + \beta_5 \ln (\text{InfrastDen}_{i,t-1}) \\ + \beta_6 \ln (\text{Primary Education}_{i,t-1}) \\ + \beta_7 \ln (\text{Tertiary Education}_{i,t-1}) \\ + \beta_8 (\text{Emp Rate}_{i,t-1}) \\ + \beta_9 \ln (\text{Emp Density}) \\ + \beta_{10} \ln (\text{Pop Density}) + \gamma_j C_j \\ + \varphi_t T_t + u_i + e_{i,t} \quad (2)$$

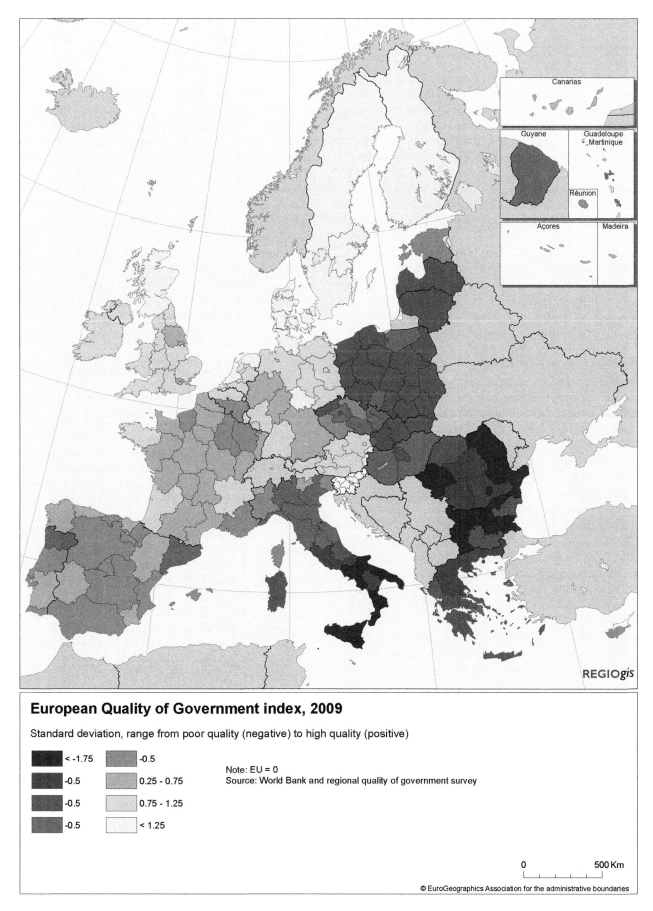

European Quality of Government index, 2009

Standard deviation, range from poor quality (negative) to high quality (positive)

■ < -1.75	▨ -0.5	
■ -0.5	▨ 0.25 - 0.75	Note: EU = 0
▨ -0.5	▨ 0.75 - 1.25	Source: World Bank and regional quality of government survey
▨ -0.5	□ < 1.25	

0   500 Km

© EuroGeographics Association for the administrative boundaries

Fig. 1. Regional quality of government combined index, 2009

Data

The main independent variable of interest, the public investments financed by the EU (*CohesionExp*), is measured over the period between 1996 and 2007. It depicts the actual payments in a given year – rather than commitments, as in a number of prior studies on the impact of Structural and Cohesion Funds – to European regions. Unfortunately, these data do not cover public investments financed by regions and by national governments. Such data exist only for a very limited number of countries. The variable thus represents a fraction of all public investment, and a highly variable fraction at that, as there are large differences in the degree to which regions draw on EU financing. These differences are explicitly addressed in some of the models below.

The quality of institutions is proxied by the use of a quality of government (*QualGov*) composite index. As indicated above, this index is constructed for 172 European regions from a survey conducted in 2009 by the Quality of Government Institute at the University of Gothenburg (see CHARRON *et al.*, 2010, for full details).

In order to transform *QualGov* into a time-variant variable, the data on government quality derived from the survey are combined with the World Bank's Global Governance Indicators. This is possible because the components included in the World Bank indicators – (1) rule of law, (2) governance effectiveness, (3) control of corruption and (4) voice and accountability – mirror those of the Quality of Government index. It is therefore assumed that the quality of government detected in every region in 2009 has evolved in a similar way as changes in governance at the national level over time (CHARRON *et al.*, 2014). Mixing both indices gives a regional indicator of quality of government that varies for the whole period of analysis.

The third key independent variable of interest is the interaction term for public investment and the quality of government (*CohesionExp**QualGov). The introduction of this interaction represents an effort to discern to what extent, if any, the impact of public investments depends on quality of government.

In addition, a number of control variables that, according to the theoretical and empirical literature, may affect regional economic performance in Europe are also considered. Data for the control variables are taken from the OECD Regional Database. The key control variables are:

- *InfrasDen*: infrastructure density defined by motorway kilometres by population.
- *Education*: the percentage of adults having either only completed primary school (*Primary Education*) or with a university degree (*Tertiary Education*) represents the proxies of the level of human capital of the workforce.
- *Emp Rate*: rate of employment in the region.
- *Density*: employment density (*Emp Density*) and population density (*Pop Density*) capture agglomeration effects and are measured as employment per square kilometre and population per square kilometre, respectively.
- GDP_{t-1}: level of GDP per capita at time $t - 1$.

The model specification considers a two-way fixed effect (FE) panel regression model, with heteroskedasticity robust estimators and country (*C*) and time (*T*) controls. The sample of regions totals 169 (three regions had to be dropped from the analysis because of gaps in the data) in 18 different countries in the EU. Most data are gathered – following the territorial division used in order to compile the Quality of Government indicator – at NUTS-2 level, with the exception of data for Belgium, Germany, Greece, the Netherlands and the UK, which refer to NUTS-1 regions. The time period covered in the analysis is limited to the years between 1996 and 2007 due to the lack of availability of World Bank Global Governance Indicators before 1996.

RESULTS OF THE ANALYSIS

Analysis for the whole sample

The empirical model is estimated including all regions considered in the analysis, regardless of the level of cohesion expenditure in each of the regions by the EU. The aim of this model is first to establish the link between investments in EU cohesion policy (Table 1, regression 1), on the one hand, and quality of government (Table 1, regression 2), on the other, with economic growth; second, to establish the same link accounting for both factors together (Table 1, regression 3); and, finally, to establish the link accounting for both main components with their interaction (Table 1, regression 4).

The analysis provides evidence that EU-financed public investment has had a positive and statistically significant link with regional growth, independently of the quality of local and regional government (Table 1, regressions 1, 3 and 4). The coefficient for the average expenditure per head per region in Cohesion Funds is always positive and significant, whereas that referring to the quality of government remains statistically insignificant (with the exception of regression 3), despite having a positive sign. The interaction between cohesion investments by the EU and the quality of government is also insignificant (Table 1, regression 4), pointing to the possibility that the investment efforts by the EU may work regardless of the quality of the government of the region where the expenditure takes place.

The relationship between the control variables and regional economic growth is generally as expected. The presence of low-skilled workers – proxied by the percentage of the adult population with low levels of educational attainment – influences growth negatively and infrastructure endowment has a positive impact. The

Table 1. Impact of public investment and quality of government on regional growth

Dependent variable GDP pc growth	(1) Two-way FE	(2) Two-way FE	(3) Two-way FE	(4) Two-way FE	(5) GMM-sys 4–7 lags	(6) GMM-sys 4–5 lags
ln GDPpc	0.00119 (0.00848)	0.00693 (0.00976)	0.000756 (0.00878)	0.000780 (0.00877)	−0.0332*** (0.00892)	−0.0328*** (0.00931)
Cohesion expenditure pc	3.16e−05** (1.15e−05)		3.05e−05** (1.20e−05)	3.10e−05** (1.24e−05)	4.44e−05** (1.84e−05)	5.25e−05*** (2.03e−05)
Quality of government		0.00384 (0.00277)	0.00380* (0.00217)	0.00392 (0.00243)	0.00137 (0.00510)	0.00178 (0.00513)
CohesionExp × QualityGov				−9.94e−07 (1.04e−05)	1.07e−05 (1.85e−05)	1.29e−05 (2.11e−05)
Primary education	−0.0847* (0.0411)	−0.0670** (0.0281)	−0.0804** (0.0379)	−0.0807** (0.0373)	−0.0325** (0.0162)	−0.0345** (0.0172)
University education	−0.0125 (0.0503)	−0.0201 (0.0453)	−0.00525 (0.0487)	−0.00543 (0.0483)		
ln Transport density	0.00275** (0.00124)	0.00238** (0.00110)	0.00253** (0.00116)	0.00253** (0.00115)		
Employment rate	0.000610 (0.000751)	−0.00142 (0.00156)	0.000752 (0.000697)	0.000746 (0.000758)	0.000550* (0.000298)	0.000495* (0.000297)
ln Employment density	−0.0544 (0.0446)	0.0314 (0.0841)	−0.0702 (0.0405)	−0.0699 (0.0435)	0.00354 (0.00241)	0.00485** (0.00234)
ln Population density	0.0566 (0.0448)	−0.0309 (0.0848)	0.0726* (0.0407)	0.0723 (0.0438)	−0.0567** (0.0254)	−0.0550* (0.0284)
ln National growth						
Constant	−0.0303 (0.115)	0.109 (0.139)	−0.0559 (0.109)	−0.0553 (0.113)	0.345*** (0.0853)	0.338*** (0.0888)
Time controls	Yes	Yes	Yes	Yes	Yes	Yes
Country controls	Yes	Yes	Yes	Yes		
Number of observations	972	1017	972	972	1125	1125
R^2	0.261	0.238	0.264	0.264		
Number of countries	18	18	18	18	18	18
p-value of Hansen test					0.353	0.006
Number of instruments					173	124

Notes: No threshold. Robust standard errors are given in parentheses.

***$p < 0.01$; **$p < 0.05$; *$p < 0.1$.

stock of the total population with a university education, employment rates and employment density are insignificant across all specifications of the model. Population density is only positive and significant in regression 3.

One potential caveat is that the results presented in Table 1 (regressions 1–4) may be affected by endogeneity. Endogeneity worries fundamentally concern the Structural Funds expenditure variable. To assess whether this is a factor in the results, the model is re-estimated using a dynamic panel analysis (generalized method of moments – GMM) (Table 1, regressions 5 and 6). GMM-system is used as it accounts better than GMM-difference for the high degree of persistence in the variables (ROODMAN, 2009a).[6] The number of time lags used as instruments is four to seven (Table 1, regression 5) and four to five (Table 1, regression 6).

The estimation of the dynamic panel analysis broadly confirms the results of the two-way fixed effect panel regression model. Expenditure in Structural Funds remains significant and positive and seems to be a more important factor determining regional economic growth than quality of government, which displays an insignificant coefficient. The interaction between both variables remains insignificant (Table 1, regressions 5 and 6).

Analysis including different cohesion expenditure thresholds

However, the results presented in Table 1 may be somewhat misleading, as the sample includes all regions in the EU and is not particularly focused on those regions that receive the bulk of the cohesion effort. Hence, the presence of a large number of regions that are relatively well-off, where EU intervention in order to achieve greater cohesion is very limited, and where the overwhelming majority of public expenditure is bound to come from local, regional and national sources, rather than from the EU, may bias the results. EU Structural Fund and cohesion intervention in most of these regions would be insufficient to make any real difference in economic performance.

As can be seen in Fig. 2, EU-financed public investment varies widely across regions and this variation is decidedly non-linear. Over the whole period of analysis, the average expenditure by the EU on Structural and Cohesion Funds was €83.23 per head per region.[7] However, the great majority of European regions are located on the left-hand side of the distribution – and well below the mean – and receive funds that normally range between €0 and €60 per inhabitant per year. By contrast, a much smaller number of regions (represented by the long tail to the right of the expenditure axis) are allocated the bulk of cohesion resources, following the principle of concentration of funds in those regions with the greatest need. These regions include the so-called 'less developed' regions – formerly known as 'Objective 1' regions – which, by definition, are considerably poorer and, in general, also tend to have greater government quality problems. These regions are, moreover, concentrated in specific parts of Europe – mainly in Central and Eastern and Southern Europe – which, as seen in Fig. 1, are precisely those with the lowest levels of quality of government. Consequently, there is some reason to believe that there may be a good deal of co-variation in the expenditure and government quality variables – that is, highly supported regions tend to be more prevalent in countries where the quality of government scores are lower.

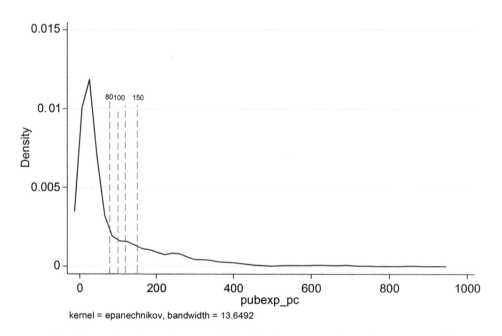

Fig. 2. Distribution of European Union funds per capita (kernel density estimate)

Given the very unequal distribution of Cohesion Funds across the regions of the EU, it is assumed that quality of government may only make a real difference for regional economic growth in those regions that received a considerable amount of funding per head per year. Therefore, the sample is divided following a series of thresholds according to the amount of money received by each region in any given year. These thresholds are established at €80, €100, €120 and €150 of regional expenditure per capita,[8] allowing one to discriminate between the effects of public investment and quality of government on regional performance in regions benefiting from different levels of public intervention. The threshold of a minimum of €100 of Structural and Cohesion Fund expenditure per capita is taken as the benchmark model for those regions receiving the bulk of the funds (Table 2), and whether the coefficients of Structural Fund expenditure and government quality, as well as their interaction, change as the level of transfers per head increases is examined (Table 3).

The results for those regions receiving a substantial amount of Structural and Cohesion Fund expenditure per capita (Table 2) differ considerably from those for the whole sample (Table 1). Although the coefficients for the control variables are, with exception of the initial GDP per capita of the region and some of the coefficients for employment and population density, virtually unchanged, the results for cohesion expenditure per capita, quality of government and their interaction tell a very different story:

- In regions where, given the level of expenditure, Structural and Cohesion Fund investments may make a real difference, the quality of government

trumps cohesion expenditure as the main variable of interest determining economic growth.

- For those regions receiving the bulk of the European cohesion effort (Table 2, regressions 2–4), the quality of the local or the regional government is an essential factor influencing economic performance.

- When cohesion expenditure, government quality and their interaction are considered together (Table 2, regression 4), the coefficients of all three variables are significant, although quality of government remains by far the most significant of the three. Cohesion expenditure has a small, positive and significant coefficient, whereas the interaction between cohesion expenditure and quality of government points in the direction of a very marginal reduction of the effect of quality of government as cohesion expenditure increases.

- As the coefficient for the interaction is negative, the positive effect of quality of government becomes smaller as the level of expenditure increases (or vice versa, expenditure has a positive effect, but that effect becomes smaller as quality of government increases). According to the coefficients of Table 2 (regression 4), this would happen when cohesion expenditure in a year exceeds €550 per capita per year, close to seven times the average expenditure per region.

In order to check whether these results are robust, Table 3 considers different expenditure thresholds for Structural and Cohesion Funds (no threshold, €80, €100, €120 and €150 per capita per annum in any given region). It is worth noting that as the threshold of structural and cohesion investments per capita per annum increases, the number of observations and the number

Table 2. Impact of public investment and quality of government on regional growth

Dependent variable GDP pc growth	(1) Two-way FE	(2) Two-way FE	(3) Two-way FE	(4) Two-way FE
ln GDPpc	−0.0494** (0.0207)	−0.0116 (0.0157)	−0.0603** (0.0202)	−0.0621** (0.0197)
Cohesion expenditure pc	2.12e−05 (1.69e−05)		1.41e−06 (1.56e−05)	1.72e−05** (6.58e−06)
Quality of government		0.0136** (0.00514)	0.0125*** (0.00336)	0.0225*** (0.00633)
CohesionExp × QualityGov				−4.39e−05** (1.50e−05)
Primary education	−0.328*** (0.0898)	−0.105* (0.0538)	−0.281*** (0.0607)	−0.286*** (0.0615)
University education	−0.189 (0.114)	0.0587 (0.0593)	−0.121 (0.0769)	−0.129 (0.0777)
ln Transport density	0.0124** (0.00474)	0.00398 (0.00365)	0.0111** (0.00401)	0.0119** (0.00379)
Employment rate	0.000967 (0.00138)	0.000570 (0.00155)	0.000933 (0.00117)	0.000987 (0.00124)
ln Employment density	−0.104 (0.0805)	−0.114 (0.0776)	−0.120* (0.0566)	−0.135** (0.0533)
ln Population density	0.111 (0.0825)	0.120 (0.0776)	0.128* (0.0574)	0.144** (0.0538)
Constant	0.546** (0.235)	0.00242 (0.200)	0.596** (0.215)	0.595** (0.224)
Time controls	Yes	Yes	Yes	Yes
Country controls	Yes	Yes	Yes	Yes
Number of observations	218	263	218	218
R^2	0.336	0.379	0.355	0.362
Number of countries	10	14	10	10

Notes: Threshold €100. Robust standard errors are given in parentheses.
   ***$p < 0.01$; **$p < 0.05$; *$p < 0.1$.

Table 3. Impact of public investment and quality of government on regional growth

Dependent variable GDP pc growth	(1) No threshold	(2) > €80	(3) > €100	(4) > €120	(5) > €150
ln GDPpc	0.000780 (0.00877)	−0.0472** (0.0182)	−0.0621** (0.0197)	−0.0816*** (0.0240)	−0.0720*** (0.0221)
Cohesion expenditure pc	3.10e−05** (1.24e−05)	1.71e−05*** (5.21e−06)	1.72e−05*** (6.58e−06)	2.54e−05* (1.17e−05)	1.48e−05 (1.65e−05)
Quality of government	0.00392 (0.00243)	0.0186** (0.00611)	0.0225*** (0.00633)	0.0258*** (0.00627)	0.0315*** (0.00721)
CohesionExp × QualityGov	−9.94e−07 (1.04e−05)	−4.07e−05*** (1.51e−05)	−4.39e−05*** (1.50e−05)	−5.49e−05*** (2.01e−05)	−6.83e−05*** (1.94e−05)
Primary education	−0.0807** (0.0373)	−0.273*** (0.0504)	−0.286*** (0.0615)	−0.311*** (0.0491)	−0.280*** (0.0502)
University education	−0.00543 (0.0483)	−0.127 (0.0729)	−0.129 (0.0777)	−0.156** (0.0660)	−0.0967 (0.0674)
ln Transport density	0.00253** (0.00115)	0.00998** (0.00363)	0.0119*** (0.00379)	0.0134*** (0.00397)	0.0144*** (0.00332)
Employment rate	0.000746 (0.000758)	0.000532 (0.00149)	0.000987 (0.00124)	0.000774 (0.00101)	−0.000369 (0.00119)
ln Employment density	−0.0699 (0.0435)	−0.112 (0.0677)	−0.135** (0.0533)	−0.113* (0.0517)	−0.0646 (0.0669)
ln Population density	0.0723 (0.0438)	0.119 (0.0688)	0.144** (0.0538)	0.122** (0.0522)	0.0715 (0.0682)
Constant	−0.0553 (0.113)	0.496** (0.223)	0.595** (0.224)	0.842** (0.304)	0.844** (0.319)
Time controls	Yes	Yes	Yes	Yes	Yes
Country controls	Yes	Yes	Yes	Yes	Yes
Number of observations	972	252	218	193	165
R^2	0.264	0.342	0.362	0.350	0.346
Number of countries	18	11	10	10	10

Notes: Different thresholds (two-way fixed effects). Robust standard errors are given in parentheses.
***$p < 0.01$; **$p < 0.05$; *$p < 0.1$.

of countries affected declines rapidly. Whereas the whole sample included a total of 972 observations and 18 countries for which a full set of variables are available, when the €80 threshold is applied only 252 observations in 11 countries remain. By the time the €150 threshold is reached, the sample is limited to 165 observations in ten countries.

The use of the different thresholds corroborates the results of the regressions for the more than €100 threshold reported in Table 2:

- Above an expenditure threshold of €80 per head per annum, the coefficient for the cohesion expenditure variable progressively loses significance as the threshold increases.
- The coefficient for cohesion expenditure is last significant at the €120 threshold. For those regions receiving more than €120 per person, additional investments in Structural and Cohesion Funds become totally dissociated from greater economic growth (Table 3, regression 5). These results stand beyond the €150 threshold presented in Table 3.

Hence, the positive and significant association between cohesion expenditure per capita and economic growth reported in Table 1 (and also in Table 3, regression 1) gradually evaporates, leading to a much stronger and significant connection between government quality and regional economic performance. Indeed, at relatively high levels of cohesion expenditure per capita, the quality of local or regional government always dominates the level of expenditure per head as the key predictor of regional economic growth. Beyond €80 of expenditure in regional development per capita per annum, the coefficient for quality of government is always highly positive and significant. And this relationship is reinforced as the threshold of expenditure is increased (Table 3, regressions 2–5). The association between quality of government and regional economic performance is considerably stronger when the threshold of expenditure is above €120 per head per annum in any given region than when the threshold is limited to €80. It is strongest for those regions receiving more than €150 per inhabitant per year and keeps on increasing beyond this threshold.

The introduction of the interaction between public investment and quality of government (Table 3) further reinforces the importance of the quality of government variable in determining regional economic performance. As seen in Table 2 and reproduced in all regressions for Table 3 – with the exception of when the no expenditure threshold is applied (regression 1) – the introduction of the interaction term reinforces the positive and significant coefficients associated to the quality of government variable.

However, the coefficient of the interaction term between cohesion investment and quality of government above the €80 per head investment threshold is

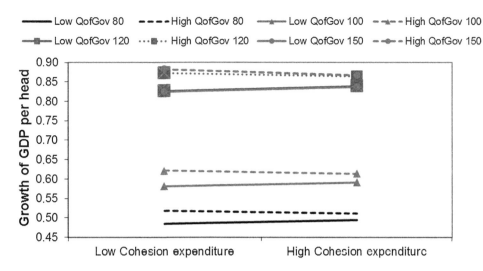

Fig. 3. Two-way interaction effect for quality of government and cohesion expenditure (unstandardized values)

always negative and significant (Table 3, regressions 2–5), at least until a €210 threshold. Nevertheless, 'the size and precise nature of this effect is not easy to divine from examination of the coefficients alone, and becomes even more so when one or more of the coefficients are negative' (DAWSON, 2014, p. 3), as is the case in the present analysis.

In order to overcome this problem and fine tune the interpretation of how the link between expenditure in cohesion and structural policies and regional economic performance is mediated by the quality of government of the different regions of the EU, Fig. 3 plots the two-way interaction effects for the unstandardized variables using the procedures of AIKEN and WEST (1991), DAWSON and RICHTER (2006), and DAWSON (2014).[9] This allows for an easy visual interpretation of the results,

> by calculating the predicted values of Y under different conditions (high and low values of the X, and high and low values of the Z) and showing the predicted relationship ('simple slopes') between the X and the Y add these different levels of Z.
>
> (DAWSON, 2014, p. 3)

In the case of Fig. 3, X represents cohesion expenditure in any given region in the EU, Y GDP growth per head, and Z quality of government.

The widespread method of setting test values that are 1 SD (standard deviation) above and below the mean is used (AIKEN and WEST, 1991; DAWSON and RICHTER, 2006). A total of 87.3% of the Structural and Cohesion Fund expenditure observations in the sample are included within this range. Also taken into account is the quality of government at the different thresholds of cohesion expenditure considered in the analysis.

Several conclusions can be extracted from Fig. 3. First of all, it is evident that the returns of European investment in regional cohesion increase as the threshold of investment per capita per annum increases. The

returns are higher at a €100 threshold than at an €80 threshold. In turn, regions that receive more than €120 of Structural and Cohesion Fund expenditure per annum do better in growth terms than those getting a minimum of €100. However, the benefits of additional Cohesion Funds stop − in agreement with the results of the regressions in Table 3 − at €120 as there is virtually no difference between the returns experienced by regions receiving more than €120 and those receiving more than €150 (note that the two lines for low quality of government for expenditure thresholds of €120 and €150 overlap). In this respect, the results confirm that poor quality of government may be at the root of what BECKER *et al.* (2012) describe as declining returns of regional development funds in Europe as the transfer intensity increases. These authors, using a radically different method, reach the conclusion that in a considerable number of European regions the transfer intensity of European regional funds exceeds what can be considered the efficiency maximizing level. They even highlight that, in some cases, a reduction of transfers would not affect regional economic performance (BECKER *et al.*, 2012).

Second, in all categories considered and for levels of expenditure ranging between 1 SD above and below the mean, regions with a higher quality of government perform significantly better at the same level of cohesion expenditure than those with a lower quality of government.

Third, although in the observations in the sample considered in Fig. 3 increasing cohesion investment helps reduce the gap in the economic returns experienced by high-quality government and low-quality government regions, this reduction is marginal and does not suffice to overcome the quality of government gap which is the main explanation behind the difference in the returns from cohesion expenditure of regions benefiting from a similar level of European regional cohesion support.

Table 4. Additional impact on regional growth of increasing Structural Fund expenditure and quality of government by 1 SD (standard deviation) in low quality of government regions (results are shown as percentages)

	> €80	> €100	> €120	> €150
Increase in Structural Fund expenditure	1.93	1.68	1.59	1.50
Increase in quality of government	6.94	6.93	5.63	6.89

To give a more precise idea of the dimension by which differences in quality of government trump the potential effects of additional cohesion investment on regional growth for these regions, some calculations based on Fig. 3 were performed.[10] The results indicate that above a certain threshold of cohesion expenditure per capita, investing more in cohesion expenditure has a positive but very limited returns on the growth of GDP per head. At levels of more than €80 in cohesion expenditure per head per annum, increasing the amount of Cohesion Funds by 1 SD in a region with a low quality of government yields an added growth of a mere 1.9% above what would have been achieved had that additional investment not taken place. The positive influence of any further cohesion investment declines as the investment threshold rises: the additional impact on growth is of 1.7% above €100 of expenditure; 1.6% above €120; and 1.5% above €150 (Table 4). By contrast, increasing the quality of government by that same standard deviation would lead to significantly higher increases in growth rates. The additional impact of improving the quality of government hovers just below 7% across all categories, with the exception of the €120 threshold (5.6%) (Table 4). The positive impact of improvements in quality of government is somewhat lower for those regions that benefit from levels of support which are considerably higher than the pre-established threshold. Yet, even in those cases, improving the quality of government would yield greater returns than continuing to increase cohesion expenditure. The additional effect of improving quality of government by 1 SD in these cases ranges between a minimum of 2.9% additional growth (above €120) and a maximum of 3.9% (above €100).

What would happen if, instead of limiting the analysis to the 87.3% of cases comprised in the range between 1 SD above and below the mean, the whole sample were taken into account? As the sign of the interaction term between cohesion investment and quality of government is always negative and significant above the €80 threshold (until the €210 threshold), there is a point where – according to the €100 threshold regression used as the benchmark model (Table 2, regression 4 or Table 3, regression 3) – the growth effect linked to pouring additional funds would offset a potentially negative growth effect of any improvements in quality

of government. As mentioned above, in our benchmark model this would happen only when cohesion expenditure exceeds €550 per capita per year. Beyond this threshold, any additional Structural Fund and Cohesion expenditure would counterbalance any potential drawbacks of having a bad government. However, this applies to a very small minority of cases – only 26 cases out of a total of 1954 years of expenditure considered in the sample (1.33% of all cases) – and fundamentally to two outlier regions: the ultra-peripheral Portuguese regions of the Azores and Madeira. In Madeira, EU expenditure exceeded the €550 threshold in 11 of the 12 years considered. In the Azores, this happened in eight years.[11] These two regions are exceptional in many ways. First, because of their island condition and ultra-peripheral status, they have been the recipients of considerably more funds than most other peripheral regions in the EU. Second, they are also the only two regions with a substantial degree of autonomy in a highly centralized country. Third, according to the data used in the analysis, they have a quality of government that is both above the national average for Portugal and that for the whole of the EU. The quality of the government is therefore much better than in other regions of Southern and Eastern Europe which have been traditionally the main recipients of Cohesion Funds. Given the special characteristics of these two regions, it may be plausible that additional funds are a better option than seeking to improve the quality of government.

Yet even in these two cases this conclusion must be treated with caution as these calculations concern only the benchmark regression. As the thresholds increase, the coefficients for cohesion expenditure decline and eventually become irrelevant beyond a €120 cohesion expenditure per capita per annum threshold, making either the coefficient of the interaction irrelevant or, at least, pushing the monetary threshold for the negative interaction effect to kick in at even higher levels, thus virtually excluding all EU regions from this possibility.

In any case, it would take an extraordinary increase in the EU budget to make a policy based on pure expenditure more efficient than one based on improvements in the quality of government of the most peripheral regions as one of its pillars. If all 71 of the regions identified as 'less developed' for the 2014–20 programming period were to be funded at this level, it would imply an expenditure of €492.8 billion. This represents multiplying the current allocation – €182.2 billion for 2014–20 – for cohesion and regional development in these regions by 2.7. Improving government quality is a far more cost-efficient and politically palatable option.

Assessing endogeneity

In order to assess whether the perception of the link between Structural Fund expenditure, quality of government and regional growth at different thresholds of

Table 5. Impact of public investment and quality of government on regional growth

Dependent variable GDP pc growth	> €80 GMM-sys	> €100 GMM-sys	> €120 GMM-sys	> €150 GMM-sys
Cohesion expenditure pc	3.14e–05** (1.54e–05)	3.82e–05* (2.21e–05)	4.06e–05* (2.27e–05)	3.47e–05* (1.94e–05)
Quality of government	0.0151*** (0.00477)	0.0147*** (0.00463)	0.0142*** (0.00471)	0.0114** (0.00451)
CohesionExp × QualityGov	−5.38e–05** (2.44e–05)	−5.23e–05** (2.25e–05)	−5.11e–05** (2.25e–05)	−3.87e–05** (1.95e–05)
ln National Growth	0.352** (0.150)	0.430** (0.171)	0.273 (0.219)	0.309 (0.229)
Constant	0.0299*** (0.00876)	0.0240** (0.0112)	0.0276* (0.0152)	0.0274* (0.0155)
Time controls	Yes	Yes	Yes	Yes
Number of observations	463	410	361	307
Number of countries	11	10	10	10
p-value of AR(4) test	0.189	0.145	0.198	0.231
p-value of Hansen test	0.372	0.427	0.602	0.769
Number of instruments	55	55	55	55

Notes. Different thresholds (GMM-sys). Robust standard errors are given in parentheses.

 ***$p < 0.01$; **$p < 0.05$; *$p < 0.1$.

Cohesion Fund expenditure is affected by endogeneity problems, this paper resorts once more to a dynamic panel data analysis (GMM-sys). As seen in Table 3, the introduction of expenditure thresholds leads to a substantial reduction in the number of observations, making it necessary to limit the number of regressors to the three key variables of the model.[12] The results of the GMM-sys analysis are presented in Table 5.

The results indicate that the direction of causality runs from cohesion expenditure and quality of government to regional economic growth, rather than vice versa. They are also broadly in line with the FE estimations presented in Table 3. Above €80 of expenditure per capita per annum in cohesion, quality of government is a more important factor for economic growth than additional cohesion expenditure. The interaction between both factors has a negative coefficient, but the coefficients show that the increase in growth associated with dedicating resources to cohesion in a region with a low quality of government vis-à-vis a region with a better government quality is marginal and incapable of overcoming the differences in economic growth impact of the variation in government quality (Table 5).

CONCLUSIONS

This article has analysed the extent to which regional growth in Europe is affected by European regional development and cohesion investment, on the one hand, and by the quality of the government of the regions receiving the funds, on the other. The capital role played by government quality on economic growth and on the returns of public policy has been strongly posited by the literature dealing with the economic implications of institutions. It has also been indirectly presumed by the EU in its structural and cohesion policy by the mere fact of having discussed a cap on the amount of resources that could be channelled

to specific regions on the basis of their capacity to absorb and adequately use funds. However, to date there has been no empirical demonstration that quality of government affects regional economic growth and may mediate the returns of European cohesion investment.

Using the quality of government index of the Quality of Government Institute at the University of Gothenburg (CHARRON *et al.*, 2010) and complementing it with World Bank Global Governance Indicators, the results of the panel data analysis for the period between 1996 and 2007 demonstrate that although at first sight quality of government does not appear to affect the economic performance of the regions in Europe, its effect kicks in above a certain threshold of expenditure. When a region receives a level of investment in cohesion and regional development which can be considered more than testimonial, the quality of the local government becomes a vital factor in determining the extent to which a region grows. This is clearly evident for regions where Structural and Cohesion Funds represent more than €80 per head per year. In these regions the importance of quality of government, both as a factor for economic growth on its own and as a mediator for an efficient use of structural Cohesion Funds, increases as the expenditure threshold rises. Beyond levels of cohesion expenditure that exceed €120 per person and per year the most efficient way to achieve greater economic and social cohesion is by improving the quality of government of any given region, except perhaps in a few minority of outlier regions, particularly the Azores and Madeira, where additional funding and cohesion expenditure would counterbalance any potential drawbacks linked to local government quality.

Hence, it can be said that both EU investments targeting regions and quality of government make a difference for regional economic growth, but above a certain threshold of expenditure (which the analysis establishes at levels of cohesion expenditure of around €120 per person per annum), the quality of government becomes – for the large majority of regions – the basic factor determining why a region grows. In many of the regions receiving the bulk of Structural Funds, greater levels of cohesion expenditure would, in the best-case scenario, only lead to a marginal improvement in economic growth, unless the quality of the government is significantly improved.

Pouring more funds into the region will only do the trick when the amount of funds devoted to regional development significantly multiplies current levels of expenditure.

Overall, the findings contribute to the rapidly expanding literature on how institutions shape economic performance and the returns of economic policy at a regional level in Europe (RODRÍGUEZ-POSE, 2013). As in the case of BEUGELSDIJK and VAN SCHAIK (2005a, 2005b) and TABELLINI (2010), it demonstrates how regional institutions in Europe are key shapers of economic performance. In particular, in has shown that, in the case of European cohesion investment, there are no shortcuts: the returns to investment do not come necessarily from the degree of investment itself, but from the quality of government of the region receiving the support and from how this government quality affects the implementation of policies. Thus, the need to address quality of government bottlenecks in order to maximize the returns of cohesion investment becomes all too evident the greater the level of investment. In these regions, simply spending greater amount of funds in areas with inefficient and/or corrupt governments may lead – without considerable improvements in government quality – to waste.

The findings give support to the broad thrust of recent EU Cohesion Policy changes aimed at shifting to 'softer' forms of infrastructure, while simultaneously setting up systems and incentives (linked to results indicators, conditionalities and greater monitoring) targeting the improvement of local governance and institutions. These are concerns that hardly featured in a past policy that was mainly devoted to improving the infrastructure endowment, human capital and innovation capacity of the regions of Europe, but which are central to the 2014 reform. In addition there are important complementarities amongst these policy domains at the local and regional levels (OECD, 2011) that can be realized by improving the quality of local and regional governments. They also raise warning signs for development policies elsewhere around the world. If development policies are to be successful, they should build in an institutional component, including promoting transparency and accountability and dealing with corruption as ways to improve government quality, as an essential part of the strategic planning process. Otherwise the implementation of one-size-fits-all policies may not yield the expected results. Taking into account place-based institutional conditions and learning how institutional quality can be consistently improved, hence

the need to become basic elements of any development strategy (BARCA et al., 2012).

Acknowledgements – The authors would like to acknowledge the conscientious work of the Editors of *Regional Studies* and of the numerous referees involved in the multiple revisions of the manuscript. They are also indebted to Philip McCann for his comments made to the very first version of the paper, to Marco Di Cataldo for help and suggestions regarding the econometric analysis, to Enrique Garcilazo's colleagues at the Organisation for Economic Co-operation and Development (OECD) for their many recommendations, and to the participants in seminars and workshops in Newcastle, Paris (twice), London, Warsaw, Padua and Brussels for numerous ideas that have helped shape this paper.

Funding – This paper would not have been possible without the financial support of the European Research Council under the European Union's Seventh Framework Programme (FP7/2007-2013)/ERC [grant agreement number 269868].

Disclosure statement – No potential conflict of interest was reported by the authors.

APPENDIX A

Table A1. *Descriptive statistics for key independent variables*

Variable	Number of observations	Mean	Standard deviation (SD)	Minimum	Maximum
ln GDP pc	2014	9.902274	0.4368569	8.49093	11.2533
Quality of government	2028	0.2945607	0.8377364	−2.448	1.629
Cohesion expenditure pc	1954	83.23541	119.0134	0	932

Table A2. *Correlations for key independent variables*

	ln GDPpc	Quality of government	Cohesion expenditure pc
ln GDP pc	1		
Quality of government	0.4433	1	
Cohesion expenditure pc	−0.2373	−0.0805	1

NOTES

1. From an institutional perspective and following the Copenhagen criteria for EU membership, the *Acquis Communautaire* implies democracy, the rule of law, a respect for human rights and the protection of minorities, and a functioning market economy.

2. Although BEUGELSDIJK and EIJFFINGER (2005) report that country-level corruption does not affect the economic returns that could be derived from EU Structural Funds.

3. There are five countries – Belgium, Germany, Greece, the Netherlands and the UK – where TL2 corresponds to NUTS-1 regions. In the rest of European countries, TL2 corresponds to NUTS-2.

4. The 27 states of the EU are covered when the World Bank Global Governance Indicators are included in the main index.

5. Recently the Quality of Government Institute has conducted the same exercise for 2013.

6. Given that the high number of years and variables included in the analysis generates a risk of instrument proliferation (ROODMAN, 2009b), the number of variables are reduced with respect to the original specification. The variables excluded are those with the greatest potential problems of multicollinearity: transport density, employment density and university education. In order to reduce further the number of instruments, only some time lags are considered as a way to identify endogenous variables. The strong persistence of some of the variables makes it advisable to avoid the second- and third-order lags and to start with the fourth-order lags. In addition, the Arellano–Bond serial correlation test (AR test) on residuals rejects the H_0 of no autocorrelation at the 5% level, but does not reject the null hypothesis from the fourth- to higher order lags. Also included is the national growth rate of ln GDP per capita as a country control.

7. The descriptive statistics and correlations for the independent variables of interest are presented in Appendix A, Tables A1 and A2.

8. Additional regressions using different thresholds (€130, €140, €170, €190, €210 and €230) were also estimated. They are not reported because of lack of space, but can be provided by the authors upon request.

9. The interpretation of the interactions in Fig. 3 is done using the simple slope tests developed by AIKEN and WEST (1991), DAWSON (2014), and DAWSON and RICHTER (2006) to plot interaction effects. As DAWSON (2014) indicates, these tests assess whether that relationship between X and Y is significant at a particular value of Z. Dawson's slope test implies 'substituting the value of Z into the regression equation, i.e., the slope is $b1 + b3\ Z$, and the standard error of this slope is calculated by $SE_s = \sqrt{s_{11} + Z^2 s_{33} + 2Z s_{13}}$, where $s11$ and $s33$ are the variances of the coefficients $b1$ and $b3$, respectively, and $s13$ is the covariance of the two coefficients' (pp. 3–4). 'The significance of a simple slope is then tested by comparing the ratio of the slope to its standard error, i.e., $(b_1 + b_3 Z)/\sqrt{s_{11} + Z^2 s_{33} + 2Z s_{13}}$ with a t-distribution with $n - k - 1$ degrees of freedom, where k is the number of predictors in the model (which is three if no control variables are included)' (p. 4). For various Excel worksheets with which to interpret these interaction effects, see www.jeremydawson.co.uk/slopes.htm/.

10. The numbers in Table 4 are derived from the Excel sheet proposed by Dawson for the assessment of interaction effects and used for the elaboration of Fig. 3 (see www.jeremydawson.co.uk/slopes.htm). They represent the additional growth in GDP per head in percentages of increasing quality of government and cohesion expenditure by 1 SD respectively in a low quality of government region at the different thresholds of cohesion expenditure considered.

11. The remaining seven cases were limited to a single year of exceptional expenditure – normally when a programming period was being closed and the regions faced the dilemma of spending the funds or returning them to Brussels – in the Greek regions of Voreia Ellada, Kentriki Ellada, Crete and the Aegean Islands; the Portuguese regions of Alentejo and Algarve; and Extremadura in Spain.

12. The number of time lags is also reduced to the fourth-order lag only as a way to keep instruments similar to the number of groups.

REFERENCES

ACEMOGLU D., JOHNSON S. and ROBINSON J. A. (2001) The colonial origins of comparative development: an empirical investigation, *American Economic Review* **91**, 1369–1401. doi:10.1257/aer.91.5.1369

AIKEN L. S. and WEST S. G. (1991) *Multiple Regression: Testing and Interpreting Interactions*. Sage, Newbury Park, CA.

AMIN A. (1999) An institutionalist perspective on regional economic development, *International Journal of Urban and Regional Research* **23**, 365–378. doi:10.1111/1468-2427.00201

AMIN A. and THRIFT N. (1994) *Globalization, Institutions and Regional Development in Europe*. Oxford University Press, Oxford.

BARCA F., McCANN P. and RODRÍGUEZ-POSE A. (2012) The case for regional development intervention: place-based versus place-neutral approaches, *Journal of Regional Science* **52**, 134–152. doi:10.1111/j.1467-9787.2011.00756.x

BECKER S. O., EGGER P. H. and VON EHRLICH M. (2012) Too much of a good thing? On the growth effects of the EU's regional policy, *European Economic Review* **56**, 648–668. doi:10.1016/j.euroecorev.2012.03.001

BEUGELSDIJK M. and EIJFFINGER S. C. W. (2005) The effectiveness of structural policy in the European union: an empirical analysis for the EU-15 in 1995–2001, *Journal of Common Market Studies* **43**, 37–51. doi:10.1111/j.0021-9886.2005.00545.x

BEUGELSDIJK S. and VAN SCHAIK T. (2005a) Social capital and growth in European regions: an empirical test, *European Journal of Political Economy* **21**, 301–324. doi:10.1016/j.ejpoleco.2004.07.004

BEUGELSDIJK S. and VAN SCHAIK T. (2005b) Differences in social capital between 54 Western European regions, *Regional Studies* **39**, 1053–1064. doi:10.1080/00343400500328040

BODO G. and VIESTI G. (1997) *La grande svolta. Il Mezzogiorno nell'Italia degli anni novanta*. Donzelli, Rome.

CHARRON N., DIJKSTRA L. and LAPUENTE V. (2014) Regional governance matters: quality of government within European union member states, *Regional Studies* **48**, 68–90. doi:10.1080/00343404.2013.770141

CHARRON N., LAPUENTE V. and ROTHSTEIN B. (Eds) (2010) *Measuring the Quality of Government and Subnational Variation*. Report for the European Commission Directorate-General Regional Policy, Directorate Regional Policy. Quality of

Government Institute, Department of Political Science, University of Gothenburg, Gothenburg (available at: http://ec.europa. eu/regional_policy/sources/docgener/studies/pdf/2010_government_1.pdf).

COLEMAN J. S. (1988) Social capital in the creation of human capital, *American Journal of Sociology* **94**(Suppl.), S95–S120. doi:10. 1086/228943

DAWSON J. F. (2014) Moderation in management research: what, why, when, and how, *Journal of Business Psychology* **29**, 1–19. doi:10.1007/s10869-013-9308-7

DAWSON J. F. and RICHTER A. W. (2006) Probing three-way interactions in moderated multiple regression: development and application of a slope difference test, *Journal of Applied Psychology* **91**, 917–926. doi:10.1037/0021-9010.91.4.917

DIAMANTI I., RAMELLA F. and TRIGILIA C. (1995) *Cultura e sviluppo*. L'associazionismo nel Mezzogiorno, Meridiana libri, Donzelli, Rome/Catanzaro.

EUROPEAN UNION (1997) *Agenda 2000: For a Stronger and Wider Union*. Office for Official Publications of the European Communities, Luxembourg.

EUROPEAN UNION (2010) *Investing in Europe's Future*. Fifth Report on Economic, Social and Territorial Cohesion. Publications Office of the European Union, Luxembourg.

GRANOVETTER M. (1973) The strength of weak ties, *American Journal of Sociology* **78**, 1360–1380. doi:10.1086/225469

GUASTI P. and DOBOVSEK B. (2011) Informal institutions and EU accession: corruption and clientelism in Central and Eastern Europe. Paper presented at the European Consortium for Political Research (ECPR) General Conference, Reykjavik, Iceland, August 2011.

HALL R. E. and JONES C. I. (1999) Why do some countries produce so much more output per worker than others?, *Quarterly Journal of Economics* **114**, 83–116. doi:10.1162/003355399555954

KAUFMANN D., KRAAY A. and MASTRUZZI M. (2009) *Governance Matters VIII: Aggregate and Individual Governance Indicators for 1996–2008*. World Bank Policy Research Working Paper No. 4978. World Bank, Washington, DC.

NORTH D. C. (1990) *Institutions, Institutional Change and Economic Performance*. Cambridge University Press, New York, NY.

ORGANISATION FOR ECONOMIC CO-OPERATION AND DEVELOPMENT (OECD) (2011) *Regional Outlook: Building Resilient Regions for Stronger Economies*. OECD Publ., Paris.

PUTNAM R. D. (1993) *Making Democracy Work: Civic Traditions in Modern Italy*. Princeton University Press, Princeton, NJ.

PUTNAM R. D. (2000) *Bowling Alone: The Collapse and Revival of American Community*. Simon & Schuster, New York, NY.

RODRÍGUEZ-POSE A. (2013) Do institutions matter for regional development?, *Regional Studies* **47**, 1034–1047. doi:10.1080/ 00343404.2012.748978

RODRÍGUEZ-POSE A. and MASLAUSKAITE K. (2012) Can policy make us happier? Individual characteristics, socioeconomic factors, and life satisfaction in Central and Eastern Europe, *Cambridge Journal of Regions, Economy and Society* **5**, 77–96. doi:10.1093/cjres/ rsr038

RODRÍGUEZ-POSE A. and STORPER M. (2006) Better rules or stronger communities? On the social foundations of institutional change and its economic effects, *Economic Geography* **82**, 1–25. doi:10.1111/j.1944-8287.2006.tb00286.x

RODRIK D., SUBRAMANIAN F. and TREBBI F. (2004) Institutions rule: the primacy of institutions over geography and integration in economic development, *Journal of Economic Growth* **9**, 131–165. doi:10.1023/B:JOEG.0000031425.72248.85

ROODMAN D. (2009a) How to do xtabond2: an introduction to difference and system GMM in Stata, *Stata Journal* **9**, 86–136. doi:10.2139/ssrn.982943

ROODMAN D. (2009b) A note on the theme of too many instruments, *Oxford Bulletin of Economics and Statistics* **71**, 135–158. doi:10. 1111/j.1468-0084.2008.00542.x

ROTHSTEIN B. and TEORELL J. (2008) What is quality of government?: a theory of impartial government institutions, *Governance – International Journal of Policy and Administration* **21**, 165–190. doi:10.1111/j.1468-0491.2008.00391.x

TÖNNIES F. (1887/1957) *Community and Society (Gemeinschaft und Gesellschaft)*, LOOMIS C. P. (Trans. and Ed.). Michigan State University Press, East Lansing, MI.

TABELLINI G. (2010) Culture and institutions: economic development in the regions of Europe, *Journal of the European Economic Association* **8**, 677–716. doi:10.1111/j.1542-4774.2010.tb00537.x

TRIGILIA C. (1992) *Sviluppo senza Autonomia. Effetti Perversi delle Politiche nel Mezzogiorno*. Il Mulino, Bologna.

VACHUDOVA M. A. (2009) Corruption and compliance in the EU's post-Communist members and candidates, *Journal of Common Market Studies* **47**, 43–62. doi:10.1111/j.1468-5965.2009.02013.x

WEBER M. (1921/1968) *Economy and Society*. G. ROTH and C. WITTICH (Trans.) Bedminster, New York, NY.

Smart Specialization, Regional Growth and Applications to European Union Cohesion Policy

PHILIP MCCANN* and RAQUEL ORTEGA-ARGILÉS†

*Department of Economic Geography, Faculty of Spatial Sciences, University of Groningen, Groningen, the Netherlands.
†Department of Global Economics and Management, Faculty of Economics and Business, University of Groningen, Groningen, the Netherlands.

McCANN P. and ORTEGA-ARGILÉS R. Smart specialization, regional growth and applications to European Union Cohesion policy, Regional Studies. The aim of this paper is to achieve two objectives. Firstly, it examines the smart specialization concept and explains the challenges involved in applying this originally sectoral concept to an explicitly spatial and regional setting. Secondly, it explains the ways in which this might be achieved so as to make the concept suitable as a building block of a reformed European Union cohesion policy.

McCANN P. and ORTEGA-ARGILÉS R. 灵活专业化、区域成长及其于欧盟凝聚政策的应用，区域研究。本文旨在达成下列两项目标。首先，本文检视灵活专业化的概念，并解释将此一源自于部门的概念应用于明确的空间及区域脉络所涉及的挑战。再者，本文解释达成上述目标的方式，使得此一概念更适合做为革新的欧盟凝聚政策之基石。

McCANN P. et ORTEGA-ARGILÉS R. La spécialisation intelligente, la croissance régionale et les applications à la politique de cohésion de l'Union européenne, Regional Studies. Les buts de ce présent article sont à deux temps. Primo, on examine la notion de spécialisation intelligente et explique les défis en jeu pour appliquer ce concept, qui à l'origine était sectoriel, à un milieu qui est explicitement spatial et régional. Secundo, on explique les manières pour y parvenir afin de rendre le concept propice comme pierre d'assise d'une politique de cohésion réformée de l'Union européenne.

McCANN P. und ORTEGA-ARGILÉS R. Intelligente Spezialisierung, regionales Wachstum und Anwendungen auf die Kohäsionspolitik der Europäischen Union, Regional Studies. Mit diesem Beitrag werden zwei Ziele verfolgt. Erstens wird das Konzept der intelligenten Spezialisierung untersucht, und es werden die Herausforderungen erläutert, die mit der Anwendung dieses ursprünglich sektoralen Konzepts auf eine ausdrücklich räumliche und regionale Umgebung verbunden sind. Zweitens wird erläutert, auf welche Weise sich diese Anwendung verwirklichen lässt, um das Konzept zu einem geeigneten Baustein für eine reformierte Kohäsionspolitik der Europäischen Union zu machen.

McCANN P. y ORTEGA-ARGILÉS R. Especialización inteligente, crecimiento regional y aplicaciones en la política de cohesión de la Unión Europea, Regional Studies. Este artículo tiene dos objetivos: primero, examinar el concepto de la especialización inteligente y explicar los retos que implica aplicar este concepto originalmente sectorial a un entorno explícitamente espacial y regional. Segundo, explicar cómo se puede conseguir esto para adaptar este concepto y convertirlo en un elemento esencial de una política de cohesión reformada de la Unión Europea.

INTRODUCTION

The *smart specialization* concept evolved as a response to the challenges associated with innovation policy design in the European context, and more recently it has become of widespread interest for a range of other Organisation for Economic Co-operation and Development (OECD) countries. The smart specialization concept contains many elements that were already evident in the innovation systems literature, the entrepreneurship and growth literatures, and in the various transactions costs literatures (OECD, 2012a). However, as the OECD (2012a) makes clear – as will be shown in this paper – the distinctive feature of the smart specialization concept is that it builds on these literatures in order to provide a clear policy-prioritization logic which is well suited to promoting innovation in a wide variety of regional settings, and in particular in the heterogeneous environment of European Union (EU) regions.

The smart specialization concept is now a major driving force behind both the new 'Innovation Union' flagship programme of the European Commission and also the EU cohesion policy reforms.[1] The aim of the Innovation Union initiative is to foster the dissemination and the realization of EU-wide economies of scale in high-technology and knowledge-intensive sectors, while the aim of the EU cohesion policy is to promote the development of many of Europe's weaker regions. These aims may at first appear to be somewhat incompatible, but as will be explained below, the way that the smart specialization concept is being applied in Europe potentially allows for both sets of objectives to be addressed. The reason is that from a regional policy perspective the smart specialization approach offers a range of advantages for the design of appropriate innovation policy-making, while allowing for the varied evolutionary nature of regional economies.

The aim of this paper therefore is to achieve two objectives. Firstly, it examines the smart specialization concept and explains the challenges involved in applying this originally sectoral concept to an explicitly spatial and regional setting. Secondly, it explains the ways in which this might be achieved so as to make the concept suitable as a building block of a reformed EU cohesion policy.

The paper is organized as follows. The next section explains the origins of the concept, and the third section outlines its early suggested links to regional issues. The fourth section examines the analytical challenges in linking the concept to economic geography and the fifth section provides a defence of the concept in a regional policy context. The sixth section discusses its future role in European cohesion policy.

THE ORIGINS OF THE SMART SPECIALIZATION CONCEPT

The smart specialization concept originated in the literature analysing the productivity gap between the United States and Europe, a gap which had become evident since 1995 (ORTEGA-ARGILÉS, 2012). This is a wide-ranging literature that attempts to identify the key factors which underpinned the increasing productivity gap (ORTEGA-ARGILÉS *et al.*, 2010, 2011). One common theme that emerged was the critical role which technological linkages and spillovers between sectors and regions, and in particular those related to information and communications technologies, play in explanations of this productivity gap. European policy attempts to close this gap were in part reflected in the European Research Area (ERA) programmes. However, a more fundamental rethinking of the productivity challenges facing Europe was undertaken by the 'Knowledge for Growth'[2] expert group (K4G) advising the former European Commissioner for Research, Janez Potočnik. This group of scholars suggested a conceptual framework for thinking about a possible policy-prioritization logic aimed at promoting EU growth, a framework which they labelled *smart specialization*.

The original smart specialization concept assumes that context matters for the potential technological evolution of innovation systems (*knowledge ecology*). In other words, the potential evolutionary pathways of an innovation system are explicitly argued to depend on the inherited structures and existing dynamics, ranging from widespread incremental change to even radical transformations of the system. As such, the smart specialization concept made explicit the implicit assumptions behind the ERA, which were that different countries and regions would tend to specialize in different knowledge-related sectors depending on their capabilities, and then proceeded to develop a policy-prioritization logic from this standpoint.

In order to develop a policy-prioritization logic aimed at promoting growth the aspatial smart specialization argument (FORAY *et al.*, 2009, 2011; DAVID *et al.*, 2009) employs the concept of a *domain*, and argues that entrepreneurs will search out the innovation opportunities within their domain. Finding ways to enhance these *entrepreneurial search* processes is essential as it is these that drive the identification and exploitation of the potential advantages of general purpose technologies (GPTs) to regenerate the targeted economic domain, often via the co-invention of new applications (DAVID *et al.*, 2009).

The smart specialization argument highlights the importance of the *relevant size* of the domain, whereby size relates not to aggregate gross domestic product (GDP), but to the range of the relevant sectors or activities in which new technological adaptations can most likely be applied and which can best benefit from knowledge spillovers (DAVID *et al.*, 2009). The original aspatial thinking in terms of potential impacts was driven primarily by the assumption of intra-sectoral spillovers, although inter-sectoral spillovers are not ruled out. Finally, as well as the promoting the entrepreneurial search processes and identifying the relevant sectors with the requisite size, the third issue to be considered is the issue of the *connectedness* of the domain. Domains that are highly connected with other domains will offer greater possibilities for learning than less connected domains, an idea which is central to all forms of network analysis.

The concept of smart specialization therefore emphasizes issues of economic potential, and the mechanisms whereby such potential is most likely be realized, and can be summarized as follows. Within a particular domain, the entrepreneurial search process leads to the identification of the *distribution* of potential opportunities for technological improvements to be embodied in a range of sectors, activities and occupations; the relevant size issue relates to the potential *magnitude* of the innovation outcomes associated with these opportunities; and the connectedness issue relates to the potential for *learning* about both these opportunities and magnitudes.[3]

A NON-SPATIAL REGIONAL INTERPRETATION OF THE SMART SPECIALIZATION LOGIC

The original smart specialization concept emerged from aspatial sectoral lines of thinking, but it increasingly shifted towards addressing regional growth issues as fundamental building blocks of national and European growth issues. In order to make the smart specialization logic applicable to a regional context, the proponents of the concept interpreted the idea of a domain in terms of that of a region, and applying the smart specialization logic in this manner, DAVID *et al.* (2009) argue that one of the features of many European regions is a weak correlation between the region's research and development (R&D) capabilities, its training specializations, and its industrial structure. A regional policy recommendation from the smart specialization proponents was therefore that rather than either pursuing 'one-size-fits-all' skills-training policies or alternatively always prioritizing high-technology sectors over others, governments should foster human capital formation for the new 'knowledge needs' of the region's *traditional* industries which are starting to adapt and apply these new technologies. As such, this argument emphasizes the critical role of knowledge diffusion processes between sectors, activities and occupations, and explicitly avoids automatically prioritizing high-technology sectors by taking a broader systems perspective.

The aim of such a policy would be, for example, to promote a local skills base that can facilitate widespread local incremental improvements across a range of the region's economic activities, as well as developing more specialized application technologies in the region. Exactly how this might be achieved is also sketched out by DAVID *et al.* (2009), who suggest that subsidizing a follower-region's access to the problem-solving expertise from researchers in a leader-region could be a fruitful way forward. Such a policy response could take the form, for example, of a network-development programme linking specialists in different regions. Obviously, inadequately designed schemes could inadvertently foster undesirable lock-in effects, becoming in effect sources of indirect subsidies to specific industries in particular regions. Therefore, in order to avoid the types of moral hazard, adverse selection and opportunism problems that could lead to such undesired outcomes, the policy needs to be carefully designed (DAVID *et al.*, 2009).

The novelty of the smart specialization concept was that although it emerged from the literature on the economics of knowledge and technology, it provided a policy-prioritization logic and a policy agenda which was rather different to most of the currently popular technology policy recommendations that tended to emphasize heavily the importance of high-technology sectors. As such, although smart specialization built on many previous literatures, it provided a major twist in terms of contemporary policy thinking, and much of this logic appeared to be highly relevant to the case of regions. However, translating the original smart specialization logic to regional policy is somewhat less straightforward than this example implies. The original sectoral concept can indeed be adapted and adopted in the regional policy context, but there are some major economic geography issues that need to be first considered in order for this to be the case.

ECONOMIC GEOGRAPHY AND THE SMART SPECIALIZATION LOGIC

The systems way of thinking underpinning the smart specialization approach explicitly acknowledges that for reasons of history and hysteresis regions vary not only in terms of their technological and industrial competences, but also in terms of their potential evolutionary trajectories. However, in order to apply the smart specialization logic to the regional context, it is necessary to translate each of the key elements of the aspatial sectoral argument – namely the entrepreneurial search process, the relevant size and the level of connectedness – into an explicitly spatial argument.

To do this one must first note that from the urban systems literature there are more or less ubiquitous features to the patterns of all spatial distributions, which are best captured by Zipf's Law (DURANTON, 2007). Core city-regions tend to be both fewer in number and also the largest and most densely populated regions. In addition, these core regions tend to be the most sectorally and structurally diversified regions. In contrast, smaller urban centres are not only much larger in number, but also they are more specialized sectorally. This combination of scale and diversity tends to imply that the larger core-region centres continuously exhibit greater knowledge-related advantages associated with the learning, sharing and matching of agents, actors and activities (DURANTON and PUGA, 2004). This is the geographical backdrop against which entrepreneurial processes operate, given that the success or otherwise of entrepreneurial processes depends on the level of credit availability, the number and variety of emerging business opportunities, the likelihood of success of these opportunities, and the scale of the markets to be reached.

Given each of these considerations, in terms of the vast literature covering the links between economic geography, entrepreneurship and innovation one can summarize broadly the overall consensus by pointing to the following five stylized facts, which although not ubiquitous are widely observed. Firstly, entrepreneurship and innovation tends to be higher in cities and more densely populated regions than in lower population density regions (ACS, 2002; CARLINO et al., 2007); secondly, entrepreneurship and innovation tends to be higher in more sectorally diversified regions (VAN OORT, 2004); thirdly, entrepreneurship and innovation tends to be higher in regions that are less dominated by a small number of large firms (CHINITZ, 1961; DURANTON and PUGA, 2001); fourthly, entrepreneurship and innovation tends to be higher in regions with large numbers of multinational companies which are internationally engaged (MCCANN and ACS, 2011); and fifthly, entrepreneurship and innovation tends to be higher in regions with large market potential. Conversely, entrepreneurship tends to be lower in regions with lower population densities, lower in regions that are more sectorally specialized, lower in regions dominated by a small number of large firms, lower in regions with firms of limited international engagement, and lower in regions with low market potential.

In addition, a sixth stylized fact is that in many parts of the world including in most OECD countries, the adoption, adaptation, and application of information and communications technologies (ICTs) across of wide range of industries appears to have *exacerbated* the differences between core and none-core regions over the last two decades (MCCANN, 2008; MCCANN and ACS, 2011). The reason for this is that ICTs are complements for knowledge-intensive activities requiring highly frequent face-to-face interactions (GASPAR and GLAESER, 1998; MCCANN, 2007), while at the same they are substitutes for routinized activities (IAMMARINO and MCCANN, 2013). The result is that a more uneven interregional and international spatial distribution of activities has emerged according to the degrees of knowledge intensity embodied in activities (MCCANN, 2008; MCCANN and ACS, 2011).

In other words, following the above terminology, the economic geography literature suggests that core regions offer greater potential rewards to the entrepreneurial search process in terms of the *distribution*, the *magnitude* and the capacity for *learning*.

Although in reality there are widespread exceptions to these stylized facts, and particularly so in the European context (STERNBERG, 2012; DIJKSTRA et al., 2013), these economic geography arguments prima facie suggest that the smart specialization logic ought naturally to favour core regions at the expense of weaker regions. This is because lagging or peripheral regions often exhibit weaknesses in entrepreneurship and innovation due to a combination of reasons, which can be variously sectoral, structural, transactional, technological, behavioural, related to resources and capabilities, related to risk and financial flows, related to externalities and issues of market failure, and also related to commercial and cultural perceptions. Typically, lagging or peripheral regions tend to face weaknesses in at least two of the three key elements of the smart specialization schema. In purely statistical or microeconomic programming terms, one would describe this problem as being one in which there are insufficient degrees of freedom, or alternatively too many variables and too few equations. In public policy terms, one might describe this problem as being one in which there are 'insufficient levers to pull' or 'too few buttons to press', given the regional challenges being faced, and more recent terminology which is currently popular in EU policy circles refers to the 'missing links' that need to be connected or to the 'bottlenecks' that need to be unblocked. However, whichever way one may wish to characterize the challenges facing these regions, it is exactly these types of areas, namely regions facing combinations of challenges, that regional policy in all parts of the world, and in the specific case of the EU, European cohesion policy, tends to target. A prima facie problem with translating the smart specialization concept of a *domain* to that of a real *region* is that everything that is known from economic geography indicates that the targets of regional policy are precisely those regional domains that tend to lack sufficient levels of at least two of the three key elements that the smart specialization schema requires in order to be an operational policy. In contrast, the regions that appear to be the most conducive and favourable for the operation of smart specialization-type processes are the buoyant core regions, and as such precisely the types of regions which EU cohesion policy does not prioritize. Moreover, the adoption and widespread adaptation of ICTs, which was one of the main catalysts for the original development of the smart specialization concept, if anything, has worsened the problem of regional disparities in many parts of the world by favouring the core regions.

All aspects of the smart specialization logic prima facie therefore appear to favour places that are not the primary target of regional policy. This apparent contradiction therefore raises the question as to whether employing a smart specialization logic in the service of regional policy is internally inconsistent and likely to undermine the very policy which it is intended to serve. If it is indeed a self-contradictory and internally inconsistent approach, then the outcomes of a combined smart specialization-regional policy approach are at best likely to be undesirable, and at worst doomed to failure. This is a real operational and implementation problem, and as such the first fundamental question regarding the application of smart specialization principles to regions is as follows:

How is the smart specialization concept to be applied as a regional policy tool when the smart specialization logic appears to favour other types of places?

If the regions that are most favourable and conducive for the operation of smart specialization processes are core regions, then this suggests that all the market signals associated with the various aspects of the smart specialization logic will favour the core regions. As price signals provide information about markets and welfare, then this fact raises doubts not only regarding the efficacy, but also the rationale for the policy, in terms of whether the wrong places are being targeted. If all aspects of the smart specialization approach naturally favour core regions rather than lagging regions, then the second question is:

Why should the smart specialization concept to be applied as a regional policy tool when the smart specialization logic favours other types of places?

In essence, the 'how' question is a positive question in that it relates primarily to the likely outcomes of the policy, given the operational and implementation challenges to be faced. In contrast, the 'why' question is essentially a normative question in that it relates to the justification for the intentions and objectives of the policy.

Taken together, these two questions raise doubts about the wisdom of promoting the smart specialization logic as a key ingredient of EU regional policy, because prima facie, the smart specialization logic appears to discriminate against lagging regions, and to contradict the design, if not the very rationale for regional policy itself. On the basis of the first how question and the second why question the third question is:

Do the answers to the first two 'how' and 'why' questions imply the death-knell of smart specialization as a regional policy tool for EU cohesion policy?

Rather surprisingly to some observers, in spite of the serious methodological and philosophical challenges posed by the first two questions, the answer to the third question is actually 'No', and that, yes, smart specialization can indeed be justified as a tool for cohesion policy.

THE JUSTIFICATION FOR USING SMART SPECIALIZATION IN REGIONAL POLICY

The justification for the defence of smart specialization as a regional policy tool actually comes in two parts. The first part of the defence addresses the second 'why'

question, while the second part of the defence addresses the first 'how' question. This section will therefore deal with the answer to the third question by dealing with the responses to the first two questions in reverse order.

Response to the why question: space-neutral versus place-based policies

In order to answer the second 'why' question it is necessary to understand that in actual fact the problems raised by the second 'why' question are not specific to the smart specialization logic at all, but relate to the more general arguments regarding the case for regional policy per se. The reasons for regional disparities are very complex, and the elements included in the smart specialization concept are only a small part of the overall story, although they are important elements. More broadly, however, the why question here relates to the much wider questions raised by the debate regarding the rationale and efficacy of space-neutral and sectoral approaches versus place-based approaches to policy (OECD, 2009a, 2009b, 2011a; BARCA *et al.*, 2012). This is a debate that is well beyond the remit or aims of this paper, but it is sufficient to say that it is this place-based approach which is the philosophical approach that underpins the current reforms of EU cohesion policy aimed at the new policy period beyond 2013.

As already shown, the smart specialization concept is essentially a way of thinking about local knowledge-enhancement and learning-enhancement systems. Therefore, the justification for using a local knowledge and learning enhancement concept such as smart specialization as part of regional policy is actually already contained in the overall justification for using a local and regional territorial place-based development policy approach to cohesion policy, rather than employing a space-neutral or purely sectoral approach. The reason is that the defence of the place-based approach already deals explicitly with these types of questions across a much broader range of issues than smart specialization alone. The place-based approach explicitly advocates employing appropriately designed local knowledge- and learning-enhancement tools in regional policy, and the smart specialization argument is one such tool. Whether it is the most appropriate regional policy tool in comparison with other alternative concepts or tools is discussed in the next section.

The important point here, however, is that the first part of the defence case for using smart specialization as part of EU cohesion policy is basically the same as that much broader defence of employing (at least in part) a place-based approach to regional development policy over a purely space neutral approach.

Response to the how question: embeddedness, relatedness and connectivity

Because regions differ so much in terms of their innovation characteristics (IAMMARINO and MCCANN,

2006), the answer to the *how* question will depend very much on the specific regional context, exactly as the place-based approach postulates. However, if one focuses on the innovation and smart growth agenda of the Europe2020 strategy, one can sketch out here the broad outlines of a general response to the first *how* question. In order to do this the OECD (2011b) typology of different types of innovation regions is followed, a typology that reflects the dominant features of the relationship between innovation and geography, and which closely mirrors the TÖDTLING and TRIPPL (2005) regional innovation classification scheme. In terms of understanding regional innovation systems, the OECD typology groups regions into three broad types, namely: knowledge regions, industrial production zones and non-science and technology (S&T)-driven regions, which typically represent the lagging regions. This classification approach is useful in demonstrating the salient and dominant features of a region's innovation system, and is also very useful in highlighting the major innovation challenges faced by the various different types of regions. For present purposes, the use of this typology also allows one to identify the key issues that need to be addressed in order to work out how a smart specialization concept could be applied to regional policy. In economic geography terminology, the key issues are embeddedness, relatedness and connectivity.

The easiest way of explaining this is by using the same domain-regeneration example originally offered by the proponents of the smart specialization concept (DAVID *et al.*, 2009), namely that of the perceived mismatch between regional skills, human capital training–provision and the demand requirements of the region. One of the central themes in regional policy concerns the need for local human capital and skills enhancement. Yet, in addition to the general level of skills, the smart specialization logic also suggests that there should be a close matching between supply of skills training and the region's medium- or long-term skills demand. But this raises the challenge of how to determine the appropriate pattern of provision of labour training so as to minimize this apparent mismatch, given that one is considering the medium- or long-term skills demands of the region driven by entrepreneurial search processes. Moreover, an additional challenge relates to the induced effect of such a programme, because it is also known that as people acquire more human capital, they become more geographically mobile, and the likelihood of such people leaving less prosperous regions and moving to buoyant regions increases (FAGGIAN and MCCANN, 2006, 2009a, 2009b). In terms of the OECD (2011b) classification above, this implies that a local skills-enhancement programme in a lagging region which is undertaken under the auspices of regional policy actually increases the likelihood of human capital outflows from this same lagging region. These human capital outflows from a lagging region

could be primarily to either industrial production zones or, more likely, to knowledge regions, but in each case the actual pattern will depend on the interregional spatial distribution of the employment possibilities. Obviously, not all recipients of local skills training will move away; a greater local skills match reduces labour outflows, whereas a greater local skills mismatch will increase outflows. However, the point remains that in terms of its intended local development objectives, the regional policy itself be undermined by the induced out-migration, unless sufficiently strong countervailing processes are also operating to ensure that enough gainful local employment opportunities are available. In other words, the relationship between skills training and regional development depends on the links between the policy and changes in the local labour supply and how these changes dovetail with the local labour demand requirements.

In terms of economic geography, less prosperous non-core regions often have more specialized industry structures, dominated by a smaller range of sectors which are highly embedded in the region, in the sense that their local input–output linkages are strong and/or longstanding. As such, in order to reduce the skills mismatch problem in these types of regions, following the smart specialization logic, one argument is that the skills-enhancement programmes should be specialized and closely allied to the requirements of the existing local industries which are already highly embedded within the region, so as also to increase the overall *embeddedness* of both the local labour force and the local industries. Here, the degree of embeddedness of local activities must be seen in the context of evolving global value chains, in which the economic linkages between regions are changing. In the case of the EU, over time its regions are becoming both more interconnected within each other and also with wider global value chains, and much of this increasing interconnection also takes place via the increasing fragmentation of value chains.

From a policy perspective, given that it is impossible to predict long-term trends, the most sensible approach is to focus on the medium-term, and here it is known that existing industrial structure is the best indicator of the medium-term regional industrial structure. The reason for this is that very few regions make fundamental structural or sectoral shifts in the short- to medium-term. The levels of embeddedness of different sectors can be identified via regional input–output models, computable regional general equilibrium (CGE) models, or more simply by means of employment patterns (MCCANN and DEWHURST, 1998). In addition, such approaches can be bolstered with information regarding the organizational (MCCANN, 1997) and institutional behaviour of the various sectors, including local university–industry links, and other regional evidence of knowledge spillovers, knowledge exchanges, or social and institutional participation. Whatever approaches are employed, another novelty of the smart specialization logic shifts local policy discussions from a tendency towards being often rather introspective and myopic to being much more explicitly.

Yet, this raises a problem. Emphasizing the regional embeddedness in the context of evolving global value chains may appear both to increase the vulnerability of the region to external shocks and also to reduce the possibilities for knowledge spillovers, precisely because it implies increasing the specialization of the region. Therefore, in order to counter these problems, it is necessary to develop a strategy to allow the less prosperous regions actually to *diversify*, not to specialize. While this may appear prima facie to run counter to the smart specialization logic, this is not the case. The smart original specialization concept promotes the idea of technological diversification within a particular domain which has a realistic specialization advantage due to its relevant scale. In a regional policy context, this implies that a labour-enhancement programme should be designed to foster the *technological diversification* strategies of the major locally embedded industries, because it is these sectors that have the relevant scale. Such a strategy is consistent with the technological relatedness argument of FRENKEN et al. (2007). This technological *relatedness* argument from evolutionary economics (FRENKEN and BOSCHMA, 2007; BOSCHMA and FRENKEN, 2011), for which there is now strong supporting empirical evidence (BOSCHMA and IAMMARINO, 2009; NEFFKE et al., 2011; BOSCHMA et al., 2012), posits that the most promising pathways forward for a region to promote its growth is by diversifying into technologies which are closely related to the existing dominant technologies. The argument here is that it allows regional assets to shift more easily between technologies because they are still able to build on their existing skills and capabilities. Inflows of new firms and the founding of new local firms are both systematically higher in fields which are technologically diversified, but also closely related to the existing dominant fields of the region, while outflows of firms or firm failures are more likely in sectors unrelated to the existing regional technological profile (NEFFKE et al., 2011). As such, it is not diversification per se that is important for growth, but the patterns of *specialized diversification* across related technologies that are important for growth. Indeed, the evidence suggests that the impact of this technological relatedness argument is even more pronounced at the regional scale than at the national scale (BOSCHMA et al., 2012). This argument is also consistent with many other findings from the regional growth literature that imply that industries which are the dominant and most relatively specialized in a region, but which also are in a region with diversified industrial structure, are likely to exhibit high growth (MAMELI et al., 2008, 2013).

Taken together, the combination of the *embeddedness* and *relatedness* principles in economic geography translates the aspatial smart specialization idea of a *relevant size* domain into a realistic set of regional policy priorities.

The third element of the aspatial-sectoral smart specialization concept that one must translate into spatial-regional terms is the issue of *connectedness*. The original connectedness idea emerged from a sectoral way of thinking, whereby the national innovation system is comprised of a set of sectoral innovation systems and inter-sectoral linkages and knowledge spillovers. Applying this sectoral approach to regions leads one to the types of networking policies suggested by DAVID et al. (2009). However, innovation-related knowledge flows are embodied in both the face-to-face interactions (MCCANN, 2007) between people and also the mobility of human capital, and as is known from New Economic Geography the Krugman shadow effect associated with centrifugal forces (KRUGMAN and VENABLES, 1995; FUJITA et al., 1999) means that policies designed to reduce spatial transactions costs may actually work in the opposite direction of the ideas suggested by DAVID et al. (2009). As such, once one moves from a sectoral to an explicitly spatial argument, it becomes clear that the smart specialization idea of connectedness does not translate so directly to a regional context, and that some additional issues need to be taken account of.

In order to consider the implications of this, one must first clarify that in economic geography the idea of connectedness is defined in terms of *connectivity*, a concept widely employed in the global cities literature (SASSEN, 2002) and originally borrowed from sociology, whereby connectivity relates to all the transactions associated with trade, transportation, passenger movements, information flows, knowledge interactions, financial flows, funds management, and international decision-making capabilities, which are situated at a particular location. From here on this paper will therefore use the terminology of connectivity (MCCANN and ACS, 2011) rather than connectedness, so as to distinguish clearly the spatial from the sectoral approach, respectively. On this point, if the knowledge inflows into regions are related to the region's existing technological fields, then this fosters growth (BOSCHMA and IAMMARINO, 2009). Setting this connectivity concept within the OECD (2011b) regional-innovation typology allows one to reconsider the role of the connectedness-connectivity element of the basic smart specialization argument.

One aspect of regional policy, exactly as the smart specialization argument posits, is to focus on a peripheral region's most connected industries, so that the regional industrial base is best able to learn from the more advanced regions. In terms of the OECD (2011b) regional-innovation typology, in the case of lagging regions this would imply ways of fostering learning-linkages with either industrial production zones or knowledge regions, whereas for industrial production zones it would imply fostering linkages with either knowledge regions or sometimes other industrial zones. Importantly, however, the networking effect must not lead to an adverse Krugman shadow effect (FUJITA et al., 1999) whereby the networking actually promotes further outflows of knowledge of skills. Therefore, in order for a smart specialization-type policy to work in a regional context, the analytical focus must centre on ways to maximize the knowledge spillovers and learning linkages within the regions which are the targets of the policy, as well as between regions.

The smart specialization-based regional policy-design challenge

The preceding discussion suggests that if smart specialization is to be successfully integrated into regional policy, it is necessary to develop regional policies that promote technological diversification amongst the most embedded industries which have the relevant scale to generate significant local impacts, whilst at the same time promoting the connectivity of the region without inadvertently creating an adverse Krugman shadow effect.

In response to this challenge, four major points can be made:

- In large and highly diversified urban centres and leading knowledge regions (OECD, 2011a) the smart specialization argument will be less relevant as almost all sectors and technological fields will be present. Moreover, in general their buoyancy implies such centres will not be a target for regional policy funding. However, for intermediate regions with both urban and rural areas, as well as for many smaller sized regions with urban centres, the smart specialization argument would seem to be very well suited. A sufficiently large population base is required in order to generate agglomeration or network effects. Moreover, intermediate and smaller regions account for well over half, and also an increasing share, of economic growth in OECD countries (OECD, 2012b), and particularly in Europe (DIJKSTRA et al., 2013). As such, both in terms of their growth potential and also the concentration possibilities offered by their spatial structure, these intermediate regions appear to be ideal targets for smart specialization policies. Of these regions, industrial production zones would be particularly suited to a mix of R&D, training and networking programmes, precisely because of their scale. For very isolated regions, however, the smart specialization argument appears to offer only very limited possibilities, because the lack of scale is likely to reduce the effectiveness of the policy approach. In these cases, rather than funding R&D, the priorities might centre on the promotion of connectivity in certain natural environmental or tourism activities, via, say, for example, wireless ICT systems

to more central core regions, so as to foster non-R&D-driven innovation in key sectors.

- The smart specialization logic applied in a regional context, in which the issues of embeddedness, relatedness and connectivity are explicitly discussed, puts the onus onto the policy designers and potential funding recipients to identify clearly the perceived market failures which are being corrected, and to justify exactly how the smart specialization approach to the tailoring and provision of public goods is to be applied, monitored and evaluated. This model is consistent with the approach of RODRIK (2004) and BARCA (2009) in which partnerships between the public and private sector are essential in order to elicit the knowledge regarding the most severe obstacles to growth, the major bottlenecks or missing links, and the optimal remedies. This form of policy-tailoring will also require appropriate results/outcome indicators to be carefully chosen which are amenable to being tracked through the life of the programme and projects.[4] This is not because the results/outcomes can be known in advance, but rather as a means to facilitate and enhance the policy process (RODRIK, 2004). As such, the smart specialization logic, when it is appropriately translated to an explicitly spatial regional context, would appear to be a powerful lens through which policy-makers can design and articulate local development policies.

- The smart specialization logic suggests that in a regional context the policy recommendations may be very different in different places, depending on the region's technological profile, its industrial structure and its geography. Relevant scale naturally points towards the agglomeration potential of bigger population centres, particularly in the dominant category of intermediate urban–rural regions, which will allow for comprehensive policy scenarios. At the same time, the possibilities offered by network systems point towards wireless information technology-based solutions in many more remote regions. There is no 'one-size-fits-all' policy, and the smart specialization logic forces priorities to be chosen amongst competing alternatives.

- The problems of local rental capture must also be addressed head on, and there are two aspects to this problem. Firstly, the smart specialization logic emphasizes prioritization and concentration of resources around key themes. As such, the framework must be translated into a policy-design logic that explicitly aims at building a policy-prioritization process based on fostering a region's technological diversification opportunities on the basis of the embeddedness, relatedness, and connectivity characteristics of the region's activities, institutions and sectors. This type of policy-process, which necessarily involves gathering evidence and data, building public–private partnerships in the policy-design stages, and also necessitates the monitoring of all policy actions and interventions, will help avoid the types of fragmented and localized sectoral rent-seeking likely to undermine the drive for resource prioritization and concentration. Secondly, it is necessary to engage with local elites in order to extract local knowledge and to tailor the policy. However, policy design at the regional level involves not only issues of externalities, but also the information asymmetries and principal-agent problems associated with engagement with local elites. The specialized diversification aspect of the smart specialization policy logic implies newness, variation and differentiation, and these very features may undermine some of the monopoly positions of local elites. As such, even if the policy is indeed translated into explicitly spatial and regional terms in the manner described here, it is necessary to ensure that the architectures of the policy-design, policy-delivery, and policy-evaluation systems are open and inclusive, and allow for a broad range of stakeholders and interested parties to participate. Otherwise they may be subject to rental capture by local elites who will subvert the process by *limiting* openness and by *restricting* the pursuit of the novelties and variations to arenas over which they maintain control. The way this can be achieved is by the use of both conditionalities and also outcome indicators, as argued on numerous occasions by The World Bank, the OECD and the European Commission, and as also discussed in detail by the BARCA (2009) report.

SMART SPECIALIZATION AND EUROPEAN UNION COHESION POLICY

In light of the regional policy-design challenges just described, this section will now examine the major elements of the smart specialization logic and it reconsiders how they might best be incorporated into a reformed EU cohesion policy. The major aim here is to design policies that will foster maximum learning linkages both within the target regions as well as between regions. In order to do this one must first translate the smart specialization logic from a sectoral innovation system approach to a regional innovation system viewpoint. In addition, it is necessary to think in terms of a national innovation system as being comprised not only of a set of distinct regional innovation systems, but also of an overarching *inter*-regional innovation system. This inter-regional element highlights the issue of how knowledge does, or does not, flow between regions, and the ways in which such flows might best be fostered and regions better connected.

Adopting a regional and interregional innovations-systems logic, if one now reconsiders both the technological aspects of diversification and also the issue of connectivity, as already shown, the original sectoral smart specialization logic, which initially emerged from the sectoral literature on the transatlantic

productivity gap, emphasized the importance of the adoption, adaptation and diffusion of general purpose technologies (GPTs), and in particular ICTs. In many cases, tailored skills training or actor-networking related to ICTs may well be a sensible regional policy priority. Moreover, such an approach is also appropriate for regions in which innovation is primarily not research based. However, on the basis of the arguments in this paper, in a regional policy setting the local adoption of ICTs may not necessarily be the priority, given that EU interregional disparities are not primarily due to ICT issues. Moreover, focusing exclusively on this ICT issue raises the risk of inadvertently subsidizing a particular sector across regions, which as noted by the proponents of the concept reflects the type of lock-in danger that must be avoided (DAVID *et al.*, 2009). As such, in addition to the ICT-related networking suggestions discussed earlier (DAVID *et al.*, 2009), other complementary approaches may be very appropriate, including the upgrading of local supply chains, the redesign of local labour-training systems, the promotion of university–industry linkages, or other local institutional reforms, exactly as recommended by the BARCA (2009) report. As such, there is no reason why the appropriate policy solutions should necessarily centre on ICT-related issues per se, although this is likely to play a key role in many policy actions.

The final issue relates to the role of entrepreneurship. In the original smart specialization logic it is the entrepreneurial search processes that are assumed to identify the medium-term smart specialization opportunities in the region. The emphasis in the smart specialization concept on promoting entrepreneurial search processes is in no way inconsistent with EU cohesion policy which is the largest source of credit to small and medium-sized enterprises (SMEs) within the EU policy portfolio. However, the fact that in the original policy concept it is the entrepreneurs and not the regional policy-makers who are assumed to be best equipped for identifying the smart specialization opportunities therefore also poses an additional policy-design challenge. In particular, designing smart specialization-based regional policies that link local SMEs and technological diversification to regional embeddedness and connectivity means that there may need to be place-specific criteria for credit availability. In particular, SME credit may need to be prioritized for firms whose entrepreneurial goals are to promote technological diversification amongst the region's most embedded industries and activities. At the same time, ironically, in order to ensure that such a policy is successful, aggregate R&D funding in its early stages would need to be explicitly space-neutral in the sense that it is *not* applied primarily to the dominant knowledge centres, but spread evenly, or at least randomly, across all places in response to funding applications. Indeed, in the United States there are National Research Council policies that work exactly according to this logic (WESSNER,

2008). Only after a peer-review performance evaluation process that takes place after a predefined period of time after the seed-funding has been granted is the continuation of funding ensured. This is both a genuinely place-neutral and also explicitly not a capital-city policy, and as such provides a powerful counter-argument to the argument that smart specialization favours strong regions.

To some observers, smart specialization may appear to raise concerns regarding 'picking winners' (DAVID et al., 2009). However, the smart specialization concept was never conceived of as a strategy for 'picking winners' or for imposing sectoral specialization by means of top-down government planning (OECD, 2012a). Rather, it was always seen as being a partnership-based policy process of discovery and learning on the part of both policy-makers and entrepreneurs, and was always framed within the recent trend towards reconsidering the role and logic of industrial (RODRIK, 2004), knowledge (TRAJTENBERG, 2009; SOETE, 2009a, 2009b), and regional (TÖDTLING and TRIPPL, 2005) policies. However, as the original smart specialization proponents themselves acknowledge (DAVID et al., 2009), the logic of the concept does imply a policy-prioritization logic based broadly on a fledgling-industry-type of argument, but with a twist. A problem with fledgling-industry arguments in general is that the medium- to long-term outcomes of the policy are by definition unknown, and as such are very risky. In contrast, however, if one applies the smart specialization logic in a regional context, emphasizing the principles of embeddedness, relatedness and connectivity, then the empirical evidence (FRENKEN et al., 2007; BOSCHMA and IAMMARINO 2009; BOSCHMA and FRENKEN, 2011; BOSCHMA et al., 2012) suggests that the policy-prioritization principles are built on a much sounder footing than the usual fledgling-industry arguments. This is a powerful argument in favour of using the smart specialization concept in regional policy design, and also makes the approach highly relevant to a wide range of regions, well beyond the core city-regions. Smart specialization as a policy-design framework therefore does not inherently favour core city-regions, but can be tailored to addressing the challenges of many types of regions. This is achieved by using the approach to consider the potential innovation and entrepreneurial opportunities associated with the region's existing characteristics, its realistic diversification potential, and to design appropriate policy interventions on the basis of these features and intended outcomes.

As well as being appropriate for a wide range of regions, the smart specialization approach also militates against recommending off-the-shelf or 'one-size-fits-all' policy solutions, and instead points to tailored policy recommendations, contingent on the region's existing knowledge assets. At the same time, the smart specialization approach also emphasized the public-

private policy-learning agenda, and this requires the use of results/outcome indicators, ongoing monitoring and evaluation, combined with pilots, policy experiments and test cases, as is made clear by the authors of the original concept (DAVID et al., 2009). These elements are all required so as to ensure that policy interventions do not in effect end up leading to the strengthening of existing monopoly positions and the associated negative lock-in effects associated with this. Making progress on these matters is an urgent issue if the policy is to be successful, and this can only be achieved if a smart specialization regional policy logic is accompanied by a rigorous self-assessment of a region's knowledge assets, capabilities and competences, the establishment of empirical baselines, and the explicit ex-ante linking of policy priorities to ongoing monitoring and the use of results/outcome indicators.

Smart specialization as a policy-prioritization logic builds on the existing regional innovation systems literature (MCCANN and ORTEGA-ARGILÉS, 2013), and many of the leading scholars in the innovation systems field have been involved in these aspects of the EU cohesion policy reforms. However, it is important to remember that while smart specialization is a major element of the overall EU cohesion policy reforms, it is one element, and other elements of the reforms are designed to deal with the associated problems of institutions, governance, cross-border cooperation, and limitations in absorptive capacity, all of which are typically faced by weaker regions attempting to upgrade their economic capabilities (MCCANN and ORTEGA-ARGILÉS, 2012).

Acknowledgements – This paper has benefitted greatly from the comments, insights, and criticisms received at various seminars and meetings offered by Fabrizio Barca, Sjoerd Beugelsdijk, Andrea Bonaccorsi, Ron Boschma, Andries Brandsma, Lewis Dijkstra, Koen Frenken, Dominique Foray, Enrique Garcilazo, Ian Gordon, Karen McGuire, Joaquim Oliveira-Martins, Andrés Rodriguez-Pose, Marcel Timmer, Bart van Ark, Frank van Oort, Attila Varga, Jouke van Dijk and Tony Venables. The opinions expressed herein are entirely those of the authors alone.

NOTES

1. See http://s3platform.jrc.ec.europa.eu/s3pguide and http://ec.europa.eu/regional_policy/newsroom/detail.cfm?id=361&LAN=EN/.
2. See http://ec.europa.eu/invest-in-research/monitoring/knowledge_en.htm/.
3. The smart specialization concept originally emphasized the importance of R&D, and in particular R&D in high-technology sectors. However, as one moves through the nine policy briefs produced by the Knowledge for Growth expert group between 2006 and 2009 and on towards the subsequent papers (DAVID et al., 2009; FORAY et al., 2011), it is possible to discern a marked shift away from the

early emphasis on R&D, and in particular on multinational R&D, through to institutional and governance issues relating to science, and finally towards technological specialization based on the adoption, dissemination and adaptation of GPTs, primarily understood as ICTs, across a wide range of sectors and activities. As such there was also an increasing emphasis on enhancing the linkages between knowledge-generation processes in all their forms (including R&D) and the promotion and dissemination of entrepreneurship and innovation across all sectors, activities and occupations within the context of global value chains.

4. In the EU context, the definitions regarding the nature and use of results indicators are contained in BARCA and McCANN (2011) and examples of such indicators are given in the two Complementary Notes on Outcome Indicators for Some EU2020 Objectives entitled 'Meeting Climate Change and Energy Objectives' and 'Improving the Conditions for Innovation, Research and Development' (see http://ec.europa.eu/regional_policy/sources/docgener/evaluation/performance_en.htm). These were subsequently updated in response to the deliberations during 2011 of the High Level Group on Outcome Indicators as 'Outcome Indicators and Targets – Towards a New System of Monitoring and Evaluation in EU Cohesion Policy', June 2011, on the DG Regio Website (see http://ec.europa.eu/regional_policy/sources/docgener/evaluation/doc/performance/outcome_indicators_en.pdf). For the most recent guidance, see http://ec.europa.eu/regional_policy/information/evaluations/guidance_en.cfm and http://ec.europa.eu/regional_policy/information/evaluations/guidance_en.cfm#1/.

REFERENCES

ACS Z. J. (2002) *Innovation and the Growth of Cites*. Edward Elgar, Cheltenham.

BARCA F. (2009) *An Agenda for a Reformed Cohesion Policy: A Place-Based Approach to Meeting European Union Challenges and Expectations*. Independent report prepared at the request of the European Commissioner for Regional Policy, Danuta Hübner. European Commission, Brussels.

BARCA F. and McCANN P. (2011) *Methodological Note: Outcome Indicators and Targets – Towards a Performance Oriented EU Cohesion Policy*. European Commission, DG Urban and Regional Policy, Brussels.

BARCA F., McCANN P. and RODRIGUEZ-POSE A. (2012) The case for regional development intervention: place-based versus place-neutral approaches, *Journal of Regional Science* 52(1), 134–152.

BOSCHMA R. A. and FRENKEN K. (2011) Technological relatedness and regional branching, in BATHELT H., FELDMAN M. P. and KOGLER D. F. (Eds) *Dynamic Geographies of Knowledge Creation and Innovation*, pp. 64–81. Taylor & Francis/Routledge, London.

BOSCHMA R. A. and IAMMARINO S. (2009) Related variety, trade linkages and regional growth, *Economic Geography* 85(3), 289–311.

BOSCHMA R. A., MINONDO A. and NAVARRO M. (2012) Related variety and regional growth in Spain, *Papers in Regional Science* 91(2), 241–256.

CARLINO G. A., CHATTERJEE S. and HUNT R. M. (2007) Urban density and the rate of invention, *Journal of Urban Economics* 61(3), 389–419.

CHINITZ B. (1961) Contrasts in agglomeration: New York and Pittsburgh, *American Economic Review* 51(2), 279–289.

DAVID P., FORAY D. and HALL B. H. (2009) *Measuring Smart Specialisation: The Concept and the Need for Indicators*. Knowledge for Growth Expert Group (available at: http://cemi.epfl.ch/files/content/sites/cemi/files/users/178044/public/Measuring%20smart%20specialisation.doc).

DIJKSTRA L., GARCILAZO E. and McCANN P. (2013) The economic performance of European cities and city-regions: myths and realities, 2013, *European Planning Studies* 21(3), 334–354.

DURANTON G. (2007) Urban evolutions: the fast, the slow, and the still, *American Economic Review* 97(1), 197–221.

DURANTON G. and PUGA D. (2001) Nursery cities: urban diversity, process innovation, and the life cycle of products, *American Economic Review* 91(5), 1454–1477.

DURANTON G. and PUGA D. (2004) Micro-foundations of urban agglomeration economies, in HENDERSON J. V. and THISSE J.-F. (Eds) *Handbook of Regional and Urban Economics, Vol. IV: Economic Geography*, pp. 2063–2117. Elsevier, Amsterdam.

FAGGIAN A. and McCANN P. (2006) Human capital flows and regional knowledge assets: a simultaneous equation approach, *Oxford Economic Papers* 58(3), 475–500.

FAGGIAN A. and McCANN P. (2009a) Human capital, graduate migration and innovation in British regions, *Cambridge Journal of Economics* 33(2), 317–333.

FAGGIAN A. and McCANN P. (2009b) Human capital and regional development, in CAPELLO R. and NIJKAMP P. (Eds) *Regional Dynamics and Growth: Advances in Regional Economics*, pp. 133–151. Edward Elgar, Cheltenham.

FORAY D., DAVID P. and HALL B. H. (2009) *Smart Specialisation – The Concept*. Knowledge Economists Policy Brief Number 9, June. European Commission, DG Research, Brussels.

FORAY D., DAVID P. and HALL B. H. (2011) Smart specialization: from academic idea to political instrument, the surprising career of a concept and the difficulties involved in its implementation. MTEI Working Paper, École Polytechnique Fédérale de Lausanne.

FRENKEN K. and BOSCHMA R. A. (2007) A theoretical framework for evolutionary economic geography: industrial dynamics and urban growth as a branching process, *Journal of Economic Geography* 7(5), 635–649.

FRENKEN K., VAN OORT F. G. and VERBURG T. (2007) Related variety, unrelated variety and regional economic growth, *Regional Studies* 41(5), 685–697.

FUJITA M., KRUGMAN P. and VENABLES A. J. (1999) *The Spatial Economy: Cities, Regions and International Trade*. MIT Press, Cambridge, MA.

GASPAR J. and GLAESER E. L. (1998) Information technology and the future of cities, *Journal of Urban Economics* 43, 136–156.

IAMMARINO S. and McCANN P. (2006) The structure and evolution of industrial clusters: transactions, technology and knowledge spillovers, *Research Policy* **35**, 1018–1036.

IAMMARINO S. and McCANN P. (2013) *Multinationals and Economic Geography: Location, Technology and Innovation.* Edward Elgar, Cheltenham.

KRUGMAN P. and VENABLES A. J. (1995) Globalization and the inequality of nations, *Quarterly Journal of Economics* **110(4)**, 857–880.

MAMELI F., FAGGIAN A. and McCANN P. (2008) Employment growth in Italian local labour systems: issues of model specification and sectoral aggregation, *Spatial Economic Analysis* **3(3)**, 343–359.

MAMELI F., FAGGIAN A. and McCANN P. (2013) The estimation of local employment growth: do sectoral aggregation and industry definition matter?, *Regional Studies* doi:10.1080/00343404.2012.756578.

McCANN P. (1997) How deeply embedded is Silicon Glen? A cautionary note, *Regional Studies* **31(7)**, 697–705.

McCANN P. (2007) Sketching out a model of innovation, face-to-face interaction and economic geography, *Spatial Economic Analysis* **2(2)**, 117–134.

McCANN P. (2008) Globalization and economic geography: the world is curved, not flat, *Cambridge Journal of Regions, Economy and Society* **1(3)**, 351–370.

McCANN P. and ACS Z. J. (2011) Globalisation: countries, cities and multinationals, *Regional Studies* **45(1)**, 17–32.

McCANN P. and DEWHURST J. H. LL. (1998) Regional size, industrial location and input–output coefficients, *Regional Studies* **32(5)**, 435–444.

McCANN P. and ORTEGA-ARGILÉS R. (2012) Redesigning and reforming European regional policy: the reasons, the logic and the outcomes, *International Regional Science Review* doi:10.1177/0160017612463234.

McCANN P. and ORTEGA-ARGILÉS R. (2013) Modern regional innovation policy, *Cambridge Journal of Regions, Economy and Society* doi:10.1093/cjres/rst007.

NEFFKE F., HENNING M. and BOSCHMA R. (2011) How do regions diversify over time? Industry relatedness and the development of new growth paths in regions, *Economic Geography* **87(3)**, 237–265.

ORGANISATION FOR ECONOMIC CO-OPERATION AND DEVELOPMENT (OECD) (2009a) *How Regions Grow.* OECD, Paris.

ORGANISATION FOR ECONOMIC CO-OPERATION AND DEVELOPMENT (OECD) (2009b) *Regions Matter: Economic Recovery, Innovation and Sustainable Growth.* OECD, Paris.

ORGANISATION FOR ECONOMIC CO-OPERATION AND DEVELOPMENT (OECD) (2011a) *Regions and Innovation Policy.* OECD, Paris.

ORGANISATION FOR ECONOMIC CO-OPERATION AND DEVELOPMENT (OECD) (2011b) *Regions at a Glance 2011.* OECD, Paris.

ORGANISATION FOR ECONOMIC CO-OPERATION AND DEVELOPMENT (OECD) (2012a) *Draft Synthesis Report on Innovation Driven-Growth in Regions: The Role of Smart Specialisation.* OECD, Paris.

ORGANISATION FOR ECONOMIC CO-OPERATION AND DEVELOPMENT (OECD) (2012b) *Promoting Growth in All Regions.* OECD, Paris.

ORTEGA-ARGILÉS R. (2012) The transatlantic productivity gap: a survey of the main causes, *Journal of Economic Surveys* **26(3)**, 395–419.

ORTEGA-ARGILÉS R., PIVA M., POTTERS L. and VIVARELLI M. (2010) Is corporate R&D investment in high-tech sectors more effective?, *Contemporary Economic Policy* **28(3)**, 353–365.

ORTEGA-ARGILÉS R., PIVA M. and VIVARELLI M. (2011) *The Transatlantic Productivity Gap: Is R&D the Main Culprit?* IZA Discussion Papers Number 5586. Institute for the Study of Labor (IZA), Bonn.

RODRIK D. (2004) *Industrial Policy for the Twenty-First Century.* Working Paper. Kennedy School of Government, Harvard University, Cambridge, MA.

SASSEN S. (2002) *Global Networks: Linked Cities.* Routledge, London.

SOETE L. (2009a) The European research area as industrial policy tool, in DELANGHE H., MULDUR U. and SOETE L. (Eds) *European Science and Technology Policy: Towards Integration and Fragmentation?*, pp. 312–327. Edward Elgar, Cheltenham.

SOETE L. (2009b) Research without frontiers, in FORAY D. (Ed.) *The New Economics of Technology Policy*, pp. 401–408. Edward Elgar, Cheltenham.

STERNBERG R. (2012) Regional determinants of entrepreneurial activities – theories and empirical evidence, in FRITSCH M. (Ed.) *Handbook of Research on Entrepreneurship and Regional Development*, pp. 33–57. Edward Elgar, Cheltenham.

TÖDTLING F. and TRIPPL M. (2005) One size fits all? Towards a differentiated regional innovation policy approach, *Research Policy* **34(8)**, 1203–1219.

TRAJTENBERG M. (2009) The rumblings of a paradigm shift: concluding comments, in FORAY D. (Ed.) *The New Economics of Technology Policy*, pp. 409–418. Edward Elgar, Cheltenham.

VAN OORT F. G. (2004) *Urban Growth and Innovation: Spatially Bounded Externalities in the Netherlands.* Ashgate, Aldershot.

WESSNER C. W. (Ed.) for the NATIONAL RESEARCH COUNCIL (NRC) (2008) *An Assessment of the Small Business Innovation Research Program.* National Academies Press, Washington, DC.

When Spatial Equilibrium Fails: Is Place-Based Policy Second Best?

MARK D. PARTRIDGE*, DAN S. RICKMAN†, M. ROSE OLFERT‡ and YING TAN§

*336 Agricultural Administration Building, The Ohio State University, Columbus, OH, USA.

†338 Business Building, Oklahoma State University, Stillwater, OK, USA.

‡101 Diefenbaker Place, Johnson–Shoyama Graduate School of Public Policy, University of Saskatchewan, Saskatoon, SK, §Business Building, Oklahoma State University, Stillwater, OK, USA.

PARTRIDGE M. D., RICKMAN D. S., OLFERT M. R. and TAN Y. When spatial equilibrium fails: is place-based policy second best, *Regional Studies*. Place-based or geographically targeted policy often is promoted to help poor regions. Based on the spatial equilibrium model, economists routinely argue that place-based policies are distortionary and only slow the needed economic adjustments. This paper reviews the empirical evidence about whether the spatial equilibrium model holds in reality and finds that, even in the United States where labour mobility is thought to be much higher than in Europe, at best weak support for the spatial equilibrium hypothesis is found. Although this suggests potential efficacy of place-based policy, the informational and political economy conditions required for place-based policy to be effective are described.

PARTRIDGE M. D., RICKMAN D. S., OLFERT M. R. and TAN Y. 当空间均衡失效时：根据地方的政策是次优的吗？区域研究。根据地方、或以特定地理为目标的政策，经常被推广来协助穷困区域。经济学者根据空间均衡模式，週而復始地主张根据地方的政策是扭曲的，且只会减缓必要的经济调整。本文回顾空间均衡模式在现实中是否成立的经验证据，并发现：即便在劳动流动性被认为远较欧洲为高的美国，也仅能发现对于空间均衡假说的微弱支持。儘管此一发现指出根据地方的政策的潜在效力，但也描绘了该政策得以生效所必须具备的资讯及政治经济条件。

PARTRIDGE M. D., RICKMAN D. S., OLFERT M. R. et TAN Y. En cas d'échec de l'équilibre spatial: une politique adaptée au milieu, est-elle une solution de second choix, *Regional Studies*. Souvent, la politique adaptée au milieu ou ciblée géographiquement est favorisée pour aider les régions en perte de vitesse. Fondées sur le modèle spatial d'équilibre, les économistes affirment régulièrement que les politiques adaptées au milieu ont des effets de distorsion et finissent par ralentir les ajustements économiques nécessaires. Cet article dresse un bilan des preuves empiriques qui laissent voir si, oui ou non, le modèle spatial d'équilibre est valable en réalité, et constate que, même aux États-Unis où la mobilité du tavail est considérée beaucoup plus élevée par rapport à l'Europe, il s'avère au mieux un soutien faible en faveur du modèle spatial d'équilibre. Bien que cela laisse supposer l'efficacité potentielle de la politique adaptée au milieu, on présente les conditions informationnelles et d'économie politique qui sont nécessaires à la réussite de la politique adaptée au milieu.

PARTRIDGE M. D., RICKMAN D. S., OLFERT M. R. und TAN Y. Wenn das räumliche Gleichgewicht scheitert: ist eine ortsbasierte Politik das Zweitbeste, *Regional Studies*. Zur Unterstützung von armen Regionen wird oft für eine ortsbasierte oder geografisch zielgerichtete Politik plädiert. Ausgehend vom räumlichen Gleichgewichtsmodell argumentieren Ökonomen gewöhnlich, dass ortsbasierte Politiken zu Verzerrungen führen und die nötigen wirtschaftlichen Anpassungen nur hinauszögern. In diesem Beitrag untersuchen wir die empirischen Belege dafür, dass das räumliche Gleichgewichtsmodell der Realität gewachsen ist, und stellen fest, dass selbst in den USA, wo von einer weitaus höheren Mobilität der Arbeitskräfte ausgegangen wird als in Europa, bestenfalls schwache Belege für die Hypothese des räumlichen Gleichgewichts zu finden sind. Obwohl dies auf eine potenzielle Wirksamkeit von ortsbasierter Politik hinweist, beschreiben wir außerdem die informationellen und wirtschaftspolitischen Voraussetzungen für eine wirksame ortsbasierte Politik.

PARTRIDGE M. D., RICKMAN D. S., OLFERT M. R. y TAN Y. Cuando el equilibrio espacial fracasa: es una política basada en áreas la segunda mejor opción, *Regional Studies*. Muchas veces se fomentan políticas orientadas geográficamente o basadas en áreas prioritarias para ayudar a las regiones pobres. Según el modelo de equilibrio espacial, los economistas habitualmente sostienen que las políticas destinadas a favorecer determinadas áreas tienen efectos distorsionadores y solamente ralentizan los ajustes económicos tan necesarios. En este artículo analizamos la evidencia empírica de si el modelo de equilibrio espacial se ve reflejado en la realidad y constatamos que, incluso en los Estados Unidos donde se considera que la movilidad laboral es mucho más alta que en Europa, existe en el mejor de los casos débiles pruebas para la hipótesis del equilibrio espacial. Aunque esto indica una posible eficacia de la política basada en áreas, describimos también las condiciones económicas informativas y políticas necesarias para que este tipo de políticas basada en áreas prioritarias sean eficaces.

Equilibrio espacial   Política basada en áreas   Movilidad laboral

JEL classifications: R12, R23, R58

INTRODUCTION

The conventional spatial equilibrium (SE) view of regional economies – at least in its strong form – precludes the need for place-based policies. With the assumptions of perfectly competitive labour and land markets and perfectly mobile factors of production, place-based policies implemented to create jobs are distortionary in the SE model (KLINE and MORETTI, 2013). Accordingly, place-based policies primarily benefit landowners and new migrants (BARTIK, 1991; PETERS and FISHER, 2004; PARTRIDGE and RICKMAN, 2006a; MORETTI, 2010). Therefore, the SE model, even in its weak form, is routinely used by economists to argue against spatially oriented economic interventions (GLAESER and GOTTLIEB, 2008).

A key feature of the SE model is the assumption of perfectly mobile labour (ROBACK, 1982). Utility differentials, such as those created by regionally asymmetric demand shocks, induce internal migration. Migration rapidly arbitrages away the utility differentials such that relative employment and real wage rates return to their equilibrium levels, capitalizing the attributes underlying the utility differentials into factor prices (PARTRIDGE and RICKMAN, 2003a). In its strongest form, the SE model implies immediate migration and an absence of utility differentials across space.

The seminal studies on US labour market adjustment by MARSTON (1985) and BLANCHARD and KATZ (1992) are routinely cited as evidence of highly geographically mobile labour and efficient regional labour markets in subsequent studies of US labour market phenomena (for example, COEN-PIRANI, 2010; ELSBY et al., 2010; HINES, 2010; SAKS and WOZNIAK, 2011; BOWMAN, 2012), supporting the SE view. Yet, many of these studies also note the contradictory evidence provided by BARTIK (1991, 1993a) and ROWTHORN and GLYN (2006) that local shocks have long-lasting or permanent effects on local labour market outcomes. Relevant to the study of the European Union, the Marston and Blanchard and Katz studies also are routinely cited by European regional labour studies as evidence of efficient US regional labour markets primarily occurring through interregional migration, which can be used to benchmark European labour market adjustment processes (BROERSMA and VAN DIJK, 2002; PEKKALA and KANGASHARJU, 2002; LÓPEZ-BAZO et al., 2005; BAYER and JÜßEN, 2007; BANDE et al., 2008; BARTZ and FUCHS-SCHÜNDELN, 2012).

An unsettled question then appears to be the degree to which the traditional SE view accurately describes the workings of regional economies. Do labour market adjustments occur? If so, do they occur in a timely manner? Evidence of efficient local labour markets not only would obviate the need for place-based policy, but also would suggest that place-based policy would likely worsen outcomes. Thus, a necessary (but not sufficient) condition for the effectiveness of place-based policy is to show that the predicted adjustments inherent in SE models are incomplete or sluggish, that is, frictions may exist in local labour markets such that there is a potential role for place-based policy (BARTIK, 1991, 1993a; MORETTI, 2010; KLINE and MORETTI, 2013).

Well-known examples of place-based policy in Canada and the United States are the long-standing Atlantic Canada Opportunity Agency (ACOA) (since 1987) and the Appalachian Regional Commission (ARC) (since 1965), respectively. Fiscal equalization also is often promoted on regional equity and efficiency grounds (BOADWAY and FLATTERS, 1982; ALBOUY, 2012). In the 2007–2013 European Union Cohesion Policy, over 80% of its budget was allocated to the 'Convergence' objective, flowing to the poorest regions in the form of 'measures to boost economic growth, including transport and other infrastructure projects' (EURACTIV, 2012). Yet, BARCA et al. (2012) argue that convergence should not be a principal development policy objective, favouring instead policies to maximize the development potential of all regions. Pervasiveness and persistence of place-targeted policies is suggestive of a perceived need for a second-best solution in the form of place-based interventions when spatial equilibration of regional economic performance fails to occur, or occurs too slowly.

This paper provides a thorough review of the empirical literature regarding the efficacy of the traditional SE view of regional economies, with an emphasis on the United States where labour is often argued to be highly mobile, though European studies are reviewed where relevant.[1] It then includes a selective review of assessments of existing place-based interventions in North America (because of the belief that the SE model mostly applies there). This is followed by an outline of the factors required for effective place-based policy. Finally, the policy implications are discussed.

LITERATURE REVIEW

Because it is thought to possess the most flexible labour market, with historically high relative migration rates (conditions required for the SE model to hold), this review pertains mostly to the US economy. Related discussion for other countries is presented when appropriate, but the key point is that if the SE model is found wanting for the United States, it is even less likely to reflect labour market adjustment in other countries. Such a finding would leave some potential scope for *effective* place-based policy.

The literature generally consists of three broad strands. First, a number of cross-sectional tests have examined the equalization of household utility and price-adjusted wages across space. Because of the difficulty in assessing the utility value of regional attributes at a point in time (GLAESER and GOTTLIEB, 2008), a potentially more fruitful way to test SE is the examination of regional labour market responses to shocks in the medium and long run. Thus, a second strand examines the persistence of differentials in key regional labour market indicators. Yet, this literature provides only indirect evidence on the research question regarding the potential need for place-based demand policies because adjustments to clearly identifiable demand shocks are not examined. A third strand examines directly the effects of regional employment growth on labour market outcomes. Because employment growth can be driven by either demand or supply forces, many studies use the shift–share model to derive an exogenous demand-based measure of employment growth.

Cross-sectional tests of spatial equilibrium

A fundamental result of the SE model is that differences in incomes do not necessarily reflect utility differentials and, alone, cannot be used to justify place-based policies. Income differences may reflect many other factors such as differential amenity attractiveness of areas. Costs of living such as housing costs also may differ, offsetting nominal income differences. To be sure, income and housing prices capitalize the values of locational attributes in SE. Property owners, rather than working households in poor areas, may be the primary beneficiaries of places receiving financial assistance (GLAESER and GOTTLIEB, 2008). Therefore, tests

of SE have examined differences in price-adjusted (real) wages and subjective measures of utility.

An extensive early literature exists on whether real wages are equalized across regions, generally finding that they are not (DICKIE and GERKING, 1989). However, the SE model posits that utility, not price-adjusted wages, will be equalized. From ROBACK (1982, p. 1260), indirect utility in an area is a function of wages (w), land rental payments (r) and amenities (s), and is equal across regions in equilibrium:

$$V(w, r; s) = k$$

where k is the equalized value. Lower rent-adjusted (real) wages reflect the existence of greater area household amenity attractiveness. Locally imbedded social capital may form a function similar to household amenities (BARCA et al., 2012). Thus, subsequent studies attempt to ascertain whether household utility is equalized across regions.

Because utility is not directly observable, tests of utility equalization examine real wages while attempting to control for differences in natural amenities. Assuming marginal differences or a Cobb–Douglas utility function, the elasticity between wages and prices across regions should be unity for utility to be equalized (WINTERS, 2009). ROBACK (1988) reports a wage-price elasticity of 0.97; using a different price index, DUMOND et al. (1999) find a wage-price elasticity of 0.46. WINTERS (2009) attributes the difference in results at least partly to the use of different price deflators in the two studies. Winters finds this elasticity depends upon the housing price measure and method of estimation. Using housing values and ordinary least squares (OLS), Winters finds the elasticity to be less than 0.50, which rises to 0.76 when housing rents are used. Including housing rents, and employing instrumental variable (IV) estimation to account for measurement error, leads to an estimated elasticity not statistically significantly different from unity, supporting the existence of an SE.

The estimated wage-price elasticity then likely depends greatly on the price deflator, estimation method and amenity measures included in the regression. Thus, more direct, self-reported measures of utility have been examined. Using the General Social Survey between 1972 and 2006, GLAESER and GOTTLIEB (2008) find that the fraction of respondents in US metropolitan areas who report being happy is unrelated to income per capita, which follows from the SE approach where utility and per capita income are not necessarily related because of amenity differences. Yet, they find large differences in reported happiness across areas, violating the utility equalization (strong) condition of the SE model.

OSWALD and WU (2011) use self-reported responses from surveys conducted by the US Center for Disease

Control (CDC) as part of the Behavioral Risk Factor Surveillance System to examine life satisfaction across states. Consistent with GLAESER and GOTTLIEB (2008), they do not find any significant correlation between self-reported life satisfaction and gross domestic product (GDP) per capita. After controlling for income though, the correlation becomes strongly negative, which the authors interpret as evidence in favour of the weak form of the compensating differential hypothesis. Yet, life-satisfaction differences remain after controlling for individuals' backgrounds and characteristics, leading the authors to reject the strong form of the compensating differential hypothesis that utility levels are equalized across states.

RICKMAN (2011) reports OSWALD and WU's (2011) state ranking of residents' average life-satisfaction level to be significantly correlated with a state population growth ranking for the period 2000–2010 ($r = 0.48$), suggesting disequilibrium adjustment based on utility differences – consistent with a weak form of the SE model. CLARK et al. (2003) derive measures of over- and under-compensation in local labour markets and use them to examine interregional migration. They find net migration towards areas where there is estimated over-compensation and away from areas where there is under-compensation. Migration, thus, worked to arbitrage away compensation differentials, consistent (at least weakly) with SE theory. Yet, over- and under-compensation in regional labour markets represent disequilibria, violating the strong condition.

BAYER et al. (2009) find that labour mobility costs preclude environmental amenities from becoming fully capitalized into factors prices. Labour mobility may be hindered because of household ties to the area and home ownership, leading hedonic analysis to undervalue environmental amenities.[2] MCGRANAHAN et al. (2011) similarly report that outdoor amenities are not fully capitalized into regional US housing prices in 1990, with effects felt for a decade afterwards. GREENWOOD et al. (1991) also find that the assumption of SE causes understatement of the equilibrium values of compensating differentials. Using the reported estimated disequilibrium gaps for 1980 by Greenwood et al., it is found that when controlling for state natural amenity attractiveness there are significantly positive relationships with population growth over both the subsequent five and ten years.[3]

Overall, as summarized in Table 1, cross-sectional tests of the predictions of the SE model find support for area household amenity differences affecting local factor prices, weakly supporting the SE view of regional economies. Little support, however, is found for the strong condition of equalized household utility levels across areas. Utility differentials routinely have been found to exist, indicative of human migration and housing price adjustments for up to a decade afterwards, leaving the door open for place-based policies contribute to equalizing household utility differentials.

Persistence of regional labour market differentials

Numerous studies have examined the reasons for regional labour market differentials and their persistence over time. Many have focused on disequilibria in regional labour markets arising from differences in labour demand, while others emphasize equilibrium explanations such as amenities and labour market policies (HOLZER, 1993; PARTRIDGE and RICKMAN, 1997a). Because of the attention given to unemployment at the national level, regional differentials in unemployment have received the most attention, with some also given to regional differentials in employment rates and poverty. For the evaluation of the SE model and place-based policy-making, the most important aspect of regional labour market differentials is the persistence of the *disequilibrium* component resulting from shocks. Early empirical investigations relied on econometrically estimated partial adjustment models, while later investigations used time-series methodology,

Table 1. Cross-sectional tests of spatial equilibrium

Study	Analysis	Finding	Spatial equilibrium
DICKIE and GERKING (1989)	Literature review of real wage equalization	Real wages not equalized	No
ROBACK (1988)	Wage-price elasticity	0.97	Yes
DUMOND et al. (1999)	Wage-price elasticity	0.46	No
WINTERS (2009)	Wage-price elasticity	0.5–1.0	Depends on estimation and housing cost measure
GLAESER and GOTTLIEB (2008), OSWALD and WU (2009)	Self-reported happiness	No relation to income/gross domestic product (GDP) per capita; significant variation in happiness levels reported	Weakly supported; strong form rejected
GREENWOOD et al. (1991), CLARK et al. (2003), RICKMAN (2011)	Migration analysis	Existence of disequilibrium gaps, related to subsequent migration	Yes, in the longer run (weak support); not in the short run (rejecting the strong form)
BAYER et al. (2009), MCGRANAHAN et al. (2011)	Hedonic estimation	Outdoor/environmental amenities only partially capitalized into factor prices	Weakly supported

which include controlling for the possibility of shifts in equilibrium differentials.

In econometrically estimated partial adjustment models, an SE of labour market outcomes is hypothesized to be determined by numerous factors, including labour demand, local labour market policies and area household amenities:

$$Y_{it}^* = \beta X_{it}$$

Deviations of labour market outcomes from the equilibrium induce adjustments in the labour market with speed α:

$$Y_{it} - Y_{it-1} = \alpha\left(Y_{it}^* - Y_{it-1}\right)$$

Substituting in the expression for the equilibrium labour market outcomes yields the econometrically estimable equation:

$$Y_{it} = (1 - \alpha)Y_{it-1} + \alpha\beta X_{it}$$

where α is the speed of adjustment, which implies that $(1 - \alpha)$ is persistence of disequilibrium; and β is long-run impact of X on Y, which is obtained as $\left(\alpha\beta/(1 - (1 - \alpha))\right)$. Correspondingly, many studies examine the role of migration in determining the speed of adjustment. More rapid adjustment supports an SE interpretation and would suggest that regional policy is less necessary.

MARSTON (1985) used a variance components method to assess the relative sizes of equilibrium and disequilibrium components of unemployment for a sample of US metropolitan areas during the 1970s. He reported that the disequilibrium component was only half as large as the equilibrium component and that it did not last for more than a year. Using a similar approach with post-Second World War data through to 1992, DAVIS et al. (1997) find much more persistence in unemployment, with the magnitudes of the coefficients on lagged unemployment suggesting that only 30% of unemployment differential is eliminated in one year. MARSTON's (1985) use of a short panel period may be one reason for the different results. DAVIS et al. (1997) report negative shocks as having a larger absolute value effect on unemployment than positive shocks.

Based on an examination of US metropolitan areas from 1976 to 1984, HYCLAK (1996) finds that about a 1 point rise in unemployment is reduced to one half by the end of four years. GORDON (1988) finds that London's unemployment differential dissipates fairly quickly following the initial rise in response to a drop in employment. The dissipation of the residual was slower during times of high national unemployment.

PARTRIDGE and RICKMAN (1997b) decomposes US state unemployment differentials into equilibrium and disequilibrium components for 1992–1994. They report that for some regions the disequilibrium component was larger, while in other regions the equilibrium component dominated. They do not address the issue of persistence in the disequilibrium component, though they find contemporaneous and lagged regional employment growth measures to be significantly related to regional unemployment.

Migration flows have also been examined in the context of interregional migration being sufficient to eliminate disequilibrium unemployment differentials. MARSTON (1985) concludes that the annual flows of people between areas is large compared with the disequilibrium component, which supports the strong form of the SE hypothesis. Yet, in examining US place-to-place migration flows during the 1980s, GABRIEL et al. (1993) conclude they were insufficient to offset shocks to the regional distribution of unemployment rates and that the primary effect was on wage differentials. TREYZ et al. (1993) estimate net migration for US states, reporting a sluggish migration adjustment process to regional imbalances in demand. They find that it took twenty years for 83.5% of a demand-induced imbalance to be eliminated through migration. Using US state data from 1976 to 1996, modelling migration as forward looking, GALLIN (2004) concludes that all the migration adjustment occurs within ten years, still a period of substantial length.

PISSARIDES and MCMASTER (1990) estimate migration and wage pooled cross-section regressions for British regions and link them to an equation for unemployment. Based on simulation of the three equations, they conclude it would take more than twenty years to eliminate a disequilibrium unemployment differential. GROENEWOLD (1997) uses three econometric equations for wages, unemployment and migration for an Australian state, reporting that adjustment through interregional migration is slow − 12.5% of a disequilibrium unemployment differential remained after fifteen years.

Although unemployment and migration have garnered most of the attention in the partial labour market adjustment literature, some attention also has been given to the persistence of regional poverty. In a series of studies using a partial adjustment model, PARTRIDGE and RICKMAN (2005, 2006a, 2007a, 2007b, 2008a, 2008b) find US regional poverty to be very persistent, in which the fraction of the regional poverty differential that is eliminated over a ten-year period ranges from 40% to 70%. The poverty adjustment process in high-poverty non-metropolitan counties, including persistently high-poverty counties, is no more sluggish than that of other non-metropolitan counties (PARTRIDGE and RICKMAN, 2005, 2007a), while poverty in metropolitan areas is at least as persistent as for non-metropolitan areas (PARTRIDGE and RICKMAN, 2008b).

More recently, studies of the persistence of unemployment and other labour market outcomes (Y) have shifted mostly to time-series analysis. Primarily, unit root tests have been performed to determine whether a shock (e) to regional unemployment has persistent effects. A unit root is said to exist if evidence is not found that the coefficient on the lagged unemployment rate (labour market outcome) (ρ) is less than 1:

$$Y_t = \mu + \rho Y_{t-1} + e_t$$

A unit root indicates persistence because a value of 1 indicates that regional unemployment will not revert back to the mean (or trend value if included in the equation) following a shock, that is, shocks have permanent effects. Values less than, but close to, 1 still imply sluggish adjustment, where the SE model would suggest a coefficient closer to zero for ρ.

BLANCHARD and KATZ (1992) perform augmented Dickey–Fuller (ADF) unit root tests for US state unemployment over the period 1972–1990, failing to reject a unit root in unemployment in all but two states. Because of the known low power of the test to reject the null hypothesis of a unit root in small samples, and based on theoretical prior beliefs of regional unemployment rates, Blanchard and Katz model them as stationary. Stationarity of unemployment implicitly forces migration to arbitrage away regional unemployment differentials (OBSTFELD and PERI, 1998), which means that their technique forces, rather than tests, SE. In comments made on the work of BLANCHARD and KATZ (1992), HALL (1992) further notes the short time-series on which their findings are based.

ROWTHORN and GLYN (2006) use a longer employment time-series that contains less measurement error and find that employment rates permanently change in response to shocks, indicating that migration plays a much smaller role in state labour market equilibration than concluded by Blanchard and Katz.

Recognizing the low power of unit root tests in small samples, PAYNE et al. (1999) use variance ratio tests. They fail to reject the null of a unit root in unemployment for all fifty US states during 1978–1996, supporting the view that shocks to state and aggregate unemployment have permanent effects. In addition, they also test for co-integration of state and national unemployment rates. The rates are co-integrated if they both share a common stochastic drift. That is, both the state (Y_i) and national unemployment (Y_n) rates are non-stationary, but a linear combination of them is stationary, that is:

$$Y_{nt} - \beta Y_{it} = u_t$$

where β is estimated and stationarity of the residual (u) indicates co-integration. Co-integration in this case implies that a state unemployment rate and the national unemployment rate follow similar long-run trends even if they deviate in the short-term. For only two states do they find co-integration between the state and national unemployment rates, indicating that the regional differentials are non-stationary. This suggests persistent disequilibrium differences in regional unemployment rates, inconsistent with stronger forms of the SE model. In contrast, in an analysis of UK regional unemployment rates for 1965–1995, MARTIN (1997) finds them to be co-integrated with the national rate. Martin estimates that divergences from long-run equilibrium are eliminated within four to six years.

Newer generations of unit root tests have been used to examine regional unemployment rates. SONG and WU (1997) test for unit roots in unemployment rates for the forty-eight contiguous US states. While they fail to reject the unit root for most states using ADF and Phillips–Perron (PP) tests, the null of a unit root is decisively rejected using a more powerful panel-based (Levin, Lin and Chu – LLC) test that imposes cross-section restrictions, casting doubt on the existence of hysteresis in state unemployment rates. Yet, a null hypothesis of the coefficient on the lagged dependent equalling zero also is rejected, indicating persistence in state unemployment rates. Using several unit root tests, including panel unit root tests, WANG and DAYANANDAN (2006) find generally that the tests support non-stationarity of poverty for most Canadian provinces between 1980 and 2003.

Unit roots are less likely to be rejected when the time-series possess structural breaks (BAYER and JÜßEN, 2007; ROMERO-ÁVILA and USABIAGA, 2007; SEPHTON, 2009). Nevertheless, the question of persistence remains. ROMERO-ÁVILA and USABIAGA (2007) find the average half-life of impulse responses to shocks in US state unemployment to be six years, with a convergence speed of 11% per year, in which the upper bound of the confidence interval exceeded twenty years in all but nine states. SEPHTON (2009) suggests that unemployment persistence diminishes after the second break that typically occurred in states around 2001. BAYER and JÜßEN (2007) in examining West German regional unemployment rates find that allowing for a structural break reduces the half-life of a shock from 5.6 to less than two years on average, concluding that small government interventions will likely be ineffective, though a regime shift suggests that a large intervention could move the economy from one equilibrium to another.[4]

In continuing developments in the time-series literature, it has been found that panel unit root tests that impose cross-sectional independence, where there is dependence, produce oversized tests. Therefore, LEÓN-LEDESMA (2002) demonstrates the importance of addressing cross-sectional dependence in panel unit root testing of unemployment rates for US states and European Union countries, failing to reject the unit root for most states and countries. CHENG et al.

(2012) provide the most recent evidence on US state unemployment persistence. They find evidence of non-stationarity when the most recent recession is included and even where there is evidence of stationarity, they find the half-life of a common component ranging from six to fourteen years.[5]

Finally, while instead constructing a 'transition probability matrix', PUGA (2002) compares the transitions from 1987 to 1995 of GDP per capita relative to the European average. Puga points to a strong persistence of relative regional income levels over this period with 83% of the regions retaining their position and only 17% showing improvement. A similar transition probability matrix for unemployment rates shows they diverged between the mid-1980s and the mid-1990s, with a relatively small number of regions retaining their relative European Union average position (OVERMAN and PUGA, 2002). Using a polarization measure, OVERMAN and PUGA (2002) report a 37% increase in polarization of unemployment rates.[6] The persistent (and by some measure increasing) inequalities within the European Union occurred despite the removal of mobility barriers as a result of the expanding union and significant structural funding, which was the inspiration for European Union Cohesion Policy.

Similar conclusions regarding the effects of removing mobility barriers on European labour market integration are reached by BARTZ and FUCHS-SCHÜNDELN (2012). These authors apply a spatiotemporal autoregressive model to EU-15 regional data for 1986–2006. A primary finding is the high inter-temporal correlation of regional unemployment rates, even after controlling for country effects. In addition, cross-country border correlations of unemployment did not change with European Union reforms, but did decrease within countries over time.

In summary (as shown in Table 2), although highly cited early studies such as those by MARSTON (1985) and BLANCHARD and KATZ (1992) suggest a highly efficient US labour market, with highly geographically mobile labour, the bulk of the evidence suggests significantly more sluggish US adjustments. Subsequent related US studies highlighted how flaws in the early studies led them to conclude incorrectly that US regional labour markets were highly efficient (for example, DAVIS et al., 1997; ROWTHORN and GLYN, 2006). A large volume of the recent literature, using time-series analysis, appears to support overwhelmingly the view of high persistence in regional labour market outcomes, including those for Europe.

Employment growth effects on regional labour market outcomes

An extensive number of studies directly examine the effects of differentials in employment growth on regional labour market outcomes. While some simply use OLS estimation of single econometric equations or reduced-form vector autoregression (VAR) equations, a common approach is to use the industry-mix component from regional shift–share analysis in IV estimation. The studies range from examining employment-induced responses in unemployment and labour force participation to assessing the employment growth effects on regional income distribution.

The industry-mix component is simply the regional employment growth rate that would occur if all of the region's industries grew at their corresponding national rates:

$$\left(\Sigma_i g_i^n * E_{i,t-1}^r\right)/E_{t-1}^r$$

where g^n is the national growth rate; i denotes industry; E^r is employment in the region (either total or industry when denoted by i); and $t-1$ denotes the beginning-period value. In addition to capturing the direct effects of having fast- or slow-growing industries, because of multiplier effects the measure also captures some growth in industries that differ from their national averages. So long as industries are not concentrated in single regions and a region's composition of industries is exogenous to subsequent regional labour market outcomes, the measure provides a useful exogenous instrument to assess regional labour market effects of labour demand shocks.

Vector autoregression (VAR) studies

Based on estimated reduced-form VARs for individual states, BLANCHARD and KATZ (1992) find that following a shock to employment, state unemployment and labour force participation rates return to their previous levels on average after five to seven years, which may be fast enough to argue that the SE model holds in a medium form. However, pooling all states for 1978–1990, using longer lags and various measures (instruments) of (for) employment growth, Blanchard and Katz find that about 15–17% of the unemployment and labour force participation responses to an employment shock remain after eight years. BARTIK (1993a) argues that large measurement error inherent in the unemployment rate and labour force participation and restrictions on lag lengths bias Blanchard and Katz's results towards no long-run effects. Using the same data as Blanchard and Katz, but testing for the optimal lag length rather than using Blanchard and Katz's restriction of two years used in the single-equation VARs, Bartik finds that after seventeen years, 25% of an employment shock is still reflected in the regional labour force participation rate.

DECRESSIN and FATÁS (1995) report similar findings for the United States, but find instead that labour force participation absorbs most of a labour demand shock in Europe, suggesting that migration is only partially returning a market to equilibrium. Changes in labour-force participation and employment rates suggest that

Table 2. Persistence of regional labour market differentials summary

Study	Geography	Period	Analysis	Focus variable	Findings	Spatial equilibrium
Econometrically estimated partial adjustment models						
MARSTON (1985)	US MSAs	1970s	Regression	Unemployment	Shock effects eliminated in a year	Yes
PISSARIDES and McMASTER (1990)	British regions	1963–1982	Regression	Unemployment	Twenty years for migration to eliminate disequilibrium unemployment differentials	No
GABRIEL et al. (1993)	US Census Divisions	1986–1987	Regression	Unemployment	Migration insufficient to offset shocks to unemployment rate	No
TREYZ et al. (1993)	US states	1971–1988	Regression	Net migration	Twenty years for migration to eliminate 83.5% of demand-induced imbalances	No
HYCLAK (1996)	US MSAs	1976–1984	Regression	Unemployment	1% rise in unemployment reduced to 0.5% after four years	Weakly
GROENEWOLD (1997)	Australian states	1978–1991	Regression	Unemployment	12.5% of a disequilibrium unemployment differential remained after fifteen years	No
DAVIS et al. (1997)	US states	1956–1992	Regression	Unemployment	30% of unemployment differential eliminated in one year	Weakly
GALLIN (2004)	US states	1976–1996	Regression	Net migration	Migration adjustment occurs within ten years	Weakly
PARTRIDGE and RICKMAN (2005, 2006b, 2007a, 2007b, 2008a, 2008b)	US counties	1979–1999	Regression	Poverty	40–70% of poverty differential eliminated within ten years	No
Time-series analysis						
BLANCHARD and KATZ (1992)	US states	1972–1990	ADF unit root test	Unemployment	Unit root in all but two states	No
SONG and WU (1997)	US states	1962–1993	Unit root test: ADF, PP, panel LLC	Unemployment	ADF and PP indicate unit root; panel LLC indicates stationarity	Weakly
MARTIN (1997)	UK regions	1965–1995	Co-integration test	Unemployment	Co-integration between regional and national unemployment rate. Divergences last for four to six years.	Weakly
PAYNE et al. (1999)	US states	1978–1996	Variance ratio test; co-integration test	Unemployment	Unit root for all fifty states; co-integration with national unemployment for only two states	No
LEÓN-LEDESMA (2002)	US states; European Union countries	1985–1999	Unit root test with cross-sectional dependence	Unemployment	Unit root for most US states and European Union countries	No
ROWTHORN and GLYN (2006)	US states	1948–2000	Fisher's λ statistic (panel test)	Employment rate	Shocks have permanent effects on employment rates	No
WANG and DAYANANDAN (2006)	Canadian provinces	1980–2003	ADF test, PP test DF-GLS test	Poverty	Poverty rates are non-stationary	No
ROMERO-ÁVILA and USABIAGA (2007)	US states	1976–2004	Unit root test with structural break	Unemployment	Convergence speed 11% per year	No
BAYER and JÜßEN (2007)	West German regions	1960–2002	Unit root test with structural break	Unemployment	Half-life of shock effects less than two years	Weakly
BARTZ and FUCHS-SCHÜNDELN (2012)	EU-15 regions	1986–2006	Inter-temporal correlation	Unemployment	High inter-temporal correlation of regional unemployment rates	No
CHENG et al. (2012)	US states	1976–2010	PANIC method; RMA data method	Unemployment	Evidence of non-stationarity; half-life of shocks six to fourteen years	No

Note: ADF, augmented Dickey–Fuller; DF-GLS, Dickey–Fuller augmented generalized least squares; LLC, Levin, Lin and Chu test; MSA, metropolitan statistical area; PANIC, panel analysis of non-stationarity in idiosyncratic and common components; PP, Phillips–Perron; and RMA, recursive mean adjusted.

some of the region's original residents benefited (or hurt) by labour demand shocks. JIMINEO and BENTOLILA (1998) find that about one-quarter of a labour demand shock effect on regional unemployment and labour force participation in Spain remains in the long run. They also report that the Spanish responses were slower than for the United States and the rest of Europe. PEKKALA and KANGASHARJU (2002) similarly find migration playing a much smaller role in regional labour market adjustment in Finland, with permanent changes found for unemployment and labour force participation in response to labour demand shocks. BROERSMA and VAN DIJK (2002) find a speed of regional labour market adjustment in the Netherlands equal to that found by Blanchard and Katz for the United States, but following other European studies, the primary adjustments occur in labour force participation rates rather than regional migration.

Contrarily, while also using the Blanchard and Katz approach, FREDRIKSSON (1999) reports that regional adjustment to labour demand shocks in Sweden is rapid, in which interregional migration is the primary adjustment and unemployment and labour force participation rates return to normal within two years. Using the Blanchard and Katz approach and assumptions to examine 166 regions in Europe for 1988–1997, TANI (2003) concludes that European workers are much more mobile than previous studies suggested, with the effects of shocks eliminated within seven years.

HUNT (2006) finds US employment and population to be co-integrated. Based on estimated vector error correction models, 53% of the impulse responses took place within twenty years, with 73% taking place within twenty-five years. These, Hunt argued, were significantly shorter than those estimated in previous studies that used levels of non-stationary variables. YEO et al. (2005) examine employment, population, and labour force participation for the state of Washington. All three variables are found to contain a unit root and are co-integrated. A shock to employment has a permanent long-run effect on labour force participation; almost 30% of the initial effect on labour force participation remains in the long run.

PARTRIDGE and RICKMAN (2003b, 2006a, 2009) construct long-run restrictions structural vector autoregression (SVAR) models to assess regional labour market dynamics. An advantage of their SVAR approach is that employment is no longer assumed solely to represent labour demand as in Blanchard and Katz and other reduced-form VAR studies. Rather, explicit recognition is given to both labour demand and labour supply; migration contains labour supply innovations and does not simply represent a response to labour demand. Among the primary findings, about 20% of a US state labour demand shock is reflected in the employment rate in the long run (PARTRIDGE and RICKMAN, 2006b), varying from a low 13% for Sunbelt states to 55% for Rustbelt states. For Canada,

about one-third of a labour demand shock is reflected in the long-run employment rate, with larger estimates for Ontario and Quebec, and little effect found for the Atlantic provinces (PARTRIDGE and RICKMAN, 2009).

Econometric equation studies of unemployment and labour force participation

One approach to examining labour supply responses to employment growth is to decompose the change in employment into the sources of supply using an identity in which changes in employment equals the sum of changes in labour force participation, changes in population and changes in the number unemployed. The supply responses then are regressed on employment growth; because of the identity, the sum of the estimated supply responses equal unity. Two primary assumptions underlie the approach: short-run fluctuations in employment are demand-driven; and labour supply contemporaneously responds to labour demand shocks without a lag (PARTRIDGE and RICKMAN, 2008d).

EBERTS and STONE (1992) use this approach in examining changes in unemployment, labour force participation and population for US metropolitan areas. They find increased labour force participation of local residents to be the primary labour supply response to increased job growth (pp. 23–24), where three-quarters of a change in employment is satisfied by individuals entering/exiting the labour force. Changes in the unemployment rate and population share account equally for the remaining supply adjustments. In subsequent analysis, using recursive identifying restrictions in estimating regional labour demand and supply, Eberts and Stone (pp. 78–83) conclude that the time for full adjustment of local labour markets toward a new equilibrium following a demand shock exceeds a decade.

Because they examined US counties, a finer level of disaggregation, PARTRIDGE and RICKMAN (2008d) added net commuting as a fourth potential source of labour supply. Based on their decomposition, they conclude that generally net commuting was the dominant supply response, limiting the benefits of job growth to the original residents. However, in non-metropolitan counties, a change in labour force participation was the primary response. Persistently high-poverty non-metropolitan counties had the smallest commuting response and largest labour force participation and unemployment responses.

In comparing London with other areas in Great Britain, GORDON (1988) finds that the unemployment rate response to a change in employment varies by size and type of area and national economic conditions. Only 17% of employment-induced change to unemployment remained after one year, where the largest response was migration. In Scotland (taken as a region), over 40% of the unemployment effect remained after one year, whereas in the typical inner borough of London, all the effect was eliminated in one year.

In a review of the early literature, BARTIK (1991, ch. 4) reports that most studies only estimated employment growth effects for short periods of time, and where longer periods were considered (ten years or greater), the studies did not distinguish short-run from long-run effects. Bartik finds that 1 percentage point employment growth effects on regional unemployment rates over long periods of time range across studies from −0.04 percentage points to no effect, while for labour force participation they range from no effect to 0.08 percentage points. The reviewed studies also failed to distinguish between whether employment growth represented demand or supply, and whether the effects varied across areas, by growth rates or across types of individuals.

In an examination of US metropolitan areas, BARTIK (1991) finds that a 1 percentage point increase in employment growth reduces unemployment by 0.06–0.07 percentage points in the long run, depending on whether micro- or aggregate data are used. The labour force participation rate is increased by 0.14%, consistent with policy having permanent effects for a region's original residents. Bartik finds generally similar effects across groups of people, though labour force participation rates of older workers are significantly more sensitive to local employment growth.

A number of studies also examined whether employment growth effects on unemployment and labour force vary by region or by source of employment growth. BARTIK (1991, ch. 4) finds no difference across metropolitan areas experiencing different growth rates. Using pooled data for thirty-eight US metropolitan areas, BARTIK (2009) finds that regional employment growth's effect on employment rates is significantly higher in the short run for metropolitan areas with initially slacker labour markets but generally not in the longer run. Yet, there is some evidence that in areas with the tightest labour markets, employment effects are smaller than the average.

PARTRIDGE and RICKMAN (1997a, 1998) find that faster US state employment growth associated with a state's composition of nationally fast-growth industries reduces unemployment rates more than growth idiosyncratic to the state. They attribute this to lesser migration in response to industry-mix employment growth because if the industries were growing faster nationally, and there was imperfect labour mobility across sectors, there would less incentive for migration. This result also was reported in the migration study of PARTRIDGE and RICKMAN (1999).[7]

Using an industry-mix employment growth measure of labour demand shocks for US metropolitan areas, NOTOWIDIGDO (2011) finds that positive shocks increase population and employment more than negative shocks reduce them. This asymmetry is particularly true for low-skilled workers. The reasons attributed to the lower mobility in declining regions are a lower elasticity of housing supply because housing stock is durable (GLAESER and GYOURKO, 2005) and social transfer payments. Because of the larger share of their budget spent on housing, low-skilled workers particularly benefit from falling housing prices in declining regions. Although social transfer payments limit labour mobility, NOTOWIDIGDO (2011) finds that even if the transfer payments were replaced by subsidies, the housing sector alone causes asymmetric population and employment responses to demand shocks in growing versus declining regions. Lower mobility in declining regions suggests that place-based policies potentially have the greatest scope to affect labour market outcomes in lagging regions permanently (though costs may be higher).

Econometric equation studies of income distribution effects

Evidence of employment growth effects on regional labour market outcomes also can be found in regional studies of income and its distribution, including poverty. The SE model suggests that demand shocks should have relatively little impact on the income distribution and poverty (PARTRIDGE and RICKMAN, 2006a). Foremost, if wages for one income group were increased, this would induce offsetting migration that would return utility to the national average. Second, the initial sorting of households (say) into poor regions suggest that they voluntarily live in places with low employment rates. Because of this relative lack of attachment to the labour market, it is unclear whether such households would take employment if a positive demand shock lifted local employment (that is, such sorting would then be a cause of high poverty pockets).

In a review and updating of previous research, BARTIK (2005) concludes that five years after a 1% increase in local employment, there is an increase in real earnings per capita that is 0.28% of local area personal income. Half of this results from area residents moving up to higher-paying occupations (the other half was attributed to increased employment rates). In further reviewing the literature, BARTIK (2012) concludes that a 1% demand shock to local employment increases local employment rates by 0.2% and occupation wages by 0.2%, for a total effect on real earnings per capita of 0.4%. If the local job mix shifts towards industries that pay more nationally, there are additional wage spillover benefits. A 1 percentage point increase in wages because of a shift in the mix of high-paying jobs increases local earnings by 2 percentage points (BARTIK, 1993b).

Regarding the distribution of income gains from employment growth, in a study of US metropolitan areas from 1979 to 1988, BARTIK (1994) finds that job growth in a metropolitan area increases the long-run share of income received by those in the lowest income quintile. Strong employment growth particularly benefits workers with the least skills and education because a tight labour market forces employers to hire them. Bartik cautions that they are beneficial only if economic development programme costs are modest and not financed by social programme cuts that benefit the poor.

Based on panel data for individuals in US metropolitan areas, BARTIK (1996) finds that a boost to employment growth of 1 percentage point reduces the probability of poverty for women by 0.33% and men by 0.20%; the same increase in metropolitan statistical area (MSA) employment growth increases average real earnings by 0.5% or 0.6%, in which half is attributable to increased annual hours worked, and the other half to greater wages. In contrast to other studies (for example, BARTIK, 1993b), blacks and whites experienced similar real earnings gains from increased MSA growth. BARTIK (2001, p. 148) concludes that 10–20% of the increase in employment and earnings may persist in the long run, in which the most important channel is poor individuals moving into higher paying jobs.

BOUND and HOLZER (2000) examine the effects of labour demand shifts for US metropolitan areas during the 1980s. They find population responses partially offset the labour market effects of demand shifts. But the more limited population responses among less-educated workers lead them to experience greater losses in work hours and earnings. Based on IV estimates (using industry-mix employment growth as the instrument), a 10% decline in an area's labour demand would reduce nominal earnings by 11% for high-school-educated workers and 6% for workers with a college degree. Most of these nominal wage declines are estimated to translate into real wage declines.

Using an equilibrium framework, LEVERNIER et al. (2000) generally do not find recent employment growth to have reduced US county poverty in 1989. Yet, they find employment to reduce poverty in counties with larger shares of African-American residents. In contrast, using a disequilibrium framework, PARTRIDGE and RICKMAN (2006a, p. 142) find a 1 percentage point increase in job growth reduces US county poverty by 0.37 percentage points in 1989 and by 0.23 percentage points in 1999.

In a study of US metropolitan areas (using a disequilibrium framework), PARTRIDGE and RICKMAN (2008b) find job growth reducing poverty, in which the effect varies across metropolitan size and county type. A 1 percentage point increase in job growth reduces poverty by 0.2 percentage points in large metropolitan area central city counties in the short run and about 0.4 percentage points in the long run. One concern is that poverty and employment growth are jointly determined. In assessing this possibility, Partridge and Rickman find that the null hypothesis of exogeneity of poverty to employment growth using the instrument of industry-mix job

growth from shift–share analysis could not be rejected. No effect is found for large metropolitan area suburban counties. For medium-sized (small-sized) metropolitan areas, a 1 percentage point metropolitan-wide increase in employment reduces poverty by 0.3 (0.3) percentage points in the short run and by 0.5 (0.6) percentage points in the long run.

In examining poverty rate changes in the 1990s for US Census tracts, CRANDALL and WEBER (2004) show that job growth reduces poverty more in high-poverty neighbourhoods. A 1 percentage point increase in employment growth rates reduces poverty by 0.011, 0.046 and 0.088 percentage points in low-, medium- and high-poverty tracts, respectively. The results are notable given the smaller geographic scale of census tracts and the higher possibility of sorting. Indeed, certain types of sorting imply that job growth would not help self-sorted households with less lower attachment to the labour market. If stronger job growth reduces poverty at the neighbourhood level, this suggests that affected households had an employment access problem. They also find that a higher initial poverty rate in a tract was associated with a greater poverty decline over the subsequent decade.

PARTRIDGE and RICKMAN (2006b, ch. 4) find an increase in current and lagged (up to two years) state employment growth of 1% reduces the poverty rate by 0.5%. They also present evidence that the effect is stronger during times of low national unemployment. The channels through which employment growth is found to affect poverty include reducing unemployment, increasing employment rates and reducing teen birth rates.

For non-metropolitan high-poverty US counties, PARTRIDGE and RICKMAN (2005) estimate that a 1 percentage point increase in employment reduces poverty by 0.11 percentage points in the long run, approximately double the magnitude of the estimate for other non-metropolitan counties. When relative employment growth is decomposed into two components using shift–share analysis, the industry-mix and competitiveness components have approximately the same poverty effect in high-poverty counties. For other counties, though, the poverty-reducing effect is four times larger for growth attributable to the county's mix of industries. Partridge and Rickman argue that the stronger industry-mix effect in non-high-poverty counties occurs because of a lesser migration response if the industries are faring poorly nationally, consistent with evidence presented above for unemployment.

In a follow-up study on persistent poverty counties, PARTRIDGE and RICKMAN (2007a) further examine the poverty-generating process in persistently high-poverty non-metropolitan counties using geographically weighted regression. They find that employment growth has three times the magnitude effect on poverty in persistently high-poverty counties relative to other non-metropolitan counties.

In a pair of papers using geographic information systems (GIS) data, PARTRIDGE and RICKMAN (2008a, 2008c) find that remoteness influences how job growth affects poverty. Using industry-mix employment as an instrument, local job growth reduces poverty only in non-metropolitan counties at a sufficient distance from the nearest metropolitan area, presumably because of lower commuting and migration responses. In fact, both studies reveal lower migration responses to employment growth the farther a non-metropolitan county is from a metropolitan area. They conclude that higher poverty in remote areas is not simply the result of the sorting of poor people into these areas, but a result of adverse labour demand shocks that do not dissipate through labour market adjustment. In addition, job growth in the nearest metropolitan area is found to reduce poverty, but the effect attenuates with distance. Such a result suggests that it is not self-sorting into remote areas that cause weak economic outcomes, but rather the lack of employment access.

In summary, studies directly examining labour demand effects on labour market outcomes perhaps provide the strongest evidence against the SE view (representative sample shown in Table 3). Labour demand shocks generally permanently raise employment rates, reduce poverty and income inequality. The ability of policies to influence labour demand is the subject of the next section.

REVIEW OF SELECTED ANALYSES OF PLACE-BASED INTERVENTIONS

Evaluations of place-based interventions are, by definition, reviews of specific programmes in particular regions, with results that may not be easily generalizable.[8] The reasons for the policy, the characteristics of the region and the outcomes are likely to be unique. Nevertheless, existing reviews or evaluations of regional development programmes may be informative regarding the general problems facing place-based policies and their evaluation.

Atlantic Canada Opportunity Agency (ACOA)

The size and diversity of Canada, along with its decentralized government, have resulted in both significant regional economic differences and a long history of national programmes to mitigate them. While regional disparities were recognized as early as the 1930s, it was not until the second half of the twentieth century that their systemic nature was formally acknowledged (BLAKE, 2003). The *Final Report of the Royal Commission on Canada's Economic Prospects* (GORDON, 1957) found that incomes and standards of living in the Atlantic region (comprised of four east coast provinces including New Brunswick, Nova Scotia, Prince Edward Island and Newfoundland) were far below the national average, suggesting that more deliberate intervention was needed. Following the Gordon Commission, the first of several explicit regional development efforts was initiated for the Atlantic region, first through existing national departments and programmes, but since 1987 through the regionally based ACOA.

The ACOA is a federal government department though its programmes may require contributions from provincial governments and local stakeholders, as well as inputs into the design of its programming. It has evolved to include an array of development programmes including: interest-free, unsecured loans to small and medium-sized businesses and not-for-profit activities; technical and financial services through community business development corporations; a non-repayable Innovative Communities Fund that consists of investments in strategic projects to build the community economies; an Infrastructure Fund; and an Atlantic Innovation Fund to encourage partnerships between businesses and research institutions with a focus on commercializing technology-based products, processes or services (GOLDENBERG, 2008). Given the breadth and long-standing nature of ACOA, it is not surprising that there have been several external reviews of the programmes, in addition to the required internal review processes.

MINTZ and SMART (2003) conducted an analysis of federal grants in Atlantic Canada over the 1988–2000 period. They describe the grant programmes as well intended, but poorly targeted. Their indictment that 'Governments are usually not good at picking winners, but losers tend to be very good at picking governments' reflects their finding that the programmes are vulnerable to serving political, rather than economic, objectives. They conclude that although the mandate of ACOA is to improve economic growth and employment in the Atlantic region, the impacts have been questionable and at a relatively significant cost. Grants are targeted at inefficient businesses resulting in higher input prices, or flow to businesses that would have undertaken the activity anyway. They propose a broad-based corporate tax reduction for the Atlantic region, another form of place-based intervention, as a superior alternative.

As a component of another Royal Commission (Royal Commission on Renewing and Strengthening Our Place in Canada), BLAKE (2003) finds that Canada's regional development strategies have been largely unsuccessful at creating long-term sustainable growth. Indeed Blake states that if one were to apply a business model to the initiatives, they would be declared an 'unmitigated disaster'. He does, however, point to significant social benefits from the resulting infrastructure and social services, concluding that the programmes are about values and social inclusion rather than about sustainable economic development. Similarly, GOLDENBERG (2008) recommends that regional development policies and programmes must

Table 3. Employment growth effects on regional labour market outcome summary

Study	Geography	Period	Methodology	Focus variable	Findings	Spatial equilibrium
Vector autoregression (VAR) studies						
BLANCHARD and KATZ (1992)	US states	1948–1990	Single-state VARs	Unemployment, labour force participation	Rates return to previous levels after five to seven years	Weakly
BLANCHARD and KATZ (1992)	US states	1978–1990	Pooled VAR	Unemployment, labour force participation	15–17% of the unemployment and labour force participation responses remain after eight years	No
BARTIK (1993a)	US states	1948–1990	Reduced-form VARs	Labour force participation	25% of an employment shock reflected in the regional labour force participation rate after seventeen years	No
JIMINEO and BENTOLILA (1998)	Spanish regions	1976–1994	Reduced-form VARs	Unemployment, labour force participation	25% of labour demand shock's effect remains in the long run	No
FREDRIKSSON (1999)	Swedish counties	1963–1993	Reduced-form VARs	Unemployment, labour force participation	Labour market adjustment completed within two years	Yes
PEKKALA and KANGASHARJU (2002)	Finnish provinces	1976–2000	Reduced-form VARs	Unemployment, labour force participation	Permanent changes	No
TANI (2003)	European Union regions	1988–1997	Reduced-form VARs	Unemployment, labour force participation	Shocks eliminated within seven years	Weakly
YEO *et al.* (2005)	Washington State	1969–1993	Reduced-form VARs	Unemployment, labour force participation, population	30% of the initial effect on labour force participation remains in the long run	No
HUNT (2006)	US states	1953–2000	VEC model	Employment, population	27% of the impulse response remains after twenty-five years	No
PARTRIDGE and RICKMAN (2006)	US states	1970–1998	SVARs	Wages, employment, population	20% of demand shock reflected in employment rate in the long run	No
PARTRIDGE and RICKMAN (2009b)	Canadian provinces	1976–2003	SVARs	Wages, employment, population	33% of demand shock reflected in employment rate in the long run	No
Econometric equation studies						
GORDON (1988)	British regions	1956–1986	Difference estimation	Unemployment	17% of effect remaining after one year	Yes
BARTIK (1991)	US MSAs	1972–1986	Panel regression	Unemployment	1% increase in employment growth reduces unemployment rate by 0.06–0.07 percentage points, and increases labour force participation rate by 0.14 percentage points	No
BARTIK (1996)	US MSAs	1979–1988	Panel regression	Real earnings, poverty	1% increase in employment reduces the probability of poverty for females by 0.33% and males by 0.20%; increases average real earnings by 0.5% or 0.6%	No
BOUND and HOLZER (2000)	US MSAs	1979–1989	IV estimation	Nominal earnings	10% decline in labour demand reduces nominal earnings by 11% for high-school-educated workers and 6% for workers with a college degree in the long run	No

(*Continued*)

Table 3. Continued

Study	Geography	Period	Methodology	Focus variable	Findings	Spatial equilibrium
CRANDALL and WEBER (2004)	US Census tracts	1990s	Spatial econometric estimation	Poverty	1% increase in employment growth rates reduces poverty by 0.011, 0.046 and 0.088 percentage points in low, medium and high poverty tracts	No
PARTRIDGE and RICKMAN (2005)	US non-metropolitan counties	1979–1999	Reduced-form regression	Poverty	1% increase in employment reduces poverty rate by 0.11 in the long run in high poverty counties, double the average	No
PARTRIDGE and RICKMAN (2006a)	US counties	1979–1999	Reduced-form regression	Poverty	1 percentage point increase in job growth reduces poverty rate by 0.37 percentage points in 1989 and by 0.23 percentage points in 1999	No

Note: IV, instrumental variable; MSA, metropolitan statistical area; SVAR, structural vector autoregression; and VEC, vector error correction.

take a holistic, community-centred, partnership approach, making strategic investments rather than remedial interventions.

Appalachian Regional Commission (ARC)

As shown in Fig. 1, the region covered by the ARC follows the Appalachian Mountains and its foothills from northwest Mississippi to southern New York. It is composed of West Virginia and parts of twelve other US states. It has 205 000 square miles with over 25 million residents.[9] The region has long been known for its lagging economy and high poverty despite its natural splendour and resource abundance in commodities such as timber and coal. The region is proximate to large Atlantic Coast metropolitan areas, but its mountainous terrain has caused isolation that has stunted its development.

The creation of the ARC gained momentum with the release of the PRESIDENT'S APPALACHIAN REGIONAL COMMISSION (PARC) (1964) report, which described the findings of a presidential commission formed by President John F. Kennedy in 1961. The PARC report documented the region's intense poverty and proposed a federal–state partnership to attack the 'common problems' of the region. The PARC report spurred the passage of the 1965 Appalachian Regional Development Act (ARDA) that created the ARC. The ARC has broadly focused on (1) building the Appalachian Development Highway System (ADHS) to reduce the region's remoteness – which is nearly complete today; and (2) providing development grants to build the region's infrastructure and to promote its socioeconomic development.[10]

The ARC, like ACOA, is a partnership of the federal, state and local governments, which is perceived to have worked well despite the jealousies that can often arise across differing levels of government. In addition, the ARC has promoted a regional approach through multi-county local development districts to coordinate

its efforts. During the administration of President Ronald Reagan in the early 1980s, the ARC was criticized for not completing its work and its federal funding for targeted development grants and programmes was sharply cut, though ADHS funding continued at relatively high levels.

There have been many evaluations of ARC programmes. Much of these are of low quality, focusing on whether stakeholders 'believe' they were effective in using ARC funding or self-reported data from employers who received assistance about how many jobs were created or retained. Instead, the focus here is on three of the more prominent (relatively higher quality) evaluations that compare economic outcomes in ARC counties with comparable counties outside of the ARC region. These studies illustrate that one of the biggest challenges facing evaluations is identifying the counterfactual of no policy intervention. The issue is whether there are comparable counties outside of the ARC region given the region's unique history and culture.

The first two studies (ISSERMAN and REPHANN, 1995; ECONOMIC DEVELOPMENT RESEARCH GROUP, INC. (ERG) and MIT DEPARTMENT OF URBAN STUDIES & PLANNING (MIT), 2007) employ a matching methodology based on control counties located at least 60 miles from the ARC; having similar 1950–1959 growth rates in personal income and earnings by sector; and possessing a similar 1959 economic structure and 1959 population. ISSERMAN and REPHANN (1995) examined the 1969–1991 period, while ERG and MIT (2007) updated their results from 1969 to 2000. The matching procedure attempts to identify 'twin counties' outside the region whose performance would be approximately equal to how the corresponding ARC counties would have fared without policy intervention. Thus, the county that contains Pittsburgh, Pennsylvania, was matched to the county that contains Buffalo, New York, and so on. GLAESER and GOTTLIEB (2008) argue that some of the matches were so

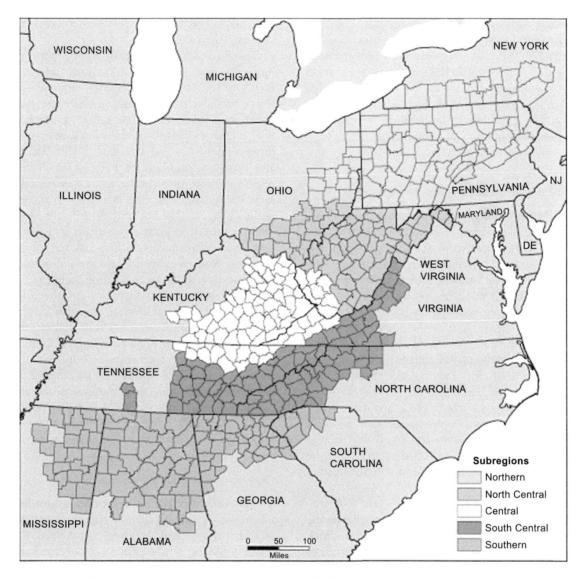

Fig. 1. Appalachian Regional Commission (ARC) and its geographic subcomponents
Source: ARC, November 2009 (available at: http://www.arc.gov/research/MapsofAppalachia.asp?MAP_ID=31)
(accessed on 19 February 2013)

geographically far from Appalachia that they would not produce credible counterfactuals.

The focus in this paper is on the work of ERG and MIT (2007) because their results are consistent with those of ISSERMAN and REPHANN (1995). ERG and MIT (2007) find that ARC counties on average had 96% faster growth in earnings, 36% faster growth in per capita income, and 9% faster growth in population than their twin counties over the 1969–2000 period. The gaps tend to apply to both metropolitan and non-metropolitan counties and are larger for those with access to the ADHS. The positive results for the highway system for Appalachia run counter to CRESCENZI and RODRÍGUEZ-POSE's (2012) negative findings for infrastructure investments made by the European Union.

GLAESER and GOTTLIEB (2008) argue that a better match would be more proximate counties in the same

state (not in the ARC) but located at least 90 kilometres from the coast. Yet, while solving the problem of using distant matches, a problem with Glaeser and Gottlieb's approach is that by definition their comparison group is not significantly distressed or they would have been designated in the ARC in the first place (or in subsequent expansions). They find that the ARC designation is positively associated with population growth during the 1970s, but is statistically insignificant between 1970 and 2000.

The present authors agree with Glaeser and Gottlieb that ERG and MIT's and Isserman and Rephann's results are too large to be credible given the relatively small financial investment made by the ARC, but Glaeser and Gottlieb's match also is far from ideal. Thus, from a reading of the broader literature, it is believed that the ARC has had net positive effects, all else being equal. One practical reason is that its non-highway system funding is in the order of only US$3 per resident and the ARC often acts more as a broker bringing together different stakeholders. With such small funding, it would be easy for the ARC to cherry-pick better funding prospects with high marginal returns than would be possible with much bigger programmes such as European Union Cohesion policy.

US Federal Empowerment Zone (EZ) Program

Federal EZs were established in 1993 for areas with high poverty and high unemployment (HANSON and ROHLIN, 2011a). There were seventy-eight applicants for EZ designation, of which parts of six large cities and three rural areas were designated. The primary incentive was a 20% wage tax credit for workers who live and work in the zone (up to US$3000), which clearly addresses the notion that the intended beneficiaries are residents. EZs also could provide incentives for capital and issue bonds on behalf of the businesses locating in the zone. EZs received a US$100 million (urban) or US$40 million (rural) block grant for social services. Almost all the unsuccessful applicants were designated as 'enterprise communities' that received considerably smaller incentives and could not use the wage tax credit. HANSON and ROHLIN (2011a) argue that the enterprise communities form a control group for comparison.

One problem with evaluating the effects of such programmes is that policy-makers may designate areas on the basis of expected under- or over-performance, which would bias traditional OLS approaches. HANSON (2009) and HANSON and ROHLIN (2011a) propose using IVs in which they find that the designation of an EZ is strongly associated with being in the district of a US House of Representative who is a member of the powerful Ways and Means Committee. The fact that the designation of EZs is closely associated with having a powerful politician illustrates a potential pitfall of all place-based policies in that politics and not economics are a driving factor. Another potential empirical problem is unmeasurable fixed effects that could bias the results. HANSON and ROHLIN (2011a) account for these by controlling for the city location of the EZ.

Using both OLS and IV approaches, HANSON and ROHLIN (2011a) find that designating an area as an EZ yielded relatively little net job creation and net-firm creation. Likewise, HANSON (2009) finds that poverty rates are not associated with the EZ designation. HANSON and ROHLIN (2011a) find that each new establishment in the EZ is associated with a US$19 million cost and each job cost about US$2.9 million, which suggests the programme was ineffective. HANSON (2009) and KRUPKA and NOONAN (2009) show that big winners were homeowners as home prices showed significant gains. Yet, it is not clear that the intended beneficiaries were homeowners versus disadvantaged workers.

There are other unintended consequences that may limit the net effects of EZs. First, HANSON and ROHLIN (2011b) use the same IV approach described above to show that industries (usually low wage) that could more easily substitute labour for capital crowd out industries where such substitution was more limited. HANSON and ROHLIN (2013) find that EZs also rearrange economic activity in which immediate neighbours lose firms to the EZ. Likewise, other poor areas within the same city lose firms to the EZ. This finding suggests that not only do EZs create few jobs, but also they apparently do so at the expense of other poor areas. While policy-makers may not mind shifting resources from wealthy to poor neighbourhoods, it is not clear that shifting activity from other poor neighbourhoods was a goal of this policy. Another implication for researchers is that if there are negative (positive) spillovers to comparison groups, estimated effects of the policy intervention will be biased upward (downward), which needs to be taken into account when deriving the counterfactual locations. Overall, these evaluations of the EZ programme are illustrative of the challenges that place-based policies face in affecting positive outcomes – especially at the neighbourhood level where spillovers could eliminate any positive net impact.

Overview of assessments of place-based policies

The assessment of place-based policies must be undertaken within the context of their *ex ante* objectives such that these should be clearly articulated. Reducing income disparities or stemming population losses from lagging regions may be appropriate indicators. As in all evaluations and impact analyses, assessment of the outcomes must be relative to a clearly articulated counterfactual – what would have been the region's trajectory in the absence of the place-based intervention? Rarely is such a complete and rigorous assessment undertaken. Further, even if there is a positive impact the full opportunity cost of this use of public funds must be considered in an environment of limited budgets and competing uses. In addition, transparency regarding social or political goals (in addition to economic targets) is an essential part of evaluating place-based interventions.

Conditions for success of place-based interventions

While the unique circumstances of individual regions and place-targeted interventions limit the extent to which generalizations can be made regarding their evaluations, a few universal inferences may be drawn. Economic efficiency considerations imply that the first requirement for place-based interventions is clear evidence that the SE forces are not adequately addressing persistent economic problems in the area. A number of indicators, including per capita incomes, poverty rates and economic growth, may be used to identify persistently lagging regions. RODRÍGUEZ-POSE (2010) points to the need also to recognize the substantial heterogeneity in the quality of institutions across space in considering place-specific policies. If locations lack quality institutions, it is hard to see how additional funding will be put to good use.

A second consideration in place-based intervention is the nature of the geographic area that is targeted. These initiatives are best directed at areas that are functional economic regions in the sense that their boundaries enclose the geographic area where people both work and spend the majority of their incomes, where the resident population accesses public and private services, such that the benefits of specific interventions are largely captured within the region. This also implies that the region is 'large' enough to meet threshold requirements for development in terms of population and labour force size. Defining the recipient region in this way will increase the probability that it has the capacity to benefit from the intervention (this especially applies to lagging rural regions).

Ensuring that place-based policy is directed at functional economic regions often requires multi-jurisdictional arrangements involving many local governments collaborating for broader regional goals rather than trying to rearrange economic activity without any *net* increase in economic activity. As the apparent success of the ARC suggests in the third section, cooperation across different levels of government also appears important to ensure that broader objectives are met rather than the narrow political interests of one level of government. Towards that end, seeking input across all levels of government and requiring matching expenditures increases accountability for all players, provides incentives for better project selection and ensures all governments strive for policy success.

Following a commitment to place-targeted intervention, the probability of success will increase if the assistance or investment is broad based (not targeting particular industries, for example), such as support for entrepreneurship in the region. This will improve the chances that individuals will choose enterprises and innovations that are consistent with the economic fundamentals of the region. Policy-makers need to avoid the trap of using sectoral policy in the guise of regional development policy – for example, claiming farm policy is rural policy or that a narrow 'cluster' helps broader regional development.

The retention and attraction of human capital to the region will be a key determinant of its long-term development. Skilled workers, and especially knowledge workers, tend to be highly mobile, so local socioeconomic conditions that make the region an attractive place to live deserve consideration. Safety, political stability, high-quality public services, good governance and a critical mass of peers will be important in this regard, in

addition to employment and income-earning opportunities.

A final condition, already reflected in some of the above is the need to tailor individual place-based intervention to the local characteristics, relying on local information, preferences and networks (BARCA, 2009; BARCA *et al.*, 2012; ORGANIZATION OF ECONOMIC DEVELOPMENT AND COOPERATION (OECD), 2009a). This includes an integrated approach to promoting the provision of public goods designed through the participation of local political institutions, and establishing linkages with other places.

Meeting these conditions does not imply that place-based policies will close the gaps between the lagging and the more prosperous regions. Nor does it speak of the cost of the intervention relative to the benefits. For public accountability purposes and flexibility in moving towards targets, benchmark values of targets should be established and periodic evaluations undertaken to ensure transparency with respect to the costs and benefits of the intervention.

DISCUSSION AND CONCLUSION

The empirical literature reviewed above suggests that the SE view of regional economies is an imperfect representation of reality. Interregional convergence either does not always occur, or if it does, the required time lag is long – perhaps intergenerational. The brief review of high visibility North American place-based interventions above suggests they may not always be successful. The question arises then as to when place-based economic policies are likely a second-best policy.

A key feature of the SE model is the implied high degree of mobility of resources. Demand or supply shocks that have differential impacts across regions will induce the flow of resources to areas of higher productivity (controlling for relative amenity appeal) increasing aggregate economic growth. In this process some regions gain, some lose, but mobile individuals and firms responding to incentives in expectation of higher levels of utility/profits are better off. Aggregate economic growth is increased. Place-targeted policy interventions that inhibit the required spatial mobility may trap individuals and firms in uneconomic regions or industries, sometimes at great expense, both directly through taxes and also through sacrificing economic growth.

But if resources are not particularly mobile, what are the policy options?[11] One set of policies relates to increasing the mobility of resources. People-based policies such as health and wellness improvements, education and training, job search incentives, subsidized moving expenses, and information and recruitment campaigns may increase mobility. The appropriate regulatory framework and removal of trade barriers between regions, for example, can facilitate the movement of financial capital. Even natural resources, the ultimate example of immobile resources, may nevertheless be mobile among uses.

There may, however, be instances where it is too costly or impractical to achieve the mobility that would be required for the poverty reduction or employment improvement goals. Even if transfer payments were replaced by subsidies to encourage mobility, durable housing may limit the population response to a negative labour demand shock (NOTOWIDIGDO, 2011). Similarly, if poverty and unemployment are concentrated among the elderly, people-based policies to improve labour mobility will be inappropriate. If education/skills, institutional, cultural or language gaps are very large, the cost of closing those gaps may be very high. Substantially 'emptying out' of regions also precludes potential future development.

Beyond cost and feasibility considerations, people-based policies to increase mobility may simply be ineffective. Financial incentives aside, historical, cultural and language barriers may inhibit mobility in a fundamental way, at least for current generations. Pockets of aboriginal populations, or immigrant populations, may not be very responsive to economic incentives designed to improve mobility. Social, historical and cultural ties may translate into very high social and personal costs. Likewise, programmes to improve skills may be ineffective, especially among older workers.

When conventional people-based policies designed to increase mobility fail to address persistently lagging regional outcomes, place-based policies may be considered in addition to, though probably not replacing, people-based policies. Place-based policies, as defined here, have two basic characteristics. First, they are policies on the part of a senior level of government for a lagging region in its jurisdiction. Local policies are always 'place-based' and are therefore not at issue. This is consistent with the original distinction between targeting 'place prosperity' versus 'people prosperity' described by WINNICK (1966) and revisited by BOLTON (1992). While improving the well-being of 'people' in the region is the ultimate target of both, targeting places may be chosen as a means to this end in a second-best world.

A second characteristic of place-based policies is that they result in immobile local investments such that the local population will benefit from the policy only while in the region. In this way, place-based policy introduces a barrier to the exit of residents of the region. Examples include physical infrastructure and support for businesses in a particular place. The geographic immobility of the object(s) of the policy is a key characteristic of place-targeted interventions. Immobility avoids outcomes such as 'brain drain' where individual recipients of people-based policies may leave the region (and be better off), though the region is worse off (ARTZ and YU, 2009; BECKSTEAD et al., 2008).

The appraisal of whether policies for lagging regions should include site-specific investments or incentives, that is, place-based policies, is complicated by the fact that existing evaluations are unique to the regions and policies that are being assessed. This review suggests that even in areas where sustained efforts have been mounted, 'success' in an absolute sense of closing gaps is elusive. The European Union Cohesion Policy is an example of the importance of objectives such as social cohesion, along with the reduction of regional disparities. Other political and social considerations may also generally play a role in the application of place-based policies.

Overall, the choice of place-based interventions will include two main considerations. First, are regional employment and poverty outcomes responsive to demand shocks? Second, will long-term benefits outweigh the costs? If increases in local jobs lead to employment of the local unemployed (rather than in-migrants or commuters) and poverty reduction, then local job stimulus may be warranted, an outcome supported by the literature review. In the long run, a thriving region will provide employment for both its own residents and for in-migrants to the region. Well-designed econometric analyses that involve a rigorous assessment of the region's response to new investments and demand will answer this question. The magnitude of the response will indicate the attractiveness of place-based investments to policy-makers.

The second criterion, comparison of the benefits and costs of place-targeted interventions, is more complex. Full opportunity cost accounting is called for as resources are shifted from (presumably) higher productivity regions/places. Both costs and benefits are likely to be distributed over decades. Current policy decisions leading to significant public regional investments will both create new opportunities and preclude others. Stimulus for developing a new industry may result in a long-term dependency (the infant industry problem). Certainly, place-specific investment will aggravate existing labour immobility. Transparency and monitoring are necessary components for public accountability and responsibility.

If place-based policies in the form of local/regional investments to create local jobs do not qualify by one or both of the above criteria, simple income transfers may be the most efficient way to address localized poverty or lagging employment. The evidence reviewed in this study and discussion suggests labour mobility is limited for reasons beyond what might be generated by income transfer payments. The costs of transfer payments arising from limited labour mobility also should be considered in setting national policies, such as those related to international trade (AUTOR et al., 2013). A reliance on household transfer payments alone is not an attractive long-term economic and political solution, however, and other options will likely need to be pursued, though they should not be at the expense of income transfer payments.

Acknowledgements – The authors would like to thank Philip McCann for suggesting the topic of the paper. They also thank the reviewers and the Editor for many helpful suggestions. Earlier versions of the paper were presented at the 59th North American Meetings of the Regional Science Association International held in Ottawa, Ontario, Canada; the 52nd Western Regional Science Association Meetings held in Santa Barbara, California, USA; and Oklahoma State University.

NOTES

1. With one exception described below, this extensive review will be at the larger regional level – say at the US county level. This paper does not review place-based (also called geographically targeted) policies at the neighbourhood or other small areas such as enterprise zones. ORGANISATION FOR ECONOMIC CO-OPERATION AND DEVELOPMENT (OECD) (2009b) provides an international overview of local development programmes.
2. PARTRIDGE and RICKMAN (1997a) find that a greater percentage of the population born in the state and greater home ownership (as measures of mobility costs) lead to persistently higher US state unemployment rates.
3. State migration estimates are derived from the US Census Bureau as the residuals of the change in population less natural population increases (see http://www.census.gov/popest/data/historical/1980s/state.html) (accessed on 14 May 2012). The respective R^2's are 0.85 and 0.75, in which the R^2's for the disequilibrium differentials used alone decreased from 0.57 to 0.48. This is suggestive of persistence in disequilibrium that diminished in the longer run, though in the longer run there is a greater chance of additional demand shocks also influencing migration.
4. GOMES and DA SILVA (2009) use an endogenous one-/ two-break Lagrange multiplier (LM) unit root test and find that the unit root null hypothesis cannot be rejected

for the major metropolitan areas of Brazil, with the exception of Rio de Janeiro. They conclude that the high persistence in Brazilian regional unemployment rates would be difficult to overcome.
5. GARCIA-DEL-BARRIOA and GIL-ALANA (2009) find that regional unemployment is persistent in Spain using panel unit root tests, regardless of whether they account for cross-sectional dependence.
6. Highlighting the importance of scale in choosing units of observation, in the context of the European Union, FAROLE et al. (2011) report that the standard deviation of per capita GDP for the constituent members declined from 12.5 in 1990 to 11.4 in 2000, but that same index increased from 26.5 to 28.5 for sub-national regions within member states.
7. PARTRIDGE and RICKMAN (1999) find that a 1% increase in competitiveness employment increased migration by 0.29 percentage points, but industry-mix employment increased it by only 0.14 percentage points. These are within the range reported by BARTIK (1991), though on the low side, being slightly lower than the estimate of TREYZ et al. (1993), which translate into a lengthy adjustment period within a stock adjustment model.
8. Indeed place-based policies are often undertaken for political reasons unrelated to spatial adjustment difficulties. They may also be designed to sustain and build on a sense of community (BOLTON, 1992). The present review focuses on interventions that have been designed to address persistent localized problems such as poverty and unemployment.
9. The source of this discussion is the ARC website (available at: http://www.arc.gov/appalachian_region/TheAppalachianRegion.asp) (accessed on 19 February 2013).
10. A good source for the historical discussion is WIDNER (1973a, 1973b, 1990). For a more critical assessment, see WHISNANT (1994).
11. This paper is silent on the mechanics of policy interventions, specifically whether they take the form of conditional transfers to regional/local governments or constitute direct involvement of the senior government. The considerations and criteria remain the same.

REFERENCES

ALBOUY D. (2012) Evaluating the efficiency and equity of federal fiscal equalization, *Journal of Public Economics* **96(9–10)**, 824–839.

ARTZ G. M. and YU L. (2009) *How You Gonna Keep 'em Down on the Farm: Which Land Grant Graduates Live in Rural Areas?* Department of Economics Staff Research Papers. Iowa State University, Ames, IA.

AUTOR D. H., DORN D. and HANSON G. H. (Forthcoming 2013) The China Syndrome: local labor market effects of import competition in the United States, *American Economic Review*.

BANDE R., FERNANDEZ M. and MONTUENGA V. (2008) Regional unemployment in Spain: disparities, business cycle and wage setting, *Labour Economics* **15(5)**, 885–914.

BARCA F. (2009) *An Agenda for a Reformed Cohesion Policy: A Place-Based Approach to Meeting European Union Challenges and Expectations*. Independent report prepared at the request of the European Commissioner for Regional Policy, Danuta Hübner. European Commission, Brussels.

BARCA F., MCCANN P. and RODRÍGUEZ-POSE A. (2012) The case for regional development intervention: place-based versus place-neutral approaches, *Journal of Regional Science* **52**, 134–152.

BARTIK T. J. (1991) *Who Benefits from State and Local Economic Development Policies?* W. E. Upjohn Institute for Employment Research, Kalamazoo, MI.

BARTIK T. J. (1993a) Who benefits from local job growth: migrants or the original residents?, *Regional Studies* **27(4)**, 297–311.

BARTIK T. J. (1993b) *Economic Development and Black Economic Success.* Upjohn Institute Technical Report Number 93-001. Report originally prepared for the US Department of Commerce, Economic Development Administration, Technical Assistance and Research Division, January.

BARTIK T. J. (1994) The effects of metropolitan job growth on the size distribution of family income, *Journal of Regional Science* **34(4)**, 483–501.

BARTIK T. J. (1996) The distributional effects of local labor demand and industrial mix: estimates using individual panel data, *Journal of Urban Economics* **40**, 150–178.

BARTIK T. J. (2001) *Jobs for the Poor: Can Labor Demand Policies Help?* Russell Sage Foundation and W. E. Upjohn Institute for Employment Research, New York, NY, and Kalamazoo, MI.

BARTIK T. J. (2005) Solving the problems of economic development incentives, *Growth and Change* **35(2)**, 139–166.

BARTIK T. J. (2009) *How Do the Effects of Local Growth on Employment Rates Vary With Initial Labor Market Conditions?* Upjohn Institute Working Paper Number 09-148. W. E. Upjohn Institute for Employment Research, Kalamazoo, MI.

BARTIK T. J. (2012) The future of state and local economic development policy: what research is needed?, *Growth and Change* **43(4)**, 545–562.

BARTZ K. and FUCHS-SCHÜNDELN N. (2012) The role of borders, languages, and currencies as obstacles to labor market integration, *European Economic Review* **56**, 1148–1163.

BAYER C. and JÜßEN F. (2007) Convergence in West German regional unemployment rates, *German Economic Review* **8(4)**, 510–535.

BAYER P., KEOHANE N. and TIMMINS C. (2009) Migration and hedonic valuation: the case of air quality, *Journal of Environmental Economics and Management* **58**, 1–14.

BECKSTEAD D., BROWN W. M. and GELLATLY G. (2008) The left brain of North American cities: scientists and engineers and urban growth, *International Regional Science Review* **31(3)**, 304–338.

BLAKE R. B. (2003) *Regional and Rural Development Strategies in Canada: The Search for Solutions.* Royal Commission on Renewing and Strengthening Our Place in Canada, Ottawa, ON.

BLANCHARD O. J. and KATZ L. F. (1992) Regional Evolutions, *Brookings Papers on Economic Activity* **1**, 1–61.

BOADWAY R. and FLATTERS F. (1982) Efficiency and equalization payments in a federal system of government: a synthesis and extension of recent results, *Canadian Journal of Economics* **15(4)**, 613–633.

BOLTON R. (1992) 'Place prosperity vs people prosperity' revisited: an old issue with a new angle, *Urban Studies* **29(2)**, 185–203.

BOUND J. and HOLZER H. J. (2000) Demand shifts, population adjustments, and labor market outcomes during the 1980s, *Journal of Labor Economics* **18(1)**, 20–54.

BOWMAN A. (2012) The mobility of immigrants and natives: evidence from internal migration following job displacement, *Regional Studies* **45(3)**, 283–297.

BROERSMA L. and VAN DIJK J (2002) Regional labour market dynamics in the Netherlands, *Papers in Regional Science* **81**, 343–362.

CHENG K. M., DURMAZ N., KIM H. and STERN M. L. (2012) Hysteresis vs. natural rate of US unemployment, *Economic Modelling* **29**, 428–434.

CLARK D. E., HERRIN W. E., KNAPP T. A. and WHITE N. E. (2003) Migration and implicit amenity markets: does incomplete compensation matter?, *Journal of Economic Geography* **3**, 289–307.

COEN-PIRANI D. (2010) Understanding gross worker flows across U.S. states, *Journal of Monetary Economics* **57(7)**, 769–784.

CRANDALL M. S. and WEBER B. A. (2004) Local social and economic conditions, spatial concentrations of poverty, and poverty dynamics, *American Journal of Agricultural Economics* **86(5)**, 1276–1281.

CRESCENZI R. and RODRÍGUEZ-POSE A. (2012) Infrastructure and regional growth in the European Union, *Papers in Regional Science* **91(3)**, 487–513.

DAVIS S. J., LOUNGANI P. and MAHIDHARA R. (1997) *Regional Labor Fluctuations: Oil Shocks, Military Spending, and Other Driving Forces.* International Finance Discussion Papers Number 578. Board of Governors of the Federal Reserve System.

DECRESSIN J. and FATÁS A. (1995) Regional labor market dynamics, *European Economic Review* **39**, 1627–1655.

DICKIE M. and GERKING S. (1989) Interregional wage differentials in the United States: a survey, in VAN DIJK J., FOLMER H., HERZOG H. W. and SCHLOTTMANN A. M. (Eds) *Migration and Labor Market Adjustment*, pp. 111–145. Kluwer, Dordrecht.

DUMOND J. M., HIRSCH B. T. and MACPHERSON D. A. (1999) Wage differentials across labor markets and workers: does cost of living matter?, *Economic Inquiry* **37(4)**, 577–598.

EBERTS R. W. and STONE J. A. (1992) *Wage and Employment Adjustment in Local Labor Markets.* W. E. Upjohn Institute for Employment Research, Kalamazoo, MI.

ECONOMIC DEVELOPMENT RESEARCH GROUP, INC. (ERG) and MIT DEPARTMENT OF URBAN STUDIES & PLANNING (2007) *Sources of Regional Growth in Non-Metro Appalachia.* Vol. 3 of Statistical Studies of Spatial Economic Relationships (available at: http://www.arc.gov/research/ResearchReports.asp?F_Category=3) (accessed on 23 July 2010).

ELSBY M. W. L., HOBIJN B. and SAHIN A. (2010) The labor market in the Great Recession, *Brookings Papers on Economic Activity* **Spring**, 1–69.

EURACTIV (2012) *EU Cohesion Policy 2014–2020.* Originally published 1 February 2011, updated November 2012 (available at: http://www.euractiv.com/regional-policy/eu-cohesion-policy-2014-2020-linksdossier-501653?display=normal) (accessed on 4 February 2013).

FAROLE T., RODRÍGUEZ-POSE A. and STORPER M. (2011) Cohesion policy in the European Union: growth, geography, institutions, *Journal of Common Market Studies* **49(5)**, 1089–1111.

FREDRIKSSON P. (1999) The dynamics of regional labor markets and active labor market policy: Swedish evidence, *Oxford Economic Papers* **51(4)**, 623–648.

GABRIEL S. A., SHACK-MARQUEZ J. and WASCHER W. L. (1993) Does migration arbitrage regional labor market differentials, *Regional Science and Urban Economics* **23(2)**, 211–233.

GALLIN J. H. (2004) Net migration and state labor market dynamics, *Journal of Labor Economics* **22(1)**, 1–21.

GARCIA-DEL-BARRIOA P. and GIL-ALANA L. A. (2009) New revelations about unemployment persistence in Spain: time series and panel data approaches using regional data, *Applied Economics* **41**, 219–236.

GLAESER E. L. and GOTTLIEB J. D. (2008) The economics of place-making policies, *Brookings Papers on Economic Activity* **Spring**, 155–239.

GLAESER E. L. and GYOURKO J. (2005) Urban decline and durable housing, *Journal of Political Economy* **113(2)**, 345–375.

GOLDENBERG M. (2008) *A Review of Rural and Regional Development Policies and Programs*. Research Report, March. Canadian Policy Research Networks, Inc.

GOMES F. A. R. and DA SILVA C. G. (2009) Hysteresis versus NAIRU and convergence versus divergence: the behavior of regional unemployment rates in Brazil, *Quarterly Review of Economics and Finance* **49**, 308–322.

GORDON I. (1988) Evaluating the effects of employment changes on local unemployment, *Regional Studies* **22**, 135–147.

GORDON W. L. (1957) *Final Report of the Royal Commission on Canada's Economic Prospects*. Queen's Printer, Ottawa, ON.

GREENWOOD M. J., HUNT G. L., RICKMAN D. S. and TREYZ G. I. (1991) Migration, regional equilibrium, and the estimation of compensating differentials, *American Economic Review* **81(5)**, 1382–1390.

GROENEWOLD N. (1997) Does migration equalize regional unemployment rates? Evidence from Australia, *Papers in Regional Science* **76(1)**, 1–20.

HALL R. (1992) Comments and discussion, *Brookings Papers on Economic Activity* **1**, 62–65.

HANSON A. (2009) Local employment, poverty, and property value effects of geographically-targeted tax incentives: an instrumental variables approach, *Regional Science and Urban Economics* **39**, 721–731.

HANSON A. and ROHLIN S. (2011a) Do location-based tax incentives attract new business establishments?, *Journal of Regional Science* **51(3)**, 427–449.

HANSON A. and ROHLIN S. (2011b) Location and employment across industry sectors: the effect of location-based tax incentives on establishment, *Public Finance Review* **39(2)**, 195–225.

HANSON A. and ROHLIN S. (2013) Do spatially targeted redevelopment programs spill-over?, *Regional Science and Urban Economics* **43(1)**, 86–100.

HINES J. R. JR (2010) State fiscal policies and transitory income fluctuations, *Brookings Papers on Economic Activity* **Fall**, 313–350.

HOLZER H. J. (1993) Structural/frictional and demand deficient unemployment in local labor markets, *Industrial Relations* **32(3)**, 307–328.

HUNT G. L. (2006) Population–employment models: stationarity, cointegration, and dynamic adjustment, *Journal of Regional Science* **46(2)**, 205–244.

HYCLAK T. (1996) Structural changes in labor demand and unemployment in local labor markets, *Journal of Regional Science* **36(4)**, 653–663.

ISSERMAN A. M. and REPHANN T. (1995) The economic effects of the Appalachian Regional Commission, *Journal of the American Planning Association* **61**, 345–364.

JIMINEO J. F. and BENTOLILA S. (1998) Regional unemployment persistence, *Labour Economics* **5**, 25–51.

KLINE P. and MORETTI E. (2013) *Place-Based Policies with Unemployment*. IZA Discussion Paper Series Number 7180. Institute for the Study of Labor (IZA), Bonn.

KRUPKA D. J. and NOONAN D. S. (2009) Empowerment zones, neighborhood change and owner-occupied housing, *Regional Science and Urban Economics* **39**, 386–396.

LEÓN-LEDESMA M. A. (2002) Unemployment hysteresis in the US states and the EU: a panel approach, *Bulletin of Economic Research* **54(2)**, 95–103.

LEVERNIER W., PARTRIDGE M. D. and RICKMAN D. S. (2000) The causes of variation of regional variations in U.S. poverty: a cross-county analysis, *Journal of Regional Science* **40(3)**, 473–497.

LÓPEZ-BAZO E., DEL BARRIO T. and ARTIS M. (2005) Geographical distribution of unemployment in Spain, *Regional Studies* **39(3)**, 305–318.

MARSTON S. T. (1985) Two views of the geographic distribution of unemployment, *Quarterly Journal of Economics* **100(1)**, 57–79.

MARTIN R. (1997) Regional unemployment disparities and their dynamics, *Regional Studies* **31(3)**, 237–252.

McGRANAHAN D. A., WOJAN T. and LAMBERT D. M. (2011) The rural growth trifecta: outdoor amenities, creative class and entrepreneurial context, *Journal of Economic Geography* **11**, 529–557.

MINTZ J. and SMART M. (2003) *Brooking No Favorites: A New Approach to Regional Development in Atlantic Canada*. C. D. Howe Institute Commentary Number 192 (available at: http://www.cdhowe.org).

MORETTI E. (2010) *Local Labor Markets*. NBER Working Paper Series Number 15947. National Bureau of Economic Research (NBER), Cambridge, MA.

NOTOWIDIGDO M. J. (2011) *The Incidence of Local Labor Demand Shocks*. NBER Working Paper Number 17167. National Bureau of Economic Research (NBER), Cambridge, MA.

OBSTFELD M. and PERI G. (1998) Regional non-adjustment and fiscal policy, *Economic Policy: A European Forum* **no. 26**, 205–247.

ORGANIZATION OF ECONOMIC DEVELOPMENT AND COOPERATION (OECD) (2009a) *How a Region Grows*. OECD, Paris.

ORGANIZATION OF ECONOMIC DEVELOPMENT AND COOPERATION (OECD) (2009b) *A Review of Local Economic and Employment Development Policy Approaches in OECD Countries*. OECD, Paris (available at: http://www.oecd.org/document/17/0,3343,en_2649_34417_42750737_1_1_1_1,00.html) (accessed on 25 July 2010).

OSWALD A. J. and WU S. (2011) Well-being across America, *Review of Economics and Statistics* **93(4)**, 1118–1134.

OVERMAN H. G. and PUGA D. (2002) Unemployment clusters across European regions and countries. *Economic Policy* 34, 115–147.

PARTRIDGE M. D. and RICKMAN D. S. (1997a) The dispersion of US state unemployment rates: the role of market and non-market equilibrium factors *Regional Studies* 31(6), 593–606.

PARTRIDGE M. D. and RICKMAN D. S. (1997b) State unemployment differentials: equilibrium factors vs. differential employment growth, *Growth and Change* 28(Summer), 360–379.

PARTRIDGE M. D. and RICKMAN D. S. (1998) Regional differences in chronic long-term unemployment, *Quarterly Review of Economics and Finance* 38(2), 193–215.

PARTRIDGE M. D. and RICKMAN D. S. (1999) A note on the benefits to current residents of state employment growth: is there an industry mix effect on migration, *Journal of Regional Science* 39(1), 167–181.

PARTRIDGE M. D. and RICKMAN D. S. (2003a) Do we know economic development when we see it?, *Review of Regional Studies* 33(1), 17–39.

PARTRIDGE M. D. and RICKMAN D. S. (2003b) The waxing and waning of regional economies: the chicken–egg question of jobs vs. people, *Journal of Urban Economics* 53, 76–97.

PARTRIDGE M. D. and RICKMAN D. S. (2005) High-poverty nonmetropolitan counties in America: can economic development help?, *International Regional Science Review* 28(4), 415–440.

PARTRIDGE M. D. and RICKMAN D. S. (2006a) *The Geography of American Poverty: Is There a Role for Place-Based Policy?* W. E. Upjohn Institute for Employment Research, Kalamazoo, MI.

PARTRIDGE M. D. and RICKMAN D. S. (2006b) An SVAR model of fluctuations in U.S. migration flows and state labor market dynamics, *Southern Economic Journal* 72(4), 958–980.

PARTRIDGE M. D. and RICKMAN D. S. (2007a) Persistent pockets of extreme American poverty and job growth: is there a place-based policy role?, *Journal of Agricultural and Resource Economics* 32(1), 201–224.

PARTRIDGE M. D. and RICKMAN D. S. (2007b) Persistent rural poverty: is it simply remoteness and scale?, *Review of Agricultural Economics* 29(3), 430–436.

PARTRIDGE M. D. and RICKMAN D. S. (2008a) Place-based policy and rural poverty: insights from the urban spatial mismatch literature, *Cambridge Journal of Regions, Economy and Society* 1, 131–156.

PARTRIDGE M. D. and RICKMAN D. S. (2008b) Does a rising tide lift all metropolitan boats? Assessing poverty dynamics by metropolitan size and county type, *Growth and Change* 39(2), 283–312.

PARTRIDGE M. D. and RICKMAN D. S. (2008c) Distance from urban agglomeration economies and rural poverty, *Journal of Regional Science* 48(2), 285–310.

PARTRIDGE M. D. and RICKMAN D. S. (2008d) Who wins from local economic development? A supply decomposition of U.S. county employment growth, *Economic Development Quarterly* 23(1), 13–27.

PARTRIDGE M. D. and RICKMAN D. S. (2009) Canadian regional labour market evolutions: a long-run restrictions SVAR analysis, *Applied Economics* 41(13–15), 1855–1871.

PAYNE J. E., EWING B. T. and GEORGE E. P. (1999) Time series dynamics of US state unemployment rates, *Applied Economics* 31, 1503–1510.

PEKKALA S. and KANGASHARJU A. (2002) Regional labor markets in Finland: adjustment to total versus region-specific shocks, *Papers in Regional Science* 81(3), 329–342.

PETERS A. and FISHER P. (2004) The failures of economic development incentives, *Journal of the American Planning Association* 70(1), 27–37.

PISSARIDES C. A. and MCMASTER I. (1990) Regional migration, wages and unemployment: empirical evidence and implications for policy, *Oxford Economic Papers* 42(4), 812–831.

PRESIDENT'S APPALACHIAN REGIONAL COMMISSION (PARC) (1964) *Appalachia: A Report of the President's Appalachian Regional Commission.* US Government Printing Office, Washington, DC.

PUGA D. (2002) European regional policies in light of recent location theories, *Journal of Economic Geography* 2, 373–406.

RICKMAN D. S. (2011) Focus on the fundamentals, in *Developing the Oklahoma Economy*, pp. 74–75. The Oklahoma Academy, Oklahoma City, OK.

ROBACK J. (1982) Wages, rent and the quality of life, *Journal of Political Economy* 90(6), 1257–1278.

ROBACK J. (1988) Wages, rents, and amenities: differences among workers and regions, *Economic Inquiry* 26(1), 23–41.

RODRÍGUEZ-POSE A. (2010) Economic geographers and the limelight: institutions and policy in the World Development Report 2009, *Economic Geography* 86(4), 361–370.

ROMERO-ÁVILA D. and USABIAGA C. (2007) Unit root tests, persistence, and the unemployment rate of the U.S. states, *Southern Economic Journal* 73(3), 698–716.

ROWTHORN R. and GLYN A. J. (2006) Convergence and stability in U.S. employment rates, *B. E. Journal of Macroeconomics: Contributions to Macroeconomics* 6(1), 1–42.

SAKS R. E. and WOZNIAK A. (2011) Labor reallocation over the business cycle: new evidence from internal migration, *Journal of Labor Economics* 29(4), 697–739.

SEPHTON P. S. (2009) Persistence in U.S. state unemployment rates, *Southern Economic Journal* 76(2), 458–466.

SONG F. M. and WU Y. (1997) Hysteresis in unemployment: evidence from 48 U.S. states, *Economic Inquiry* 35(2), 235–243.

TANI M. (2003) Have Europeans become more mobile? A note on regional evolutions in the EU: 1988–1997, *Economics Letters* 80(1), 23–30.

TREYZ G. I., RICKMAN D. S., HUNT G. L. and GREENWOOD M. J. (1993) The dynamics of U.S. internal migration, *Review of Economics and Statistics* 75(2), 209–214.

WANG B. and DAYANANDAN A. (2006) Unit root tests of Canadian poverty measures, *Economics Bulletin* 9(2), 1–7.

WHISNANT D. E. (1994) *Modernizing the Mountaineer.* University of Tennessee Press, Knoxville, TN.

WIDNER R. R. (1973a) Evaluation of the administration of the Appalachian Regional Development Program, *Growth and Change* **4**, 25–29.

WIDNER R. R. (1973b) Transport investment and Appalachian development, *Public Administration Review* **33**, 225–235.

WIDNER R. R. (1990) Appalachian development after 25 years: an assessment, *Economic Development Quarterly* **4**, 291–312.

WINNICK L. (1966) Place prosperity vs people prosperity: welfare considerations in the geographic redistribution of economic activity, in *Essays in Urban Land Economics in Honor of the Sixty-fifth Birthday of Leo Grebler*, pp. 273–283. Real Estate Research Program, University of California at Los Angeles, Los Angeles, CA.

WINTERS J. V. (2009) Wages and prices: are workers fully compensated for cost of living differences?, *Regional Science and Urban Economics* **39**, 632–643.

YEO J. H., SUNG K. A. and HOLLAND D. W. (2005) Labor market behavior in Washington: a cointegration approach, *Annals of Regional Science* **39**, 317–335.

The Potential Application of Qualitative Evaluation Methods in European Regional Development: Reflections on the Use of Performance Story Reporting in Australian Natural Resource Management

FRANK VANCLAY

Department of Cultural Geography, Faculty of Spatial Sciences, University of Groningen, Groningen, the Netherlands.

VANCLAY F. The potential application of qualitative evaluation methods in European regional development: reflections on the use of Performance Story Reporting in Australian natural resource management, *Regional Studies*. This paper argues that qualitative evaluation methods potentially have a useful role in the assessment of regional development projects in Europe. It outlines several evaluation methods used in outcomes assessment, specifically Most Significant Change Technique, Performance Story Reporting and Collaborative Outcomes Reporting. An example of the practical application of these methods in Australia is provided along with a consideration of their applicability in the European context. The paper discusses issues related to the evaluation of rural and regional development programmes and concludes that qualitative evaluation using story-based approaches provides a rigorous way of assessing the performance of projects and programmes.

VANCLAY F. 质化评估方法在欧洲区域发展上的可能应用：奥地利自然资源管理使用绩效叙述报告的反思，区域研究。本文主张，质性研究评估方法在评价欧洲区域发展计画上具有潜在的用处。本文概述运用于成果评量的部分评估方法，特别是"最重要的变化技术"、"绩效叙述报告"以及"协作成果报告"。我将提供这些方法在奥地利的实际运用案例，并考量它们在欧洲脉络的适用性。本文探讨乡村与区域发展计画评估的相关议题，并做结道：运用根据叙述方法的质化评估，提供了评价计画与方案绩效的严谨方法。

VANCLAY F. L'application éventuelle des méthodes d'évaluation qualitative dans l'aménagement du territoire en Europe: des réflexions sur l'emploi du Performance Story Reporting quant à la gestion des ressources naturelles en Australie, *Regional Studies*. Cet article affirme que les méthodes d'évaluation qualitative jouent un rôle utile dans l'évaluation des projets d'aménagement du territoire en Europe. On esquisse plusieurs méthodes d'évaluation employées dans l'évaluation des résultats, notamment la Most Significant Change Technique (Technique de changement le plus significatif), Performance Story Reporting (Tableau de bord permettant de mesurer la progression vers les objectifs et les priorités) et Collaborative Outcomes Reporting (Rapport collaboratif sur les résultats). On fournit un exemple de l'application pratique de ces méthodes en Australie et on prend également en considération leur applicabilité dans un cadre européen. L'article discute des questions qui se rapportent à l'évaluation des programmes d'aménagement ruralo-régional et conclut qu'une évaluation qualitative qui emploie des façons axées sur les histoires fournit un moyen exhaustif d'évaluer les projets et les programmes.

VANCLAY F. Die potenzielle Anwendung von qualitativen Bewertungsmethoden in der europäischen Regionalentwicklung: Überlegungen über den Einsatz von Performance Story Reporting im Bereich der Naturressourcenverwaltung in Australien, *Regional Studies*. In diesem Beitrag wird die These aufgestellt, dass qualitative Bewertungsmethoden eine potenziell nützliche Rolle bei der Bewertung von regionalen Entwicklungsprojekten in Europa spielen können. Beschrieben werden mehrere Methoden zur Ergebnisbewertung: die 'Most Significant Change Technique', das 'Performance Story Reporting' und das

'Collaborative Outcomes Reporting'. Der Beitrag enthält ein Beispiel für die praktische Anwendung dieser Methoden in Australien sowie eine Untersuchung ihrer Anwendbarkeit auf den europäischen Kontext. Ebenso erörtert werden Aspekte im Zusammenhang mit der Bewertung von Programmen zur ländlichen und regionalen Entwicklung; das Fazit lautet, dass eine qualitative Bewertung mit Hilfe von Story-Ansätzen eine präzise Methode zur Untersuchung der Leistung von Projekten und Programmen bietet.

VANCLAY F. La posible aplicación de métodos cualitativos de evaluación en el desarrollo regional europeo: reflexiones sobre el uso de los informes sobre el desempeño en la gestión de recursos naturales en Australia, *Regional Studies*. En este artículo se argumenta que los métodos de evaluación cualitativa tienen potencialmente un papel útil en la valoración de los proyectos de desarrollo regional en Europa. Se destacan varios métodos de evaluación que se utilizan en la valoración de resultados, especialmente la 'técnica del cambio más significativo', los 'informes sobre el desempeño' y los 'informes sobre los resultados de colaboración'. Se muestra un ejemplo de la aplicación práctica de estos métodos en Australia junto con una consideración de su aplicabilidad en un contexto europeo. Se analizan las cuestiones relacionadas con la evaluación de los programas de desarrollo rural y regional y se concluye que la evaluación cualitativa, en la que se utilizan planteamientos basados en historias, ofrece un método riguroso de valorar el desempeño de proyectos y programas.

INTRODUCTION: THE NEED FOR QUALITATIVE EVALUATION

The attempt to identify what works and why are perennial questions for evaluators, programme and project managers, funding agencies, and policy-makers (GREENE, 2000; FELLER, 2007). Policies, programmes, plans and projects (hereafter all 'programmes' for convenience) all start with good intent, often with long-term and usually over-optimistic goals. An important issue is how to assess the success of these programmes during their life, often before their goals have been fully achieved. Thus, some sense of interim performance is needed to provide feedback to fine-tune the programme, to determine whether subsequent tranche payments should be made, and also to assist in decision-making about whether similar programmes should be funded.

Evaluation in such circumstances is complex. How can the achievement of goals be assessed if they are long-term? Evaluation cannot wait years to determine whether a programme has been successful. Thus, evaluation needs to consider carefully the programme logic, whether interim steps have been achieved, and whether there are signs that longer-term objectives and goals are likely to be achieved. But this is not straightforward. All programmes, especially long-term ones, should incorporate a degree of adaptive management or reflexivity into them allowing them to respond to feedback along the way. Final success therefore is not just whether the original plan was correct, but the extent to which a programme has effective monitoring and is capable of adapting to feedback as it progresses. Depending on the context, it may also be the case that various external factors have changed and the

original goals and/or programme logic need to be revised to accommodate the changed circumstances. Any programme seeking to contribute to high-level goals like enhanced community well-being, social sustainability, regional development potential, innovativeness, etc., is likely to be affected by a changing context. Therefore, a key factor for success (and thus for evaluation) is the ability of the programme to be responsive to change. How is this adaptivity to be evaluated?

It is increasingly evident that standard ex-post quantitative evaluation techniques are not adequate to deal with these matters. Standard approaches to evaluation cannot deal with long lag times, they cannot cope with multi-causality, and they cannot cope with a changing operating environment. Qualitative methods, on the other hand, offer a way of collecting evidence about the performance of a programme or project. They also enable the collection of feedback to assist in modifying the programme. They can work in tandem with quantitative indicators, playing a complementary but different although equally important role. This paper, which is based on a report developed at the request of the European Commission's Directorate General for Regional Policy (VANCLAY, 2012a), explores issues associated with the evaluation of regional development programmes in Europe and elsewhere. Using an example from Australia, the paper highlights how qualitative methods can be used to assess the performance of regional development programmes. The paper attempts to provide a possible different way of thinking about how the performance of regional development interventions might be assessed. Comments about their possible application in the European context are provided at the end of the paper.

ISSUES FACING PROGRAMME EVALUATION

Many programmes facilitate the provision of a broad range of social benefits that were not necessarily the core purpose of the programme, and frequently there can be many other unanticipated spin-off benefits as well. Collectively these may contribute significantly to the perceived success of the programme, especially by programme beneficiaries. Should evaluation consider the success of a programme on the basis of unintended consequences? At face value, many key decision-makers might say no. But, on the other hand, it is unlikely that a programme would be considered successful if it caused a lot of unanticipated harm in addition to still achieving its narrow goals. Evaluation therefore must take an holistic approach considering the potential for good as well as the potential for harm, and it needs to consider the unanticipated consequences as much as the intended goals (ESTEVES and VANCLAY, 2009; JOÃO et al., 2011; VANCLAY, 2003).

Another issue is that an evaluation cannot simply measure whether goals (that is, desired results) were achieved. If so, how would the evaluation establish causality? Could the observed change have been the result of other things occurring at the same time? What if there were underlying trends in a community/region anyway? In the field of social impact assessment, the concept of baseline is extended beyond being a single data point fixed in time. Instead, it is argued that the meaningful comparison is not time $(t + 1)$ against time $(t0)$; but rather a comparison at a point in time against what would have happened without the programme (ESTEVES et al., 2012). The baseline is thus the line (not point) of expected trending without the programme. In European policy circles, this is called the 'counterfactual' (EVALSED, 2012) – a term borrowed from psychology where it has a slightly different meaning, that is, a mental representation or image of an alternative trajectory, past or future (ROESE, 1997). Thus, programmes can still be regarded as 'successful' if an indicator at a future time is worse than it was at commencement, providing that there is a reasonable analysis to establish that there were other changes taking place such that the programme made the community better off than it would have been without the programme.

In considering a wide range of outcomes, and with the realization that many of the broader social benefits of programmes are subjective, the adage normally attributed to Albert Einstein that 'not everything that counts can be counted' becomes important (VANCLAY, 2012b). Particularly in cases of the enhanced well-being type of programmes referred to above, the additional benefits may be in terms of an improvement in how people feel about where they live and their lives in general, about how they feel about the future of their community, and about how different groups in a community cooperate or at least get on with each other. While not necessarily impossible to measure, these high-level goals are difficult to measure, and are not normally included in routine data-collection processes.

The issue of high-level, broader social benefits raises the question of attribution. How can the evaluator know whether an observed effect was due to the programme? A short and simple answer might be that they cannot. A more complex answer questions whether simplistic assumptions of direct cause and effect are appropriate. Big programmes with high-level outcomes do not have simple cause-and-effect relationships; they have complex interconnecting multi-causal linkages. A deeper understanding of the nexus of these relationships is needed. Such systems are dynamic, are mediated by iterative feedback processes, are confounded by inhibiting and enabling mechanisms, and are potentially affected by catalytic relationships (including non-linear and exponential effects) between system elements.

It is important to realize that these debates have existed in the field of evaluation for decades (for a discussion on the purpose and history of evaluation, see GREENE, 2000). While some evaluators have attempted to persist with ever-improving and ever-more-sophisticated empirical quantitative techniques (for example, LEEUW and VAESSEN, 2009), many other evaluation experts fundamentally disagree that such methods can address the complexity of the programmes being considered (for example, GUIJT et al., 2011). Instead, they advocate the use of robust qualitative measures arguing that qualitative methods are more valid, give better information, are more efficient, include the potential for unanticipated factors to be included and address causality.

A final argument in favour of qualitative methods (especially narrative approaches) is that they can yield powerful stories that are not only useful for media reports, but also often frequently preferred by politicians and other decision-makers (DENNING, 2007; KURTZ, 2009; MAYNE, 2004). It is an illusion of scientists that hard data are the only convincing evidence. As Benjamin Disraeli (or at least Mark Twain) implied many years ago with the now famous 'lies, dammed lies and statistics' aphorism, a statistic (data, evidence) is only as accurate as the reliability of the processes used to collect it and the extent to which it faithfully represents reality (its validity). But reliability, validity and significance, the once all-important cry of quantitative social researchers has now been replaced by other criteria. With so much data, evidence, information and knowledge everywhere, the key concerns of the users of information are no longer the old ideal concerns of purist statisticians, but the pragmatic considerations of salience, credibility and legitimacy (CASH et al., 2003). Users of information want to know: Is it relevant information?; Is it useful information?; and Do I believe it? – which is partly based on its credibility to them as individuals (in other words, is consistent with their worldview) and partly on the extent to which they trust the source of that information. Very often, a story conveys this information much more effectively (that is, convincingly) than other forms of evidence (DENNING, 2007; FISHER, 1989; KURTZ, 2009; LABONTE, 2011; SANDELOWSKI, 1991; SHAW et al., 1998).

A NOTE ON TERMINOLOGY: OUTPUTS AND OUTCOMES

Programme logic refers to the perceived causal understanding of how the different components of a programme (specifically inputs and activities) work together to produce outputs and outcomes. Outcomes are generally conceived as being immediate, intermediate and ultimate (MAYNE, 2004). Programme logic:

> captures the rationale behind a program, probing and outlining the anticipated cause-and-effect relationships between program activities, outputs, intermediate outcomes and longer-term desired outcomes. A program logic is usually represented as a diagram or matrix that shows a series of expected consequences, not just a sequence of events.
>
> (ROUGHLEY, 2009, p. 7)

MAYNE (1999) presents a good model illustrating the complexity of programme logic (Fig. 1).

Another significant concept in the field of evaluation (especially in the area of agricultural extension) is 'Bennett's hierarchy' (BENNETT, 1975). Bennett championed the phrase 'up the hierarchy' as a reaction to the excessive attention being given to inputs (for example, dollars spent, hours consumed), activities (for example, numbers of workshops held), and people

involvement (for example, numbers of people attending), arguing that more attention needed to be given to a range of higher-order considerations. Bennett's model, usually represented as a ladder or staircase, went as follows:

- Inputs (resources expended).
- Activities (what was done).
- People involvement (who and how many people involved).
- Reactions (what they thought of it, immediate reactions as might be measured by exit surveys).
- KASA change (that is, changes after a period of time in the knowledge, attitudes, skills and aspirations of participants).
- Practice change (changes in the behaviour of people).
- End results (or ultimate outcomes, that is, what long-term difference did it make).

Bennett's model is not a programme logic model; rather it is a conceptualization of the different stages of a project that should be considered by evaluation. Bennett's argument was that instead of measuring the easy-to-measure things low down in the hierarchy like the inputs, activities and people involvement normally addressed, evaluators should go up the hierarchy and consider all stages. However, because measuring end results (ultimate outcomes or goals) may be difficult especially in short timeframes, measuring KASA change and practice change provides interim indicators of the effectiveness (or likely effectiveness) of a project or policy. Together with a programme logic model and a theory of change, some evidence of the likelihood of success can be gained by having adequate people involvement (in terms of the target group), positive reactions from participants, some evidence of KASA change and some evidence of practice change. Empirical

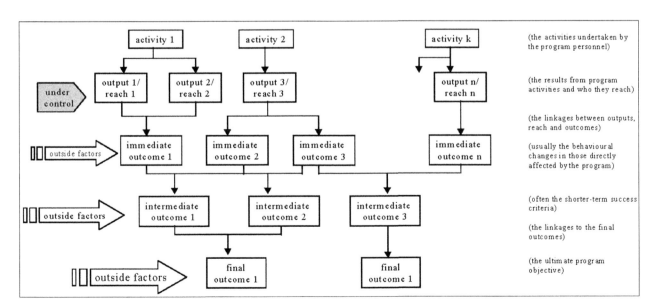

Fig. 1. Generic depiction of programme logic
Source: MAYNE (1999, p. 9)

evidence may be hard to collect, especially if external conditions are changing, but stories of change from (a selection of) participants can be readily collected. If the majority of participants report that the activity has led to KASA change and has led to practice change, then that is reasonable evidence of success.

THE ADDED VALUE OF QUALITATIVE METHODS IN EVALUATION

In general, qualitative research tends (adapted primarily from PADGETT, 2012, and a range of other sources):

- To focus on meaning and on the 'why' rather than on 'how many'.
- To focus on issues where deeper understanding is required rather than on confirming prior hypotheses.
- To be inductive rather than deductive.
- To be open rather than closed.
- To seek to discover the 'insider' rather than 'outsider' perspective.
- To be person-centred rather than variable-centred.
- To take a humanistic or phenomenological perspective rather than a positivist perspective.
- To be constructivist rather than naturalistic.
- To promote joint learning by all participants rather than just the learning of the researcher.
- To be holistic rather than particularistic.
- To be contextual (situated, embedded) rather than decontextual (distant, removed or detached).

In evaluation, qualitative research is used specifically to consider the why and how questions that quantitative methods typically cannot answer, for example (adapted from ROYCE et al., 2001; and ANATAS, 2004):

- Why does the programme work (or not work)?
- How does the programme achieve its goals?
- Why does it work for some clients (or in some situations) and not others?
- What are/were the needs of the clients that were not anticipated by programme developers?
- What were the additional unintended and/or unexpected positive or negative consequences?

Thus, qualitative methods are a valuable and important contribution to project and programme evaluation, especially when the focus is formative (how can the project or programme be improved) rather than summative (asking whether a project or programme was a success).

A SHORT HISTORY OF QUALITATIVE EVALUATION

GUBA and LINCOLN (1989) described four 'generations' in the history of evaluation: measurement, description, judgement and constructivist evaluation. Perhaps 'paradigms' or 'modalities' would have been more appropriate

words to use than 'generations', at least in terms of what they mean. A major criticism of this temporal overview of the field of evaluation is that the extent to which the phases (generations) actually existed as discrete time periods is exaggerated – as can be demonstrated by the observation that the earlier generations are still very much in existence. Nevertheless, after a period of methodology battles or paradigm wars/clashes (WADSWORTH, 2005), the dominant culture of evaluation is changing. While the division between summative evaluation and formative evaluation is widely accepted, evaluation is now developing a greater focus as being creative (PATTON, 1981), qualitative (PATTON, 1990), participatory (JACKSON and KASSAM, 1998; WHITMORE, 1998), utilization-focused (PATTON, 1997), constructivist or fourth generation (GUBA and LINCOLN, 1989), empowering or fifth generation (FETTERMAN et al., 1995; LAUGHLIN and BROADBENT, 1996; FETTERMAN, 2000), and as a form of action research (WHYTE, 1990). Evaluation is now viewed as research for informing decision-making at all phases of the project, programme or policy (VANCLAY et al., 2004). Instead of just being ex-post assessment or audit, evaluation is now understood to contribute to all stages of project or programme development. Rather than being solely the domain of independent experts, evaluation is now widely seen as a participatory approach that empowers and builds capacity within institutions and amongst all programme and project partners. Evaluation is now seen as a form of action research that informs project and programme design. Ongoing evaluation and adaptive management are essential parts of being innovative and a learning organization. Evaluation is your friend (VANCLAY et al., 2004).

Monitoring and evaluating the performance of rural development programmes in developing countries has been an area where much innovation has taken place in evaluation methods, largely because of the inappropriateness of many traditional quantitative means of evaluation and because of the strong interest by funders in knowing whether their funding was being used effectively (GUIJT et al., 2011). Many external evaluators and programme managers have grappled with how to design fair methods that adequately capture the changes brought about by development interventions, especially when empirical indicators were not available, were too broad, or not sufficiently sensitive to change.

While there were several story-based approaches to evaluation in the 1990s, two of the main proponents were Rick Davies and Jessica Dart. Although originally going by a variety of terms, in 2000 Davies and Dart settled on 'Most Significant Change Technique' (MSC) as the term for the emergent method (DART and DAVIES, 2003; DAVIES and DART, 2005). Since then, the approach has become firmly established in the evaluation and development cooperation professions, and as at July 2013 the term 'most significant change technique' had over 52 000 hits on Google. Some evaluations using this approach include WILDER and WALPOLE (2008) and WATERS et al. (2011).

Performance Story Reporting (PSR) is similar to and derives from the MSC. Dart attributes the actual name 'performance story' to John Mayne of the Canadian Auditor General's Office (MAYNE, 2004; DART and MAYNE, 2005). Arguably PSR overcomes some of the criticisms of MSC (WILLETTS and CRAWFORD, 2007) and in particular removes concern about any bias implied by the name and the (mis)perception that the method only looked for positive stories potentially with atypical results. PSR has improved procedures to MSC which means that it provides a more sophisticated, yet still workable tool. While not yet widely represented in the scholarly literature, it is well known in the evaluation field (DART and MAYNE, 2005) and as at July 2013 had over 9000 hits on Google.

Collaborative Outcomes Reporting (COR) is the latest incarnation of these story-based approaches to evaluation. Similar to PSR (in fact Dart provides her PSR work as examples of COR), the technique was renamed because of resistance to the word 'story' by some evaluation clients (Jessica Dart, personal communication, 20 April 2011) and because COR emphasizes integrating empirical and qualitative data and does not rely on the story alone. There are a range of other refinements, but these are minor so information about MSC and PSR is essentially still relevant to COR. As at July 2013, 'collaborative outcomes reporting' had over 27 000 hits on Google and had been presented to a number of evaluation conferences.

There are many other story-based or narrative approaches to evaluation that are championed by various people including LABONTE et al. (1999), WADSWORTH et al. (2007), KURTZ (2009), MAXSON et al. (2010) and WITHERS (2010). One of the well-known approaches is that of the Cynefin framework which is implemented in a range of settings with SenseMaker software (KURTZ and SNOWDEN, 2003; SNOWDEN and BOONE, 2007). The US Centers for Disease Control and Prevention (CDCP) advocate a 'success story' approach (CDCP, 2007; LAVINGHOUZE et al., 2007). Stories and vignettes are also widely used in social research in a range of ways (for example, DARE et al., 2011; HOWDEN and VANCLAY, 2000; HUGHES and HUBY, 2002; SANDELOWSKI, 1991; VANCLAY and ENTICOTT, 2011; ENTICOTT and VANCLAY, 2011).

AN EXAMPLE APPLICATION OF PERFORMANCE STORY REPORTING AT THE PROGRAMME LEVEL

Background to the Australian context

The Australian government funds a range of natural resource management (NRM) programmes and projects collectively known as 'Caring for Our Country' (http://www.nrm.gov.au) (for a history, see HAJKOWICZ, 2009). For the five-year period from 2008 to 2013, the total value of the government's investment in this programme was about A$2.25 billion (COMMONWEALTH OF AUSTRALIA, 2008). Investments in the two previous five-year periods totalled A$1.5 billion and A$1.3 billion, respectively (AUDITOR GENERAL, 2008). A further A$2.2 billion has been committed for the five-year period to 2018 (COMMONWEALTH OF AUSTRALIA, 2012).

The programme is currently undergoing considerable change, amidst much criticism (for example, ROBINS and KANOWSKI, 2011; TENNENT and LOCKIE, 2013). It is very broad and supports various efforts to improve NRM across the whole of Australia, depending on the specific needs of each locality/region. It has supported a range of disparate projects often in conjunction with local community (Landcare) groups and individuals (who often have considerable personal investment and commitment to the activities) and may include small grant programmes, co-funding programmes, and support for project staff and project costs. Issues addressed include biodiversity, habitat and remnant vegetation protection and restoration; the establishment of wildlife corridors; water quality and stream health issues; methods to address salinity, acidity and acid sulphate soils and soil erosion; tree-planting activities; weed removal and feral animal issues; and whatever else local regions determine are appropriate and consistent with the government's terms of reference for the programme. PRAGER and VANCLAY (2010) provide a comparison of these land management issues between Germany and Australia. Specific information about the types of activities funded is available from the Australian government's *One Land – Many Stories: Prospectus for Investment* (COMMONWEALTH OF AUSTRALIA, 2012).

While the objectives are now very clear (COMMONWEALTH OF AUSTRALIA, 2008) and there is a clearly elaborated programme logic (ROUGHLEY, 2009), earlier versions of the programme did not have clearly identified intended outcomes. While anecdotal evidence suggested that there was much benefit from the programme (CURTIS and LOCKWOOD, 2000; PRAGER and VANCLAY, 2010), various official reports were dubious about the benefits. The AUDITOR GENERAL's (2008, p. 16) report, for example, concluded that there were 'significant areas of noncompliance by State agencies' (in relation to their obligations in terms of the Commonwealth–State agreements that underpinned the programme), and that:

> the quality and measurability of the targets in the regional plans is an issue for attention and … should be considered nationally – especially as the absence of sufficient scientific data has limited the ability of regional bodies to link the targets in their plans to program outcomes.

This context of official concern about the alleged benefits of the programme, but strong public and political support for the programme led to a real need to prove that the programme was being successful, especially in the knowledge that empirical indicators were unlikely to reveal results in the short-term. It was also an impetus to experiment with new evaluation techniques, since existing methods had failed.

Dart had been experimenting with the MSC and PSR for some time, first in the early to mid-1990s in developing country contexts and later in an agricultural extension context in Australia. Dart's work was known by various people in the Australian government, especially in NRM circles, and it became evident that PSR might be a good way to assist the government in its need to capture the impacts of its NRM investments.

The government's Bureau of Rural Sciences (now part of the Australian Bureau of Agricultural and Resource Economics and Sciences; http://www. abares.gov.au) conducted a feasibility assessment of the use of story-based approaches (CARR and WOOD-HAMS, 2008). That feasibility assessment (or 'independent review' as they claimed) considered three questions (CARR and WOODHAMS, 2008, p. 3):

1) Are qualitative approaches such as MSC a) useful and b) appropriate as evidence of outcomes, including intermediate and other outcomes?
2) What are the strengths and weaknesses of using PSR to report by outcomes?
3) Could MSC and PSR be used by NRM regions in Australia as a form of participatory evaluation for producing program performance reports by outcomes.

Based on four pilot applications of the method, the feasibility assessment concluded that:

Qualitative approaches to participatory evaluation such as MSC are both useful and appropriate as evidence of outcomes at multiple levels in NRM program logic hierarchies, including intermediate outcomes. Not only are qualitative approaches a valuable source of evidence of the changing human dimension of NRM, they are frequently a profound source of insight and sometimes the only kind of evidence available of the type of practice and attitudinal changes taking place. ...

Four key strengths of PSR were mentioned in reflective interviews: engagement, capacity building, problem-sharing and adaptive learning. These strengths were primarily associated with the MSC phase of the PSR process. Identifying and engaging evaluation stakeholders was seen as a major strength of PSR and was the strength most frequently mentioned by interviewees. Many of the regional staff who took part in the MSC process appreciated the chance to build relationships with resource managers and develop their personal interviewing skills. The MSC process also increased communication about shared experiences and approaches to NRM problems that, in turn, led to an adaptive approach to natural resource management.

Arguably, there are two other key strengths of PSR. First, it integrates qualitative and quantitative evidence.

Second, performance story reports rely upon participatory processes using program logic, which allows progressive collection and testing of evidence throughout the life of the investment program.

There are three key challenges for PSR: time and resources; data, results and interpretation; and complexity and preparedness. The biggest challenge across all stages of PSR was a perceived lack of time and resources to conduct the PSR process. Such comments came from all interviewees, consultants, regions and Australian Government representatives. At the regional level, interviewees were concerned that the goodwill and involvement from resource managers and regional staff would start to wane if the process was repeated each year without sufficient resources or local incentive.

(CARR and WOODHAMS, 2008, p. 61)

As a result of the positive feasibility assessment, the PSR approach was rolled out across Australia with the Australian government publishing a 'user guide': *Developing a Performance Story Report* (ROUGHLEY and DART, 2009). In total, around thirteen project-level PSR reports were prepared (the exact number is hard to determine). While not all these reports are publicly available on the internet (for one that is available, see DART and O'CONNOR, 2008), a limited number of hardcopies and PDFs of the reports are in circulation, having being distributed to participants and others who expressed an interest at the time. The PSR method has also been used to assess other programmes and projects, especially in the NRM domain (for example, CLEAR HORIZON and ENVIRONMENT VICTORIA, 2010).

Description of how to undertake a performance story report evaluation

The Australian government's *User Guide* (ROUGHLEY and DART, 2009) and various other instruction manuals (for example, DART et al., 2000; DAVIES and DART, 2005; SILVER et al., 2009) provide instructions on conducting evaluations using PSR. ROUGHLEY and DART (2009, p. 12) suggest that a typical report is between ten and thirty pages long and comprises five parts:

Program context – background information about the program and the context in which it operates (how the program began, its location, objectives and key strategies, funding sources, structure and expected achievements), as well as an outline of the objectives and boundaries of the performance story evaluation and a summary of key outcomes and what has been learned.

Evaluation methodology – a brief overview of the process used in undertaking the evaluation.

Results – a listing of the most relevant and rigorous sources of evidence against the outcomes from the program logic hierarchy. This includes data as well as stories of change which are excerpts from interviews that best illustrate change that has occurred as a result of the program.

Findings and implications – a discussion framed by the evaluation questions that covers how the study has illustrated the program's impact (intended and unintended outcomes), the progress it has made towards its expected outcomes and how it has contributed to the long-term outcomes of NRM or a large NRM initiative. This part also includes recommendations for applying the findings to future phases of the program.

Index – a list of all the sources of evidence considered in the evaluation, including any additional references and the categories of interviewees and study participants.

ROUGHLEY and DART (2009, p. 15, slightly modified) describe the seven steps to produce a report:

- Scoping – inception or planning meetings are held to determine what will be evaluated, to develop the programme logic (if not already existing), set evaluation questions, and identify sources of existing evidence and possible people to interview.
- Evidence gathering – an 'evidence trawl' is conducted to identify existing data that will provide the best evidence of expected outcomes. This is followed by the social inquiry process, where interviews are conducted with people who can provide additional information about programme outcomes. Specific questions are asked and recorded to provide stories of significant changes that have occurred as a result of the programme.
- Integrated data analysis – quantitative and qualitative data are analysed to identify evidence corresponding to the outcomes in the programme logic and integrated within the results chart.
- Expert panel – people with relevant expertise assess the evidence of outcomes that has been gathered. They judge and make statements about the extent to which the evidence is adequate to assess the progress the programme is making towards its stated outcomes. The panel should also identify any further evidence that might be needed to make a conclusive statement about the achievement of programme outcomes. Following the panel meeting, the evaluator integrates all of the analysed evidence and assesses the amount and quality of evidence available for each outcome in the programme logic to inform a draft set of recommendations.
- Summit meeting – all evaluation participants come together to consider and discuss the findings, nominate the stories that best illustrate the impact of the programme, and make recommendations.
- Integration, report and communications – the evaluator prepares the PSR report, which is a synthesis of all the above steps including the recommendations from summit meeting participants. The findings of the evaluation are communicated to all stakeholders.
- Revising the programme logic – programme managers, staff and other stakeholders meet to consider the report and to revise the programme logic and implementation accordingly.

The *User Guide* (ROUGHLEY and DART, 2009) describes the process of selecting and interviewing respondents. It suggests that programme (project) participants, strategic informants (such as project managers, programme coordinators) and scientific experts who are in a position to comment about likely changes be interviewed. It suggests that depending on the context, between twenty and fifty people need to be interviewed 'to gain an in-depth view of how participants have experienced the program' (p. 23). The *User Guide* also describes the social inquiry process suggesting that questions should focus on outcomes and stories of change. Ultimately the interviewer/ evaluation team construct narratives/vignettes/performance stories based on the answers to the questions asked. The interviewer has a responsibility to ensure that the right questions have been asked to allow the participant to provide the information to construct the stories. The stories are in the 'voice' and words of the participants as much as possible, but are edited to ensure that the story is an effective way of explaining what happened. As with all social research, the stories (transcripts) should be given back to the participant for them to approve and edit as they see fit. This process of constructing narratives/vignettes by modifying the actual transcript but remaining true to the intent is not uncommon in social research (for other examples, see DARE *et al.* 2011; and VANCLAY and ENTICOTT, 2011). Three or so stories that best illustrate 'an important change that has occurred as a result of the program' (ROUGHLEY and DART, 2009, p. 46) are selected in a participatory process in the summit meeting (the fifth step). The summit meeting participants also discuss the main issues that emerged and develop recommendations.

The project-level PSR reports can be aggregated into a higher level evaluation or meta-evaluation. One example of this is the assessment of NRM outcomes in the State of South Australia for the period 2001–2008, which drew on several PSR reports that were conducted in that state (DEPARTMENT OF WATER, LAND AND BIODIVERSITY CONSERVATION (DWLBC), 2009).

While the Australian government's *User Guide* makes specific recommendations as to how PSR reports should be presented, arguably they could be presented in a variety of formats, including as conventional consultancy reports, websites, DVDs, posters, brochures, or as mixed media with video and/or audio files. One of the more creative PSR reports contained an appendix comprising a newsletter that had been widely circulated. The newsletter was comic book style, but instead of caricature drawings used real photographs of people in outdoor settings with speech bubbles indicating their name and role which were hot-linked to a website where the reader could listen to an audio file recording of that person's comments (BESSEN CONSULTING SERVICES, 2009).

An assessment of the Australian experiment

As far as can be determined, there has been no publicly available, official, ex-post assessment of the effectiveness of the PSR method or an overall summary of the state of NRM in Australia based on the thirteen or so PSR case studies that were claimed to have been undertaken. Instead, in 2012 the Australian government initiated a completely separate review of the Caring for Our Country programme containing no (or very little) mention of the earlier PSR experiment. The PSR reports that are accessible on the internet in general give a positive impression of both the method and the particular project being evaluated. It is reasonable to suspect that the PSR reports that are not readily accessible were either not favourable towards the specific NRM project being evaluated, and/or demonstrated problems with the application of the method such that the results would be contestable. At some locations, there was cynicism by some members of the expert panels and others with the process. There was also concern by the regions about how time consuming the process was.

The government has since made many changes to the Caring for Our Country programme which have led to much criticism from a range of commentators (for example, ROBINS and KANOWSKI, 2011; TENNENT and LOCKIE, 2013). Whether the non-carry forward of the performance story approach was because of inherent problems with the method or because of the way it was implemented (see below) – or conversely because of the fact that it may have revealed things that the government did not want to hear or to be told – cannot be adequately determined from available sources. It is important to appreciate that the time period in question was politically delicate in Australian politics, particularly with a minority government holding power only with the support of a few independent politicians or minor parties, and a disposing of a sitting prime minister by his (and again later her) own party. What is interesting to note is that while there has been a marked reduction of interest in PSR at the federal level, many local-level agencies have become strongly committed to PSR and continue to produce PSR reports. Therefore, reasonable academic reflection on what has transpired in Australia would suggest that the fact that the government has not continued with PSR is not indicative of a problem with the method.

For the purposes of this paper, it does not actually matter what ultimately happened in Australia. The Australian case is being presented as proof that qualitative evaluation can be applied in practice. While there may be areas for possible improvement with the method (see discussion below), these do not fundamentally detract from its potential value in Australia, in Europe, or elsewhere. Qualitative evaluation methods are being outlined in this paper as being of potential use (something to consider), and this paper is not necessarily specifically recommending the PSR approach in exactly the way implemented in the Australian context. It does however recommend the approach in general.

CRITICAL REFLECTIONS ON THE PERFORMANCE STORY REPORTING METHOD

The commentary provided here draws on a cursory review of the PSR reports available to the author, discussions with various participants and stakeholders in the PSR approach and NRM in Australia, and the author's personal experience in participating in a summit meeting. The author, an experienced social research methodologist and rural sociologist/geographer, has been an observer of NRM in Australia for over three decades (for example, VANCLAY, 2004). He relocated from Australia to the Netherlands in 2010. While there is no claim that this is a thorough review, the observations below are likely to be indicative of the issues that would need to be considered in any further utilization of the method.

In comparison with the MSC, in PSR ironically the role of stories has been downplayed, and the importance of programme logic and the capacity of PSR to be an integrative approach to evaluation using qualitative and quantitative data has been emphasized. This is even more so the case in COR, the next incarnation of the method. It is likely that there was scepticism about the story-based approach in official and scientific circles in Australia, and it is possible that, as a result, the method was (re)designed in an attempt to maximize its perceived credibility to the key stakeholders (that is, the auditor-general and political detractors). The inclusion of an expert panel is one example of the attempt to increase the legitimacy of the method in the eyes of the cynics. For people committed to participatory approaches and/ or who are accepting of qualitative methods, the expert panel is unnecessary and perhaps undesirable, and is not likely to be effective or useful. However, where an overseeing or monitoring function is needed, they could be used. However, a problem arises when the expert panel does not fundamentally believe in the process, or when their views are markedly different to those of the project participants. Arguably, the stakeholder panel alone should be a sufficient validation process.

Curiously, PSR was used in Australia because there was no pre-existing programme logic and little capacity to utilize data other than the performance stories. The unique value of the method which led to its use was its ability to be a retrospective assessment and to provide some evidence of change in the absence of baseline data. The stories of participants gave a sense of the multifaceted nature of the outcomes, were able to adjust for the confounding effects of external events (such as the drought most of Australia experienced for much of the previous decade), and detailed the unanticipated benefits that were experienced.

Anecdotal evidence suggests that involvement in the PSR process was very rewarding for participants. They learned things about what they were doing that they had not thought of before. This enabled them to consider this aspect of their activities and to enhance upon it. The programme evaluation was also done after an extended dry period, when many farmers and rural residents were hurting and many NRM schemes (tree planting etc) were not particularly effective. Instead of the evaluation process proving that the schemes were yet another failure leading to further disappointment (and mental health deterioration) to participants (HUNT et al., 2011), the evaluations revealed to the participants that there were benefits from these programmes anyway. Thus, it was a valuable self-validation process. Project managers and NRM agency staff also mentioned that they learned about the factors and inputs that contributed to change and outcomes in ways that survey-type evaluations would not have achieved. And because of the participatory process, these findings were self-realizations (personal learnings) rather than the conclusions of some external expert which would not necessarily be accepted by the audience. As mentioned above, many managers at the regional level have become strong supporters of the PSR approach and continue to use it in their agencies, despite lack of interest at the Australian federal level.

There is no doubt that the majority of participants in the process thought it valuable and worthwhile. In general, they thought that the story approach was refreshing and that it validated their personal views. Bureaucrats, especially those not familiar with qualitative research methodologies, were unimpressed. They did not accept that the stories were evidence of outcome, and they were worried about a potential bias in the selection of stories favouring atypical positive stories. The implication of this observation is that there is no point in using the PSR method, unless process work is done with key stakeholders to ensure that they understand how the method works and so that they accept the legitimacy of the approach.

While the use of the method was arguably successful in the Australian context (despite its later abandonment), there were some issues that could be addressed should the methodology be used again in the future in Australia or elsewhere. The PSR method has some inherent limitations. For example, there is potential for considerable variation in the way the stories are compiled especially when multiple interviewers are used. It is necessary to ensure good training, supervision and monitoring of the interviewers so that they are relatively consistent in the way stories are collected and to ensure that the stories are effective as stories and valid as a fair reporting of participant experience. Given that the procedure allows for a degree of editing of the transcripts (see p. 37 of the User Guide for precise statements about this), it is quite likely that there will be variation in the extent to which this occurs.

From a social research perspective, the analysis should be done on all the available data using all interview transcripts that are available, not just the stories selected for inclusion in the report. Using qualitative data analysis software (for example, NVivo) to code the original interview transcripts (rather than the enhanced stories) would be appropriate. The selected stories are intended only to exemplify the information in the evaluation report and do not constitute the data or the analysis. Therefore, it might be argued that there is no harm in the stories being modified or enhanced, or even combined to produce indicative narratives (DARE et al., 2011) rather than attempt to be faithful to the notion of being interview transcripts. The method of selecting and ratifying the stories used as vignettes in the summit meeting provides a quality control to ensure that the vignettes are legitimate and authentic even if they are not the actual words of a single person. The PSR method (as strictly outlined in the User Guide) is a hybrid approach and is confused in its methodological positioning. Conceivably the expert panel and the rules about the stories are about ensuring the external legitimacy of the process, rather than necessarily being about the integrity of the data or the analysis.

Notwithstanding the above criticisms, the key point is that story-based evaluation is an effective way of collecting evidence of change, especially in contexts where there are not adequate empirical indicators, where causality is hard to establish, and where there may be external factors that influence the outcomes. In these contexts, the stories of participants provide a means of determining success. Similar to all qualitative social research, the robustness of the method is established through the professionalism of the researchers, and the consistency of stories from multiple sources (triangulation), allowing of course for different perspectives from different stakeholders. It is clear that story-based evaluation could be an appropriate approach in the context of European Union Cohesion Funds, especially as an augmentation to other forms of evaluation.

SPECULATION ON THE FEASIBILITY OF STORY-BASED EVALUATION IN THE CONTEXT OF EUROPEAN UNION COHESION POLICY

The application of a story-based approach to evaluation in the Australian NRM context establishes the potential of the approach. There is nothing particularly unusual about the Australian situation that would mean that it would apply there but not elsewhere such as in Europe or North America. Indeed, it has been used in many other contexts, including in developing countries (WILLETTS and CRAWFORD, 2007), in Canada where it was used to evaluate the effectiveness of the various cultural programmes undertaken by the City of Surrey as part of its Cultural Capital of Canada Award

(WITHERS, 2010), and in the USA where a similar approach is promoted by the US Department of Health through the CDCP (2007). Thinking about the European situation and the types of interventions typically funded suggests the following observations may be appropriate.

- Local development interventions in an urban or rural setting – this seems to be an ideal situation for the use of story-based evaluation. Because of the disparateness of the range of activities, selecting common indicators could be difficult. Story-based evaluation would enable the collation of evidence of change even where the on-ground activities varied considerably.
- Innovation support and/or enterprise support – companies and other organizations (for example, universities) could create stories about what they used the support for and what difference the support made. In these cases, empirical indicators may be available – at least in terms of the improvement in the financial performance of profit-oriented companies; however, the stories are likely to highlight additional added-value dimensions that are not revealed through the numbers alone.
- Support for dynamic systems involving numerous different stakeholders such as clusters – measurement in such contexts is always difficult because of differing units of analysis. The dynamic nature implies that the system is in a state of flux such that movement on any one indicator does not necessarily explain what is happening. Stories have a greater potential to explain how the funding support made a difference to different stakeholders in the system.
- Incentive grants and loans intended to stimulate behaviour change – potentially these initiatives are difficult to evaluate with existing indicators because they are often quite specific. Nevertheless, often ad hoc indicators can be developed that measure the changed behaviour, especially where the behaviour relates to consumption. However, where the behaviour change is not immediate, it may be harder to identify appropriate indicators. Here story-based evaluation can assist. Qualitative approaches might also provide a greater understanding about why the programme led to changed behaviour. Perhaps the grant or loan was not the main cause and the measured relationship was spurious. Qualitative evaluation would also be able to provide a sense of whether the size of the grant or loan was appropriate to have the necessary stimulus effect, or whether it needed to be increased to expand uptake, or whether it could be decreased without sacrificing its effectiveness.
- Training and capacity building – measures of investment for training and capacity building can readily assess the numbers of people attending activities, and where there are assessment (examination) processes, the number who passed. Satisfaction surveys can also be undertaken. However all these measures are low down on Bennett's hierarchy, that is, they are largely measures of inputs, activities, outputs, or satisfaction and are not adequate measures of ultimate, intermediate or even immediate outcomes. The outcomes of training should focus on what difference the training makes to the lives of those who did the training. Story-based evaluation is likely to provide much more information about the outcomes of training and capacity building programmes than any empirical measure can.
- Investment in infrastructure (roads, rail, environmental infrastructure) – it is worth highlighting that story-telling approaches might reveal many more benefits (and potentially problems) about improvements in infrastructure. Improved public transport, for example, not only reduces journey-to-work time, but by making it accessible to mobility-restricted people potentially makes a world of difference to them enabling them to get jobs, have a wider range of entertainment, better access to shopping, and greater autonomy over their lives. The crude empirical indicators give no sense of the richness and value that increasing transport options can have.

Thus, in all types of European Union funding, whether or not empirical indicators are available, story-based approaches will always provide additional information. In a summative context, story-based approaches will provide additional evidence especially of the extra 'social return on investment'. In a formative context, story-based and qualitative evaluation will provide more information about how the programme can be improved.

CONCLUSION

There is ample testament to the power of stories. Tell a person an isolated alleged 'fact', and they wonder about its veracity. Tell a person a proper story, and it will likely be accepted. Stories are more engaging; stories are more meaningful; stories are more real; stories convey information more effectively and are more likely to be remembered than facts.

An effective story, however, has to be a proper story. It cannot be an inchoate amalgam of odd ideas. To be an effective story, it needs to conform to the standard basic elements of all stories. It needs to have a beginning, a middle and an ending. It needs to have a coherent and credible storyline. It needs to be multidimensional, but the different components need to be interconnected and the causal relations between the components need to become clear in the course of the story. It needs to be personal and emotional. KURTZ (2009) provides much advice on how to construct good stories.

Telling stories as a means of effecting behaviour change is an ancient art. Biblical parables, children's fables, classic mythology and good literature all seek to influence their readers. Using stories to understand, analyse and make sense of things in a formal way is relatively recent, but has been part of strategic planning in business for some decades. Using stories as an evaluation methodology is more recent, but has much appeal and, as demonstrated by the Australian experience, has the potential to be effectively implemented.

It is not intended that story-based approaches replace quantitative indicators where they are available. The intention is that the stories complement the quantitative indicators and that they add value to those indicators by providing additional meaning and interpretation. Big programmes are subject to long lag times, and can be subject to the influence of multiple external influences. It is naïve to think that having a list of simple indicators will reveal the complex processes taking place. Stories are therefore a much more effective way of understanding what is happening.

Acknowledgements — The document on which this paper is based was prepared at the request of the European Commission's Directorate-General for Regional Policy. Significant comments on it and/or drafts of this paper and their associated presentations were received from (in alphabetical order): Fabrizio Barca, Veronica Gaffey, Phillip McCann and Marielle Riche. Thanks to Jessica Dart for agreeing to be interviewed. Thanks also to many Australian natural resource management (NRM) stakeholders with whom these issues were discussed. The original document is available from the DG-Regio website at: http://ec.europa.eu/regional_policy/sources/docgener/evaluation/doc/performance/Vanclay.pdf

REFERENCES

ANATAS J. (2004) Quality in qualitative evaluation: Issues and possible answers, *Research on Social Work Practice* **14(1)**, 57–65.

AUDITOR GENERAL (2008) *Regional Delivery Model for the Natural Heritage Trust and the National Action Plan for Salinity and Water Quality*. Audit Report Number 21 2007–08). Australian National Audit Office, Canberra, ACT (available at: http://www.anao.gov.au/uploads/documents/2007-08_Audit_Report_21.pdf) (accessed on 11 April 2012).

BENNETT C. (1975) Up the hierarchy, *Journal of Extension* **13(2)**, 7–12.

BESSEN CONSULTING SERVICES (2009) *Performance Story Report: Evaluation of Investment in the Dugong and Marine Turtle Project*. North Australian Indigenous Land and Sea Management Alliance, Darwin, NT (available at: http://www.savanna.org.au/nailsma/publications/downloads/Dugong-and-Marine-Turtle-Project-PSR.pdf) (accessed on 28 April 2013).

CARR A. and WOODHAMS F. (2008) *Monitoring, Evaluating, Reporting and Improving (MERI) Natural Resource Management: Making MERI in Australia*. Bureau of Rural Sciences, Canberra, ACT.

CASH D., CLARK W., ALCOCK F., DICKSON N., ECKLEY N., GUSTON D., JÄGER J. and MITCHELL R. (2003) Knowledge systems for sustainable development, *Proceedings of the National Academy of Sciences, USA* **100(14)**, 8086–8091.

CENTERS FOR DISEASE CONTROL AND PREVENTION (CDCP) (2007) *Impact and Value: Telling Your Program's Story*. CDCP, National Centers for Chronic Disease Prevention and Health Promotion, Division of Oral Health, Atlanta, GA (available at: http://www.cdc.gov/oralhealth/publications/library/pdf/success_story_workbook.pdf) (accessed on 28 April 2013).

CLEAR HORIZON AND ENVIRONMENT VICTORIA (2010) *Regional Sustainable Living Program: Performance Story Report*. Environment Victoria, Melbourne, VIC (available at: http://environmentvictoria.org.au/sites/default/files/RSL%20Whole%20of%20Program%20Report%20-%20public%20version.pdf) (accessed on 28 April 2013).

COMMONWEALTH OF AUSTRALIA (2008) *Caring for Our Country Outcomes 2008–2013*. Commonwealth of Australia, Canberra, ACT (available at: http://nrmonline.nrm.gov.au/catalog/mql:1887) (accessed on 28 April 2013).

COMMONWEALTH OF AUSTRALIA (2012) *One Land – Many Stories: Prospectus for Investment*. Australian Government Department of Sustainability, Environment, Water, Population and Communities, Canberra, ACT (available at: http://www.environment.gov.au/biodiversity/publications/prospectus/index.html) (accessed on 25 July 2013).

CURTIS A. and LOCKWOOD M. (2000) Landcare and catchment management in Australia: Lessons for state-sponsored community participation, *Society and Natural Resources* **13(1)**, 61–73.

DARE M., VANCLAY F. and SCHIRMER J. (2011) Understanding community engagement in plantation forest management: Insights from practitioner and community narratives, *Journal of Environmental Planning and Management* **54(9)**, 1149–1168.

DART J. and DAVIES R. (2003) A dialogical, story-based evaluation tool: the Most Significant Change Techniquef, *American Journal of Evaluation* **24(2)**, 137–155.

DART J., DRYSDALE G., COLE D. and SADDINGTON M. (2000) *The Most Significant Change Approach for Monitoring an Australian Extension Project*. PLA Notes Number 38, pp. 47–53. International Institute for Environment and Development, London.

DART J. and MAYNE J. (2005) Performance story, in MATHISON S. (Ed.) *Encyclopedia of Evaluation*, pp. 307–308. Sage, Thousand Oaks, CA.

DART J. and O'CONNOR P. (2008) *Performance Story Report: A Study of the Mount Lofty Ranges Southern Emu-Wren and Fleurieu Peninsula Swamps Recovery Program and How it Contributed to Biodiversity Outcomes in the Adelaide and Mount Lofty Ranges Natural Resources Management Region*. Commonwealth of Australia, Canberra, ACT (available at: http://nrmonline.nrm.gov.au/catalog/mql:2167) (accessed on 11 April 2012).

DAVIES R. and DART J. (2005) *The 'Most Significant Change' (MSC) Technique: A Guide to its Use* [self-published manual for a consortium of development agencies] (available at: http://www.mande.co.uk/docs/MSCGuide.pdf) (accessed on 11 April 2012).

DENNING S. (2007) *The Secret Language of Leadership: How Leaders Inspire Action through Narrative*. Jossey-Bass, San Francisco, CA.

DEPARTMENT OF WATER, LAND AND BIODIVERSITY CONSERVATION (DWLBC) (2009) *Our Changing Environment: Outcomes and Lessons from Investment in South Australia's Natural Resources 2001–2008*, Government of South Australia, Department of

Water, Land and Biodiversity Conservation, Adelaide, SA (available at: http://nrmonline.nrm.gov.au/catalog/mql:2677) (accessed on 10 October 2013).

ENTICOTT G. and VANCLAY F. (2011) The moral accountability of agricultural scripts: an analysis of farmers' talk about animal health risks, *Health Risk and Society* **13(4)**, 293–309.

ESTEVES A. M., FRANKS D. and VANCLAY F. (2012) Social impact assessment: the state of the art, *Impact Assessment and Project Appraisal* **30(1)**, 35–44.

ESTEVES A. M. and VANCLAY F. (2009) Social development needs analysis as a tool for SIA to guide corporate–community investment: applications in the minerals industry, *Environmental Impact Assessment Review* **29(2)**, 137–145.

EVALSED (2012) *EVALSED: The Resource for the Evaluation of Socioeconomic Development* (available at: http://ec.europa.eu/regional_policy/sources/docgener/evaluation/guide/guide2012_evalsed.pdf) (accessed on 14 September 2013).

FELLER I. (2007) Mapping the frontiers of evaluation of public sector R&D programs, *Science and Public Policy* **34(10)**, 681–690.

FETTERMAN D. M. (2000) *Foundations of Empowerment Evaluation*. Sage, Thousand Oaks, CA.

FETTERMAN D. M., KAFTARIAN S. J. and WANDERSMAN A. (Eds) (1995) *Empowerment Evaluation*. Sage, Thousand Oaks, CA.

FISHER W. R. (1989) *Human Communication as Narration: Toward a Philosophy of Reason, Value, and Action*. University of South Carolina Press, Columbia, SC.

GREENE J. C. (2000) Qualitative program evaluation: practice and promise, in DENZIN N. K. and LINCOLN Y. S. (Eds) *Handbook of Qualitative Research*, pp. 530–544. Sage, Thousand Oaks, CA.

GUBA E. and LINCOLN Y. (1989) *Fourth Generation Evaluation*. Sage, Newbury Park, CA.

GUIJT I., BROUWERS J., KUSTERS C., PRINS E. and ZEYNALOVA B. (2011) *Evaluation Revisited: Improving the Quality of Evaluative Practice by Embracing Complexity (Conference Report)*. Centre for Development Innovation, Wageningen University and Research Centre, Wageningen (available at: http://capacity.org/capacity/export/sites/capacity/documents/topic-readings/110412-evaluation-revisited-may-2010_small-version.pdf) (accessed on 11 April 2012).

HAJKOWICZ S. (2009) The evolution of Australia's natural resource management programs: towards improved targeting and evaluation of investments, *Land Use Policy* **26(2)**, 471–478.

HOWDEN P. and VANCLAY F. (2000) Mythologization of farming styles in Australian broadacre cropping, *Rural Sociology* **65(2)**, 295–310.

HUGHES R. and HUBY M. (2002) The application of vignettes in social and nursing research, *Journal of Advanced Nursing* **37(4)**, 382–386.

HUNT W., VANCLAY F., BIRCH C., COUTTS J., FLITTNER J. and WILLIAMS B. (2011) Agricultural extension: Building capacity and resilience in rural industries and communities, *Rural Society* **20(2)**, 112–127.

JACKSON E. T. and KASSAM Y. (Eds) (1998) *Knowledge Shared: Participatory Evaluation in Development Cooperation*. Kumarian, West Hartford, CT.

JOÃO E., VANCLAY F. and DEN BROEDER L. (2011) Emphasising enhancement in all forms of impact assessment, *Impact Assessment and Project Appraisal* **29(3)**, 170–180.

KURTZ C. (2009) *Working with Stories in your Community or Organization* (available at: http://www.workingwithstories.org) (accessed on 11 April 2012).

KURTZ C. and SNOWDEN D. (2003) The new dynamics of strategy: sense-making in a complex and complicated world, *IBM Systems Journal* **42(3)**, 462–483.

LABONTE R. (2011) Reflections on stories and a story/dialogue method in health research, *International Journal of Social Research Methodology* **14(2)**, 153–163.

LABONTE R., FEATHER J. and HILLS M. (1999) A story/dialogue method for health promotion knowledge development and evaluation, *Health Education Research* **14(1)**, 39–50.

LAUGHLIN R. and BROADBENT J. (1996) Redesigning fourth generation evaluation, *Evaluation* **2(4)**, 431–451.

LAVINGHOUZE R., PRICE A. and SMITH K. (2007) The program success story: a valuable tool for program evaluation, *Health Promotion Practice* **8(4)**, 323–331.

LEEUW F. and VAESSEN J. (2009) *Impact Evaluations and Development: NONIE Guidance on Impact Evaluation. The Network of Networks on Impact Evaluation*. c/- Independent Evaluation Group, The World Bank, Washington, DC (available at: http://siteresources.worldbank.org/EXTOED/Resources/nonie_guidance.pdf) (accessed on 11 April 2012).

MAXSON M., GUIJT I., *et al.* (2010) *The 'Real Book' for Story Evaluation Methods*. GlobalGiving Foundation (available at: http://www.globalgiving.org/jcr-content/gg/landing-pages/story-tools/files/-story-real-book--2010.pdf) (accessed on 11 April 2012).

MAYNE J. (1999) *Addressing Attribution through Contribution Analysis: Using Performance Measures Sensibly (Discussion Paper)*. Office of Auditor-General of Canada (available at: http://dsp-psd.pwgsc.gc.ca/Collection/FA3-31-1999E.pdf) (accessed on 11 April 2012).

MAYNE J. (2004) Reporting on outcomes: setting performance expectations and telling performance stories, *Canadian Journal of Program Evaluation* **19(1)**, 31–60.

PADGETT D. K. (2012) *Qualitative and Mixed Methods in Public Health*. Sage, Thousand Oaks, CA.

PATTON M. Q. (1981) *Creative Evaluation*. Sage, Beverly Hills, CA.

PATTON M. Q. (1990) *Qualitative Evaluation and Research Methods*. Sage, Newbury Park, CA.

PATTON M. Q. (1997) *Utilization-Focused Evaluation*. Sage, Thousand Oaks, CA.

PRAGER K. and VANCLAY F. (2010) Landcare in Australia and Germany: comparing structures and policies for community engagement in natural resource management, *Ecological Management and Restoration* **11(3)**, 187–193.

ROBINS L. and KANOWSKI P. (2011) 'Crying for our Country': eight ways in which 'Caring for our Country' has undermined Australia's regional model for natural resource management, *Australasian Journal of Environmental Management* **18(2)**, 88–108.

ROESE N. (1997) Counterfactual thinking, *Psychological Bulletin* **121(1)**, 133–148.

ROUGHLEY A. (2009) *Developing and Using Program Logic in Natural Resource Management: User Guide*. Australian Government, Canberra, ACT (available at: http://nrmonline.nrm.gov.au/catalog/mql:2164) (accessed on 11 April 2012).

ROUGHLEY A. and DART J. (2009) *Developing a Performance Story Report. User Guide*. Australian Government, Canberra, ACT (available at: http://nrmonline.nrm.gov.au/catalog/mql:2162) (accessed on 11 April 2012).

ROYCE D., THYER B. T., PADGETT D. K. and LOGAN T. K. (2001) *Program Evaluation: An Introduction*, 3rd Edn. Brooks/Cole, Pacific Grove, CA.

SANDELOWSKI M. (1991) Telling stories: narrative approaches in qualitative research, *Image: Journal of Nursing Scholarship* **23(3)**, 161–166.

SHAW G., BROWN R. and BROMILEY P. (1998) Strategic stories: how 3M is rewriting business planning, *Harvard Business Review* **76(3)**, 41–50.

SILVER M., RICHARDS R. and COWELL S. (2009) *A Guide to Designing and Implementing Performance Reporting to Increase the Confidence of Conservation Investors*. Bush Heritage Australia, Melbourne, VIC (available at: http://lwa.gov.au/files/products/reporting/pn30209/pn30209.pdf) (accessed on 11 April 2012).

SNOWDEN D. and BOONE M. (2007) A leader's framework for decision making, *Harvard Business Review* **85(11)**, 69–76.

TENNENT R. and LOCKIE S. (2013) Vale Landcare: the rise and decline of community-based natural resource management in rural Australia, *Journal of Environmental Planning and Management* **56(4)**, 572–587.

VANCLAY F. (2003) International principles for social impact assessment, *Impact Assessment and Project Appraisal* **21(1)**, 5–11.

VANCLAY F. (2004) Social principles for agricultural extension to assist in the promotion of natural resource management, *Australian Journal of Experimental Agriculture* **44(3)**, 213–222.

VANCLAY F. (2012a) *Guidance for the Design of Qualitative Case Study Evaluation: A Short Report to DG Regio* (available at: http://ec.europa.eu/regional_policy/sources/docgener/evaluation/doc/performance/Vanclay.pdf) (accessed on 17 May 2012).

VANCLAY F. (2012b) The potential application of Social Impact Assessment in coastal zone management, *Ocean and Coastal Management* **68**, 149–156.

VANCLAY F. and ENTICOTT G. (2011) The role and functioning of cultural scripts in farming and agriculture, *Sociologia Ruralis* **51(3)**, 256–271.

VANCLAY F., LANE R., WILLS J., COATES I. and LUCAS D. (2004) 'Committing to Place' and evaluating the higher purpose: Increasing engagement in natural resource management through museum outreach and educational activities, *Journal of Environmental Assessment Policy and Management* **6(4)**, 539–564.

WADSWORTH Y. (2005) 'Gouldner's child?': some reflections on sociology and participatory action research, *Journal of Sociology* **41(3)**, 267–284.

WADSWORTH Y., WIERENGA A. and WILSON G. (2007) *Writing Narrative Action Evaluation Reports in Health Promotion: Manual of Guidelines, Resources, Case Studies and QuickGuide*, 2nd Edn. State of Victoria, Department of Human Services and the University of Melbourne, Melbourne, VIC.

WATERS D., JAMES R. and DARBY J. (2011) Health promoting community radio in rural Bali: An impact evaluation, *Rural and Remote Health* **11(1)**, article #1555 (online journal available at: http://www.rrh.org.au/articles/subviewnew.asp?ArticleID=1555) (accessed on 11 April 2012).

WHITMORE E. (Ed.) (1998) *Understanding and Practicing Participatory Evaluation: New Directions for Evaluation*. Jossey-Bass, San Francisco, CA.

WHYTE W. F. (Ed.) (1990) *Participatory Action Research*. Sage, Newbury Park, CA.

WILDER L. and WALPOLE M. (2008) Measuring social impacts in conservation: experience of using the Most Significant Change method, *Oryx* **42(4)**, 529–538.

WILLETTS J. and CRAWFORD P. (2007) The most significant lessons about the Most Significant Change Technique, *Development in Practice* **17(3)**, 367–379.

WITHERS D. (2010) *Narrative Evaluation: City of Surrey's Cultural Capital of Canada Award Program* (available at: http://denisewithers.files.wordpress.com/2011/02/surreycccreport1.pdf) (accessed on 28 April 2013).

RHOMOLO: A Dynamic General Equilibrium Modelling Approach to the Evaluation of the European Union's R&D Policies

ANDRIES BRANDSMA and D'ARTIS KANCS

DG Joint Research Centre, European Commission, IPTS, Seville, Spain.

BRANDSMA A. and KANCS D'A. RHOMOLO: a dynamic general equilibrium modelling approach to the evaluation of the European Union's R&D policies, *Regional Studies*. European integration changes the prospects of regional economies within the member states of the European Union in many ways. Cohesion Policy is the European Union's instrument to influence and complement the efforts made at the national level to ensure that the gains of economic integration reach everyone, and there are no regions left behind. This paper presents and applies a spatial general equilibrium model RHOMOLO to assess the impact of regional policy in the European Union. The presented simulation results highlight strengths of the approach taken in RHOMOLO in handling investments in research and development (R&D), infrastructure and spillovers of investments in the innovation capacity of the regions, both of which cannot be captured by models in which the spatial structure is not present.

BRANDSMA A. and KANCS D'A. RHOMOLO：一个评估欧盟研发政策的动态一般均衡模型，区域研究。欧盟整合，以诸多方式改变欧盟成员国内的区域经济前景。凝聚政策，是欧盟影响、并补充在国家层级上力图确保每人皆能分享经济整合的果实、且没有任何区域被遗落的政策工具。本文呈现、并应用空间一般均衡模型 RHOMOLO，对欧盟区域政策的影响进行评估。本文所呈献的模拟结果，强调 RHOMOLO 所採取的方法，在处理研发（R&D）与基础投资，以及区域创新能力投资的外溢方面的优势，而上述两者皆无法以不具备空间结构的模型捕捉之。

BRANDSMA A. et KANCS D'A. L'évaluation des politiques de l'Union européenne en matière de R et D: la méthode de modélisation en équilibre général dynamique RHOMOLO, *Regional Studies*. L'intégration européenne modifie de manières différentes les perspectives d'avenir des économies régionales des pays-membres de l'Union européenne. La politique de cohésion constitue l'outil de l'Union européenne qui a pour objet d'influencer et de compléter les efforts faits au niveau national afin d'assurer que les gains de l'intégration économique s'avèrent avantageux pour tout le monde, et que personne n'a du retard. Ce présent article cherche à présenter et à appliquer le modèle d'équilibre général spatial RHOMOLO pour évaluer l'impact de la politique régionale dans l'Union européenne. Les résultats de simulation presentés ici mettent en relief les atouts de la méthode employée par RHOMOLO pour traiter les investissements dans la recherche et le développement (R et D), l'infrastructure et les retombées des investissements dans la capacité d'innovation des régions. Les modèles au sein desquels il manque une structure spatiale ne peuvent capter ni l'un, ni l'autre.

BRANDSMA A. und KANCS D'A. RHOMOLO: ein Ansatz für ein dynamisches allgemeines Gleichgewichtsmodell zur Bewertung der F&E-Politik der Europäischen Union, *Regional Studies*. Durch die europäische Integration ändern sich die Aussichten der regionalen Ökonomien innerhalb der Mitgliedstaaten der Europäischen Union auf vielerlei Weise. Die Kohäsionspolitik ist das Instrument der Europäischen Union zur Beeinflussung und Ergänzung der Bemühungen auf nationaler Ebene, um sicherzustellen, dass der Nutzen der wirtschaftlichen Integration jeden erreicht und keine Regionen zurückbleiben. In diesem Beitrag wird das räumliche allgemeine Gleichgewichtsmodell RHOMOLO zur Untersuchung der Auswirkung der Regionalpolitik in der Europäischen Union vorgestellt und angewandt. Die vorgestellten Ergebnisse der Simulation verdeutlichen die Stärken des von RHOMOLO verfolgten Ansatzes beim Umgang mit Investitionen in Forschung und Entwicklung (F&E) und in die

Infrastruktur sowie mit den Übertragungseffekten der Investitionen in die Innovationskapazität der Regionen, welche sich beide nicht mit Modellen erfassen lassen, in denen die räumliche Struktur nicht vorhanden ist.

BRANDSMA A. y KANCS D'A. RHOMOLO: un planteamiento de modelo dinámico de equilibrio general para la evaluación de las políticas de I+D de la Unión Europea, *Regional Studies*. A través de la integración europea se cambian de muchas maneras las perspectivas de las economías regionales en los Estados miembros de la Unión Europea. La política de cohesión es el instrumento de la Unión Europea que orienta y amplía los esfuerzos realizados en el ámbito nacional con el objetivo de garantizar que las ventajas de la integración económica lleguen a todos y ninguna región quede rezagada. En este artículo presentamos y aplicamos el modelo espacial de equilibrio general RHOMOLO para evaluar el efecto de la política regional en la Unión Europea. Los resultados presentados de la simulación ponen de relieve las ventajas del planteamiento de RHOMOLO en lo que respecta a la gestión de las inversiones en investigación y desarrollo (I+D) y en la infraestructura, así como de los efectos indirectos de las inversiones en la capacidad de innovación de las regiones, los cuales no pueden ser captados por modelos en los que no esté presente la estructura espacial.

INTRODUCTION

The geographical distribution of the gains from economic integration has been a concern of decision-makers since the early beginnings of the European Union (EU). Cohesion Policy is the EU's instrument for reducing regional disparities and stimulating the economic development of regions that are lagging behind (EUROPEAN COMMISSION, 2014). EU support to regions is provided as a financial contribution to programmes negotiated with the member states. The Structural and Cohesion Funds amount to roughly one-third of the EU budget, which means that between 0.3% and 0.4% of the EU's gross domestic product (GDP) is redistributed over member states and regions through Cohesion Policy. At the receiving end – for the less developed regions – the inflow of funds can be a very substantial part of regional income, even though there is a maximum of about 4% of GDP to the funding received by any member state in a given year.

There is a wide range of activities that are supported by Cohesion Policy, varying from the building of motorways to training programmes, such as, for instance, helping Bulgarian magistrates to improve their knowledge of EU law. The multitude and diversity of the projects and interdependencies between regions make it difficult to evaluate the effects of Cohesion Policy at any aggregate level. Nevertheless, this is what EU policy-makers are required to do in order to be able to compare the returns on different types of investment, taking into account the externalities that would justify making the public investment at the EU level. How the funding assists the regions in increasing their capacity for growth and to what extent the impact spreads across regions are major issues of Cohesion Policy evaluation.

The present study proposes a spatial computable general equilibrium (SCGE) approach to policy impact assessment. In order to demonstrate the strengths of this approach, this paper takes the example of two broad categories of investment – Research, Technological Development and Innovation (RTDI), on the one hand, and Infrastructure (INF), on the other – and looks at the possible impact on EU regions. In doing so, it addresses a point made in the 6th Cohesion Report that even though the infrastructure connecting the EU-15 – the member states forming the EU before enlargement in 2004 – had largely been completed, there was still a great need to improve transport links to the EU-12 – the 12 member states that joined in the last rounds of EU enlargement.[1] The 6th Cohesion Report also argued that support to enterprises and research and development (R&D) in the EU-15 should not go at the expense of other types of investment, pointing out that investments in human capital and innovation might be more appropriate for the less developed regions in the EU-15.

Running simulations with the 2014–20 Cohesion Policy expenditure data for RTDI and INF until 2025, this paper shows how the approach taken in RHOMOLO[2] can help to identify the potential impact of policy interventions at the regional level and the shift of the pattern of the impact between regions and sectors over time. In order to assess the possible impact of investments in RTDI and infrastructure over time, the RHOMOLO model is used in combination with the Commission's QUEST model (VARGA and IN'T Veld, 2010). The sophisticated dynamics and inter-temporal optimization in a multi-country setting of QUEST allows for a calibration of RHOMOLO with respect to the macro-dynamics of QUEST. While the approach taken is not new and essentially follows the concept of Geographic Macro and Regional modelling (VARGA, 2015), what RHOMOLO adds is an empirically based coverage of changes in relative prices taking agglomeration and dispersion forces into account. The RHOMOLO dataset is complete for all NUTS-2 regions and consistent with national accounts and international trade data. Key parameter values for each type of policy intervention are taken from the empirical literature and, whenever warranted, estimates are made on the basis of regional data. In RHOMOLO the regional differentiation accounts for the level of economic development and, in the case of RTDI, also for the distance to the technological frontier in sectors of the economy.

The simulation results presented in this paper highlight the choices that policy-makers are facing in the allocation of funds to regions of member states and to broad categories of investment covering all EU regions. Ideally, this approach should also help to find combinations of allocations to regions and categories of investment that would make all EU regions better off, but the results at this stage suggest that this would be asking too much in view of the complexity of the geographic interactions and the uncertainty surrounding the key parameters.

In developing a spatial CGE approach, implementing it empirically for the whole EU at the regional level and demonstrating how it is operated, the paper partly fills the gap identified in the literature (BROECKER et al., 2001; BROECKER and KORZHENEVYCH, 2013; VARGA, 2015). The closest model to RHOMOLO is CGEurope (BROECKER and KORZHENEVYCH, 2013). Whereas CGEurope is more sophisticated along the spatial dimension, RHOMOLO provides a greater sectoral detail. Each of the 267 NUTS-2 regional economies is divided into six (NACE 1) economic sectors. In addition, RHOMOLO includes the labour market and migration for different levels of skills. This makes it a comprehensive tool for assessing the impact of the whole of Cohesion Policy at the regional level, which amounts to roughly €50 billion of spending via the EU budget per year.

The paper is structured as follows. It first presents the background and main features of RHOMOLO. The third section describes the data used for empirical implementation, calibration and empirical validation of the model. Two scenarios are set up in the fourth section with simulation results discussed in the fifth section. The sixth section has concluding remarks.

THE RHOMOLO MODEL[3]

The domestic economy (which corresponds to the EU) consists of $R - 1$ regions $r = 1, \ldots, R - 1$, which are included into M countries $m = 1, \ldots, M$. The rest of the world is introduced in the model as a particular region (indexed by R) and particular sector (indexed by S). Sector S differs from domestic sectors in that it

only has one variety which is exclusively produced in region R. Formally, there are $N_{S,r} = 0$ and $N_{s,R} = 0$ for all r and s; and $N_{S,R} = 1$. The foreign variety of final good is used as the numéraire.

The final (and intermediate) goods sectors include $s = 1, \ldots, S$ different economic industries in which firms operate under monopolistic competition à la DIXIT and STIGLITZ (1977). Each firm produces a differentiated variety which is considered as an imperfect substitute to other varieties by households and firms. Goods are either consumed by households or used by other firms as intermediate inputs or as investment goods. The number of firms in sector s and region r is denoted by $N_{s,r}$. It is large enough so that strategic interactions between firms is negligible. The number of firms in each region is endogenous and to a large extent determines the spatial distribution of economic activity.

Trade between (and within) regions is costly, implying that the shipping of goods between (and within) regions entails transport costs which are assumed to be of the iceberg type, with $\tau_{s,r,q} > 1$ representing the quantity of sector's s goods that needs to be sent from region r in order to have one unit arriving in region q (e.g. KRUGMAN, 1991). Transport costs are assumed to be identical across varieties but specific to sectors and trading partners (regions). They are related to the distance separating regions r and q but can also depend on other factors, such as transport infrastructure or national borders. Finally, transport costs can be asymmetric (i.e. $\tau_{s,r,q}$ may differ from $\tau_{s,q,r}$). They are also assumed to be positive within a given region (i.e. $\tau_{s,r,r} \neq 1$), which captures, among others, the distance between customers and firms within the region.

R&D is modelled as one additional sector of the economy producing innovation. The national R&D sector sells R&D services to local final and intermediate goods firms within the same country and uses regional input. Hence, there are M national R&D sectors that produce new knowledge using a bundle of high-skill labour rented from the different regions of the country. The demand for R&D depends on the relative unit price of R&D with respect to unit prices of other production factors.

The production (and purchase) of R&D services produces a positive externality to all the sectors in the country. The production process of R&D services features learning by doing, as labour productivity is positively related to the existing stock of R&D. The knowledge production function displays constant returns to scale and prefect competition. Government can affect innovative activity through taxes and/or subsidies. In addition, the supply of high-skill labour determines the innovation capacity of the R&D sector.

The wage of high-skill workers employed in the R&D sector is equalized across regions in a country and there is imperfect substitution between high-skill R&D workers in a region (earning the national R&D wage) and high-skill workers in the others sectors of the regional economy, whose wage is determined regionally. Each national sector buys national R&D services at the same price; there are no trade costs for R&D services: R&D services are traded within countries, but not internationally.

In RHOMOLO there are international technological spillovers in the sense that the national R&D sector absorbs part of the technology produced in the other $M - 1$ countries, which results in international knowledge spillovers from the stock of accumulated R&D in other countries. In other words, together with labour, material and capital service inputs, the production functions of each sector display a total factor productivity (TFP) parameter, which shifts the production function depending on the stock of R&D.

Each region is inhabited by H_r households, which are mobile between regions. They partly determine the size of the regional market.[4] The income of households consists of labour revenue (wages), capital revenue and government transfers. It is used to consume final goods, pay taxes and accumulate savings.

Finally, in each country there is a public sector that levies taxes on consumption and on the income of local households. It provides public goods in the form of public capital which is necessary for the operation of firms. It also subsidizes the private sector, including the production of R&D and innovation, and influences the capacity of the educational system to produce human capital.

The detailed regional and sectoral dimensions of RHOMOLO imply that the number of (non-linear) equations to be solved simultaneously is relatively high. Therefore, in order to keep the model manageable from a computation point of view, its dynamics are kept relatively simple. Three types of factors (physical capital, human capital and knowledge capital) as well as several types of assets are accumulated between periods. Agents are assumed to save a constant fraction of their income in each period and form their expectations based only on the current and past states of the economy. The dynamics of the model are then described as in a standard Solow model, i.e. a sequence of short-run equilibria that are related to each other through the build up of physical and human capital stocks.

RHOMOLO contains several endogenous agglomeration and dispersion forces affecting the location choices of firms (see DI COMITE and KANCS, 2014, for a formal description of endogenous location in RHOMOLO). Three effects drive the mechanics of endogenous agglomeration and dispersion of economic agents in RHOMOLO: the market access effect, the price index effect and the market crowding effect. The market access effect captures the fact that, everything else being equal, in the presence of the mentioned endogenous agglomeration and dispersion forces firms in large/central regions would have higher profits than firms in small/peripheral regions, and hence the tendency of firms to locate their production in large/

central regions and export to small/peripheral regions. The price index effect captures the impact of firms' location and trade costs on the cost of living for workers, and the cost of intermediate inputs for producers of final demand goods. The market crowding effect captures the fact that because of higher competition on input and output markets, firms may prefer to locate in small/peripheral regions with fewer competitors.

RHOMOLO contains three endogenous location mechanisms that bring the agglomeration and dispersion of firms and workers about: the mobility of capital, the mobility of labour and vertical linkages. Following the mobile capital framework of MARTIN and ROGERS (1995), it is assumed that (1) capital is mobile between regions; and (2) the mobile capital repatriates all its earnings to the households in its region of origin. Following the mobile labour framework of KRUGMAN (1991), it is assumed that workers are spatially mobile (though the mobility is not perfect); mobile workers not only produce in the region where they settle (as the mobile capital does), but also they spend their income there (which is not the case with capital owners); workers' migration is governed by differences in the expected income and by differences in the costs of living between regions (the mobility of capital is driven solely by differences in the nominal rates of return).[5] Following the vertical linkage framework of VENABLES (1996), it is assumed that, in addition to the primary factors, firms use intermediate inputs in the production process; similarly to final goods consumers, firms value the variety of intermediate inputs; trade of intermediate inputs is costly.

DATA AND EMPIRICAL IMPLEMENTATION

Dimensions of RHOMOLO

RHOMOLO covers 267 NUTS-2 regions in the EU-27, which are disaggregated into six NACE Rev. 1.1 sectors (Table 1 and Fig. 1, respectively).[6] The extensive regional and sectoral disaggregation implies considerable data needs. In particular, for the empirical

Table 1. Sectoral disaggregation of the RHOMOLO model

Code	Sector description
AB	Agriculture, Hunting and Forestry
CDE	Mining and quarrying, Manufacturing, Electricity and gas
F	Construction
GHI	Wholesale and retail trade, Repair of motor vehicles, motorcycles, Personal and household goods, Hotels and restaurants, Transport and communications
JK	Financial intermediation, Real estate and business services
LMNOP	Non-market services

Source: Authors' aggregation based on the NACE Rev. 1.1 classification.

Fig. 1. Spatial disaggregation of the RHOMOLO model

implementation of the RHOMOLO model, data for all exogenous and endogenous variables at the regional (and sectoral) level for the base year (2007) and numerical values for the behavioural parameters are required.

The base year (2007) data are compiled in the form of a regionalized social accounting matrix (SAM) (see POTTERS *et al.*, 2013; and THISSEN *et al.*, 2014, for details). For the construction of SAMs for the member states, data are taken from the World Input Output Database (WIOD) project and the Global Trade Analysis Project (GTAP). The WIOD database consists of International Input–Output tables, International and National Supply and Use tables, National Input–Output tables, and Socio-Economic and Environmental Accounts, covering all EU-27 countries and the rest of the world for the period from 1995 to 2009. An attractive feature of the WIOD data is that an attempt is made to identify and take out re-exports before calculating the total value of exports. Generally, the WIOD data are available for 59 NACE Rev. 1.1 sectors, which, for present purposes, are aggregated into the six macro-sectors used in RHOMOLO. The SAMs are constructed at the national level, based on the Supply and Use tables, and then regionalized while keeping national aggregates, such as on value added and employment, as constraints.

Data for inter-regional variables

The inter-regional labour migration pattern is captured in RHOMOLO by data on net changes in the regional labour force (see BRANDSMA *et al.*, 2014, for details). The relocation of workers between any two regions is modelled as a function of expected income and distance; for the estimation of the elasticities data are required on labour migration, regional GDP and unemployment. EUROSTAT's Regional Migration Statistics provides

data on migration within member states. The national totals are brought in line with Organisation for Economic Co-operation and Development (OECD) data on migration in OECD countries, providing data on migration flows between countries. The Household Income and Active Population data are again extracted from EUROSTAT. Together with data on unemployment and wages, which are extracted from the labour force survey, the constructed data on inter-regional migration flows provide the necessary input to the analysis of labour market and migration features in the RHOMOLO model.

Inter-regional trade flows are estimated using detailed inter-regional transport and freight data from THISSEN *et al.* (2013, 2014). These data are aligned with the available macro-data: the distribution of production and consumption over the EU regions and the national SAMs to ensure consistency with the rest of the RHOMOLO database. The regionalized SAMs were used for the construction of the regional production and consumption constraints. Inter-regional trade costs come from the TRANSTOOLS database, which add up to the country level trade flows from the COMEXT international trade statistics.

Data for inter-temporal variables

Knowledge capital enters RHOMOLO through region-specific R&D intensities (expenditures on R&D divided by GDP), which are available at the national and regional levels from EUROSTAT's Science and Technology Indicators database. Whereas R&D data by sector are available at the national level, comparable data are not available at the regional level for most of the countries. EUROSTAT distinguishes four sectors of performance: governments, higher education institutions, business sector and private non-profit organizations, but they do not correspond to the six sectors in RHOMOLO. Given the sectoral aggregation adopted in RHOMOLO (Table 1), all expenditures on R&D outside the business sector fall under non-market services. The sectoral disaggregation is made by using the gross fixed-capital formation by NACE sector calculated at the regional level.[7]

The regional stock of human capital is proxied in the RHOMOLO database by three different levels of education: low skill (isced0_2), medium skill (isced3_4), and high skill (isced5_6). Wages are differentiated on the basis of the corresponding categories of education levels to account for the decision of households to spend time on education. Data for this are available in the Labour Force Survey (LFS) and the EU KLEMS database.

Data on the regional stock of physical capital are constructed using the perpetual inventory method (PIM). This approach starts with an estimate of the initial stock by country and industry, regionalized by share in gross value added (GVA) in the year 1995 and calculates the final capital stock by region and by industry in 2007 by adding the yearly capital investments and making assumptions on depreciation. The following data are generated: gross fixed-capital formation by sector at the NUTS-2 level in current prices for the years 1995–2010; price deflators for conversion into constant prices; and initial stocks for calculating the net capital stocks for each year by applying the PIM from the EU KLEMS database. These data are available at the national level, which were regionalized by GVA share; depreciation rates are calculated by weighing the average service life of each of the six types of assets for each country (according to the ESA95 classification).

Model parameters

In order to parameterize the RHOMOLO model, all key structural parameters are estimated econometrically; others are drawn from the literature (OKAGAWA and BAN, 2008). For example, all parameters related to inter-regional labour migration are estimated in a panel data setting for each country (BRANDSMA et al., 2014; PERSYN et al., 2014). Similarly, all parameters related to the elasticities of substitution on both the consumer and producer sides are being estimated econometrically. For the purpose of this paper, which is focused on the spatial pattern of the effects rather than the sectoral, the elasticities of substitution are the same for all sectors and regions.

Finally, as usual in spatial CGE models, all shift-and-share parameters are calibrated to reproduce the base year (2007) data in the SAMs. In order to determine the sensitivity of simulation results with respect to the implemented parameters in RHOMOLO, extensive sensitivity analysis and robustness checks were performed. Among others, the sensitivity analysis allows one to establish confidence intervals (in addition to the simulated point estimates) for RHOMOLO's simulation results.

COHESION POLICY AND SCENARIO CONSTRUCTION

European Cohesion Policy (ECP)

In January 2014 the European Commission adopted the framework budget of Cohesion Policy for 2014–20.

The new package is focused on the 'Europe 2020' objectives and mainly target growth and jobs. The total Cohesion Policy expenditure of €342 billion is divided over 123 lines of expenditure in the 2014–20 programming period. A closer inspection of the 123 expenditure categories shows that modelling of each expenditure category separately is hardly feasible given the multi-interpretable and often overlapping description of the lines of expenditure.[8] Therefore, for the purpose of simulations presented in this paper, the 123 expenditure categories are regrouped into five broad categories in order to match parameters in the model. Table 2 provides an overview of the expenditures per type of region and aggregate expenditure category. The last column shows that around two-thirds (68%) of the ECP funds is reserved for the less developed regions. The category 'Infrastructure' covers almost half of all ECP funds (49%).

Research and technological development scenario

The construction of a research and technological development scenario, which can be simulated in RHOMOLO, involves the following three (four) steps: (1) aggregating all relevant ECP expenditure lines into one broad RTDI category; (2) specifying the parameter or set of parameters through which the policy shock will be applied in RHOMOLO; (3) estimating the size of the shock in each region and the pattern by which it is spread over time; and (4) (if necessary) making further adjustments to correct for any known deficiencies of the model vis-à-vis the scenario at hand.

In order to construct a research and technological development scenario, which can be simulated in RHOMOLO, in a first step all relevant ECP expenditure lines were aggregated into the total 'RTDI expenditures' per region (category RTDI in Table 2).[9] According to the third column in Table 2, for the 2014–20 period, almost €42 billion have been allocated to lines of expenditure that can be associated with support to RTDI. This corresponds to around 12% of the total ECP expenditures. Around 60% of the total RTDI expenditures (€25 billion) will be allocated to the less developed regions (Table 2).

Table 2. Breakdown of Cohesion Policy expenditures for 2014–20 (€, millions)

Type of region	Number	RTDI	IND	INF	HC	A	Total	Share
Less developed regions	65	25 250	27 127	129 128	38 408	12 162	232 075	0.68
Transition regions	51	5772	6218	14 339	10 201	1585	38 115	0.11
More developed regions	151	10 916	9101	24 167	24 196	2954	71 335	0.21
Total	267	41 938	42 447	167 634	72 805	16 701	341 525	1.00
% of total European Cohesion Policy (ECP)		0.12	0.12	0.49	0.21	0.05	1.00	

Notes: Number = the number of regions per category of region types (267 = total number of regions in RHOMOLO); INF, Infrastructure; HC, Human Capital; RTDI, Research, Technological Development and Innovation; IND, Industry and Services; and A, Technical Assistance.
Source: EUROPEAN COMMISSION (2014).

In a second step, the relevant parameters through which the RTDI policy shock will be applied in RHOMOLO are specified. The nested production structure of RHOMOLO contains many different entries for TFP shocks. However, they are activated in a rather constrained way in the present simulation, which applies the same TFP shock to all sectors in the region.[10] For the purpose of the present exercise, an increase in productive public capital and TFP improvements are the two main conduits through which the support to RTDI is modelled in RHOMOLO.[11]

In a third step, the size of the shock in each region and the pattern by which it is spread over time is estimated econometrically. For the purpose of this study, these estimates are readily available from DI COMITE et al. (2015) and KANCS and SILIVERSTOVS (2015). The estimates of KANCS and SILIVERSTOVS (2015) suggest a plausible range of 20–30% (Fig. 2).[12] This is close to the estimates used also in the QUEST model (MCMORROW and ROGER, 2009), and therefore adopted in the present simulations. In order to ensure robustness of the simulation results, extensive sensitivity analysis is performed for a plausible range of all R&D parameters.

As a result, a research and technological development scenario of the ECP investments is obtained that can be readily implemented and simulated in RHOMOLO. The RTDI scenario is summarized in Table 3 and Fig. 3.[13] The middle panel represents the exogenous policy shock used as input in the model. The left and right panels are reported only for background information, and for a better understanding of differences between regions.

The left panel in Fig. 3 reports the ECP expenditure on RTDI in millions of euros from Table 2. Applying the econometrically estimated elasticities, the information contained in the left map is transformed into region-specific productivity improvements (middle map). Fig. 3 shows a clear correlation between the left and middle maps. Any differences between the two maps can be attributed to spatial knowledge spillovers.

The right map in Fig. 3 is another way to express the estimated productivity impact of RTDI expenditure – here it is expressed per €1 invested. The map shows a very different pattern from the left and middle maps because of spatial knowledge spillovers; the lagging behind regions (mainly in South and East Europe) benefit more than proportionally from RTDI policies (the rate of return is higher). A visible outlier from this general pattern is North Italy, which is both relatively well developed (in terms of technology) and has a high productivity multiplier in the right panel. This result may be driven, for example, by interactions of spatial knowledge spillovers, absorptive capacity and investments in RTDI.

Transport infrastructure scenario

In order to construct a transport infrastructure scenario, which can be simulated in RHOMOLO, in a first step an aggregate measure of the total ECP expenditure on *transport infrastructure* is constructed for each region. For this purpose, all policy instruments directly affecting transport infrastructure are aggregated into total 'INF expenditures' per region. No weights are applied at this stage of aggregation, although the literature (EUROPEAN COMMISSION, 2011a) suggests that there could be substantial differences in the expected impact per component.[14]

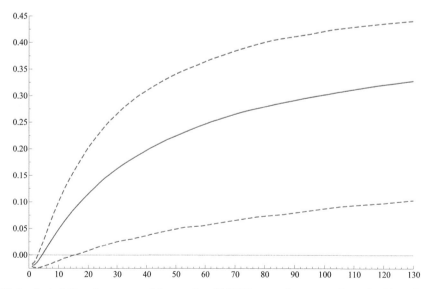

Fig. 2. Research, Technological Development and Innovation (RTDI) scenario construction: elasticity of total factor productivity (TFP) (y-axis) with respect to research and development (R&D) intensity (x-axis). Dashed lines: bootstrapped 90% confidence interval based on 1000 replications
Source: Authors' estimations based on KANCS and SILIVERSTOVS (2015) data

Table 3. Research, Technological Development and Innovation (RTDI) scenario construction: European Cohesion Policy (ECP) expenditure on RTDI in 2014–20 (€, millions) and estimated impact on regions' productivity (%)

Region	€	TFP	Region	€	TFP	Region	€	TFP	Region	€	TFP
AT11	23.2	0.118	DEC0	50.2	0.120	GR25	50.5	0.180	PT11[a]	1486.7	2.219
AT12	69.0	0.050	DED1	269.6	0.626	GR30	199.4	0.118	PT15	52.4	0.528
AT13	6.5	0.004	DED2	294.0	0.775	GR41	15.6	1.450	PT16[a]	977.2	1.113
AT21	51.7	0.150	DED3	156.4	0.496	GR42	3.6	0.094	PT17	134.2	0.144
AT22	94.7	0.108	DEE0	373.5	0.403	GR43	49.1	0.152	PT18[a]	234.6	1.941
AT31	63.4	0.053	DEF0	83.2	0.107	HU10	86.3	0.099	PT20[a]	24.2	1.345
AT32	6.5	0.014	DEG0	268.9	0.036	HU21[a]	182.4	0.979	PT30	23.6	0.122
AT33	14.3	0.036	DK01	34.9	0.013	HU22[a]	115.0	0.817	RO11[a]	82.5	0.189
AT34	9.1	0.010	DK02	22.2	0.033	HU23[a]	199.6	2.833	RO12[a]	69.7	0.144
BE10	16.4	0.015	DK03	30.3	0.019	HU31[a]	276.4	2.658	RO21[a]	121.9	0.316
BE21	24.5	0.021	DK04	27.9	0.018	HU32[a]	240.5	2.287	RO22[a]	84.6	0.206
BE22	33.1	0.083	DK05	13.3	0.009	HU33[a]	316.4	0.864	RO31[a]	97.0	0.131
BE23	13.4	0.017	EE00[a]	600.6	1.981	IE01	46.3	0.025	RO32	31.8	0.023
BE24	11.2	0.016	ES11	550.9	1.085	IE02	152.2	0.024	RO41[a]	68.8	0.186
BE25	20.2	0.041	ES12	78.5	0.304	ITC1	193.8	0.282	RO42[a]	54.5	0.086
BE31	9.9	0.033	ES13	85.5	0.287	ITC2	5.8	0.080	SE11	7.0	0.002
BE32	95.8	0.287	ES21	155.6	0.173	ITC3	89.4	0.065	SE12	46.3	0.053
BE33	40.6	0.166	ES22	23.3	0.103	ITC4	138.4	0.031	SE21	26.6	0.048
BE34	12.0	0.211	ES23	13.5	0.081	ITD1	7.0	0.038	SE22	8.1	0.008
BE35	18.2	0.017	ES24	56.6	0.043	ITD2	3.9	0.006	SE23	29.2	0.026
BG31[a]	50.0	1.798	ES30	99.7	0.022	ITD3	134.6	0.050	SE31	119.6	0.330
BG32[a]	49.7	2.001	ES41	178.8	0.251	ITD4	51.8	0.064	SE32	117.8	0.736
BG33[a]	50.8	1.923	ES42	356.2	0.849	ITD5	64.8	0.024	SE33	177.5	0.190
BG34[a]	57.6	0.929	ES43[a]	225.2	0.484	ITE1	164.7	0.131	SI01[a]	329.0	0.842
BG41[a]	66.3	0.557	ES51	348.7	0.110	ITE2	75.0	0.220	SI02	241.9	0.468
BG42[a]	84.4	0.938	ES52	494.2	0.400	ITE3	74.5	0.076	SK01	142.9	0.322
CY00	54.2	0.178	ES53	30.2	0.049	ITE4	180.0	0.108	SK02[a]	331.2	0.850
CZ01	30.5	0.043	ES61	1078.4	0.847	ITF1	49.6	0.301	SK03[a]	309.0	1.925
CZ02[a]	297.3	0.711	ES62	173.0	2.374	ITF2	19.5	0.140	SK04[a]	410.6	1.608
CZ03[a]	314.3	1.734	ES63	3.9	0.000	ITF3[a]	1681.2	1.640	UKC1	95.9	0.219
CZ04[a]	325.3	2.168	ES64	6.7	0.000	ITF4[a]	835.6	2.651	UKC2	122.9	0.536
CZ05[a]	447.5	1.854	ES70	319.8	0.354	ITF5[a]	37.8	0.409	UKD1	16.9	0.069
CZ06[a]	424.5	1.683	FI13	109.3	0.258	ITF6[a]	519.8	1.896	UKD2	23.8	0.022
CZ07[a]	371.0	2.281	FI18	52.9	0.035	ITG1[a]	1068.9	1.963	UKD3	136.4	0.114
CZ08[a]	339.8	0.766	FI19	70.4	0.156	ITG2	62.1	0.025	UKD4	71.6	0.095
DE11	14.6	0.005	FI1A	120.4	0.501	LT00[a]	882.8	1.491	UKD5	88.8	0.245
DE12	10.5	0.006	FI20	1.2	0.010	LU00	16.6	0.018	UKE1	31.2	0.075
DE13	8.7	0.008	FR10	29.9	0.004	LV00[a]	632.0	1.476	UKE2	11.8	0.026
DE14	7.0	0.004	FR21	80.9	0.146	MT00	39.2	0.395	UKE3	50.0	0.057
DE21	33.1	0.015	FR22	112.7	0.149	NL11	22.7	0.046	UKE4	91.7	0.067
DE22	15.2	0.027	FR23	115.4	0.124	NL12	31.6	0.118	UKF1	63.2	0.045
DE23	11.6	0.019	FR24	82.5	0.095	NL13	23.6	0.096	UKF2	59.7	0.079
DE24	13.1	0.020	FR25	85.3	0.183	NL21	20.2	0.029	UKF3	42.8	0.107
DE25	21.2	0.021	FR26	58.3	0.071	NL22	28.8	0.033	UKG1	29.0	0.040
DE26	15.3	0.018	FR30	268.0	0.225	NL23	11.1	0.043	UKG2	67.9	0.063
DE27	25.0	0.020	FR41	120.0	0.187	NL31	7.9	0.005	UKG3	161.5	0.092
DE30	269.7	0.339	FR42	31.8	0.064	NL32	15.0	0.007	UKH1	19.8	0.015
DE41	149.0	0.667	FR43	51.6	0.087	NL33	24.3	0.012	UKH2	11.5	0.008
DE42	38.8	0.126	FR51	150.5	0.116	NL34	1.9	0.005	UKH3	17.4	0.005
DE50	40.2	0.065	FR52	100.3	0.121	NL41	25.4	0.014	UKI1	14.6	0.004
DE60	4.6	0.002	FR53	64.6	0.095	NL42	16.6	0.008	UKI2	19.6	0.006
DE71	32.1	0.014	FR61	207.9	0.226	PL11[a]	612.7	1.009	UKJ1	1.3	0.001
DE72	9.0	0.016	FR62	147.7	0.302	PL12	749.7	0.688	UKJ2	2.6	0.002
DE73	12.2	0.018	FR63	31.4	0.037	PL21[a]	915.1	2.211	UKJ3	2.2	0.002
DE80	212.5	0.789	FR71	117.2	0.075	PL22[a]	1076.1	1.432	UKJ4	2.5	0.002
DE91	80.1	0.097	FR72	55.2	0.110	PL31[a]	638.9	4.276	UKK1	17.4	0.013
DE92	98.9	0.117	FR81	141.0	0.184	PL32[a]	662.4	4.970	UKK2	10.4	0.037
DE93	56.6	0.101	FR82	166.9	0.368	PL33[a]	399.8	3.263	UKK3[a]	83.4	0.642
DE94	80.7	0.067	FR83	20.0	0.006	PL34[a]	378.1	3.292	UKK4	18.9	0.059
DEA1	130.5	0.038	GR11[a]	89.7	1.066	PL41[a]	746.0	1.350	UKL1[a]	380.9	0.716
DEA2	67.2	0.031	GR12[a]	167.5	0.590	PL42[a]	390.3	2.850	UKL2	53.4	0.077
DEA3	46.6	0.040	GR13	11.2	0.180	PL43[a]	237.9	1.802	UKM2	81.0	0.116
DEA4	31.1	0.026	GR14[a]	107.6	0.877	PL51[a]	562.3	1.460	UKM3	210.0	0.376
DEA5	103.0	0.058	GR21[a]	63.5	1.879	PL52[a]	311.1	1.922	UKM5	14.8	0.209

(Continued)

Table 3. Continued

Region	€	TFP	Region	€	TFP	Region	€	TFP	Region	€	TFP
DEB1	34.1	0.071	GR22	23.1	0.921	PL61[a]	516.3	2.168	UKM6	37.9	0.477
DEB2	7.7	0.027	GR23[a]	92.9	0.922	PL62[a]	387.0	3.042	UKN0	98.5	0.016
DEB3	39.5	0.042	GR24	20.7	0.135	PL63[a]	570.9	0.762			

Notes: Aggregate Cohesion Policy expenditure on RTDI for the entire 2014–20 period (€, millions); TFP, estimated increase in total factor productivity (%).

[a]Less developed regions.

Source: Authors' estimates based on EUROPEAN COMMISSION (2014) data.

Next, the spatial dimension of the ECP transport infrastructure investment is approximated based on the region-specific expenditures calculated in the first step. Given that information on region-pair-specific transport cost reductions is not available, it needs to be determined how region-specific expenditure is converted into region-pair-specific expenditure. The spatial dimension is important because transport infrastructure improvements affect not only the region where the money is spent, but also all other regions with which it trades. The adopted bilateral transformation of transport infrastructure investments accounts both for the intensity of the ECP expenditure and for the proximity of regions where the investment takes place. The adopted measure introduces a spatial structure (economic geography) in the bilateral measure of transport infrastructure investment by weighting the proximity of regions, implying that the further away are the trading regions (trade is more costly), the less weight will be attributed to the transport infrastructure improvements between the two regions. The weighting implies that the further away are the two regions, the lower impact will a fixed amount of expenditure have (1 km of road can be improved much more than 10 km of road by the same amount of expenditure).

In a third step, INF$_{od}$, which is a bilateral measure of expenditure in millions of euros, is transformed into changes in bilateral trade costs between regions, which are measured as a share of trade value. This is done by pre-multiplying the bilateral measure of transport infrastructure investments, INF$_{od}$, by an elasticity measuring the effectiveness of transport infrastructure investments. The elasticity of trade costs with respect to the quality of infrastructure is retrieved from studies on TEN-T infrastructure (EUROPEAN COMMISSION, 2009, 2011b), because no comparable elasticities are available for ECP investments in transport infrastructure. These elasticities are of the same order of magnitude as those estimated in the literature for other countries. For example, according to the estimates of FRANCOIS *et al.* (2009), the elasticity of trade costs with respect to the quality of infrastructure is in the range of −0.02 to 0.60 – see Fig. 4, where the elasticities of trade costs are plotted against GDP per capita for countries at different stages

of economic development: from developing (left) to developed (right) countries.

The elasticities reported in Fig. 4 suggest that the importance of transport infrastructure with respect to trade costs is decreasing in the level of GDP per capita, implying that the marginal impact of an additional unit of investment in public infrastructure in more developed countries/regions (with more developed infrastructure) is smaller than in less developed countries/regions (with less developed infrastructure). The inverse relationship between the elasticity of trade costs with respect to the quality of infrastructure and the GDP per capita suggests using region-specific elasticities depending on regional GDP: higher for less developed regions and lower for more developed regions.

As a result, a transport infrastructure scenario of the ECP investments is obtained that can be readily implemented in RHOMOLO. The constructed scenario is summarized in Table 4 and Fig. 5; the left panel shows the expenditure in millions of euros; the total impact on accessibility is shown in the middle panel of Fig. 5. The right panel maps the marginal impact on accessibility, which is calculated as changes in regions' accessibility per euro of Cohesion Policy investment.

In line with expectations, the left and middle panels in Fig. 5 show very similar patterns. The right panel shows that the same investment in transport infrastructure has a larger marginal impact in the more developed regions (darkly shaded regions) than in the less developed regions (lightly shaded regions). Fig. 5 confirms that transport cost reductions in the less developed regions have an impact on the accessibility of the transition regions and the more developed regions. Even if there would be zero investment in the more developed regions, they still would benefit from improved access to markets in the less developed regions, making their marginal impact per euro invested obviously much higher than for the less developed regions.[15]

SIMULATION RESULTS[16]

RTDI versus INF scenario

Simulation results – the ECP-induced GDP growth effects compared with the baseline – are presented

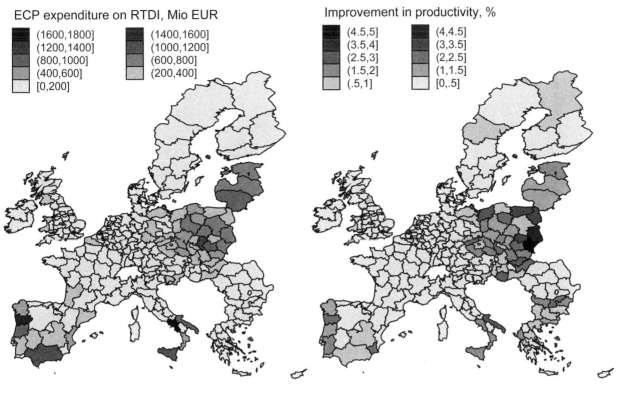

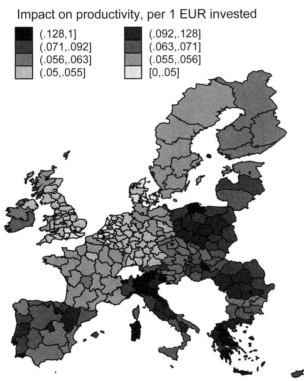

Fig. 3. Research, Technological Development and Innovation (RTDI) scenario construction (exogenous policy input into simulations): (left) European Cohesion Policy's (ECP) expenditure on RTDI in 2014–20 (€, millions); (right) estimated improvement in regions' productivity due to the ECP's investments in RTDI in 2014–20 (changes in per cent); and (bottom) estimated marginal improvement in regions' accessibility due to the ECP's investments in RTDI in 2014–20 per €1 of investment. The middle panel represents the policy shock used as the input in model simulations; the left and right panels are reported only for background information
Source: Authors' estimations based on EUROPEAN COMMISSION (2014) DG REGIO data

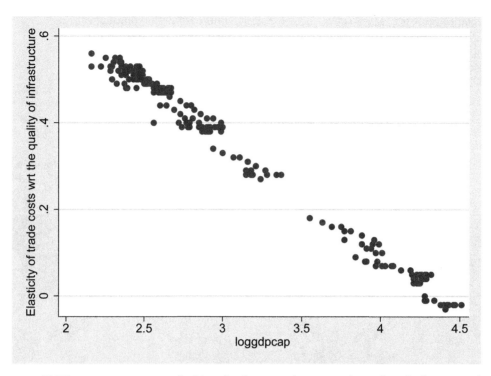

Fig. 4. Infrastructure (INF) scenario construction: elasticity of trade costs with respect to the quality of infrastructure (y-axis) and log of per capita gross domestic product (GDP) (2010 €) (x-axis)
Source: Authors' estimations based on FRANCOIS *et al.* (2009) data

Table 4. Infrastructure (INF) scenario construction: European Cohesion Policy (ECP) expenditure on INF in 2014–20 (€, millions) and estimated impact on regions' accessibility (%)

Region	€	Tcost	Region	€	Tcost	Region	€	Tcost	Region	€	Tcost
AT11	0.7	1.664	DEC0	2.6	1.506	GR25	51.0	2.507	PT11[a]	359.6	9.045
AT12	3.9	1.751	DED1	49.0	2.810	GR30	232.1	6.683	PT15	17.9	1.655
AT13	2.1	1.773	DED2	53.4	2.930	GR41	17.7	1.675	PT16[a]	210.3	5.820
AT21	1.1	1.552	DED3	26.8	2.236	GR42	16.2	1.659	PT17	111.5	3.668
AT22	2.0	1.641	DEE0	57.2	2.964	GR43	55.5	2.464	PT18[a]	53.2	2.418
AT31	1.7	1.612	DEF0	6.7	1.622	HU10	161.0	5.602	PT20[a]	31.4	1.587
AT32	0.7	1.549	DEG0	50.1	2.765	HU21[a]	148.1	5.301	PT30	30.7	1.638
AT33	1.9	1.536	DK01	1.9	1.470	HU22[a]	124.4	4.693	RO11[a]	126.0	4.119
AT34	0.6	1.493	DK02	1.6	1.452	HU23[a]	156.2	5.331	RO12[a]	114.1	3.782
BE10	1.3	1.455	DK03	1.6	1.478	HU31[a]	217.0	6.873	RO21[a]	199.6	5.538
BE21	2.2	1.480	DK04	1.5	1.454	HU32[a]	269.7	8.046	RO22[a]	139.4	4.220
BE22	2.9	1.490	DK05	0.7	1.420	HU33[a]	224.5	6.947	RO31[a]	160.0	4.711
BE23	1.1	1.431	EE00[a]	221.9	6.196	IE01	15.3	1.333	RO32	52.1	2.507
BE24	0.5	1.425	ES11	176.3	5.122	IE02	9.1	1.226	RO41[a]	114.5	3.801
BE25	1.6	1.434	ES12	25.7	1.905	ITC1	32.0	2.174	RO42[a]	79.8	3.120
BE31	0.8	1.452	ES13	8.6	1.529	ITC2	1.0	1.460	SE11	1.3	1.198
BE32	7.3	1.583	ES21	22.7	1.860	ITC3	10.0	1.644	SE12	2.6	1.215
BE33	3.5	1.512	ES22	4.9	1.457	ITC4	22.0	1.951	SE21	3.5	1.229
BE34	1.1	1.461	ES23	2.6	1.411	ITD1	2.8	1.548	SE22	2.4	1.261
BE35	1.5	1.461	ES24	24.5	1.886	ITD2	1.3	1.505	SE23	2.4	1.240
BG31[a]	65.6	2.943	ES30	28.4	1.971	ITD3	22.9	2.016	SE31	8.8	1.299
BG32[a]	64.9	2.904	ES41	55.4	2.557	ITD4	6.9	1.651	SE32	7.8	1.245
BG33[a]	65.3	2.895	ES42	45.0	2.308	ITD5	8.4	1.627	SE33	10.5	1.251
BG34[a]	73.5	3.050	ES43[a]	106.2	3.640	ITE1	27.4	2.045	SI01[a]	93.2	3.700
BG41[a]	84.0	3.322	ES51	78.3	3.105	ITE2	9.0	1.647	SI02	68.8	3.110
BG42[a]	105.9	3.781	ES52	105.5	3.645	ITE3	10.3	1.664	SK01	35.1	2.569
CY00	23.7	1.673	ES53	7.6	1.452	ITE4	41.4	2.353	SK02[a]	285.3	8.708
CZ01	69.1	3.737	ES61	407.3	9.936	ITF1	7.5	1.594	SK03[a]	267.9	8.227
CZ02[a]	137.0	5.381	ES62	57.2	2.580	ITF2	3.0	1.493	SK04[a]	356.8	10.222

(*Continued*)

Table 4. Continued

Region	€	Tcost	Region	€	Tcost	Region	€	Tcost	Region	€	Tcost
CZ03[a]	150.9	5.436	ES63	1.9	1.335	ITF3[a]	339.7	9.023	UKC1	5.1	1.465
CZ04[a]	160.0	5.703	ES64	3.1	1.291	ITF4[a]	223.4	6.389	UKC2	6.5	1.492
CZ05[a]	203.2	6.780	ES70	122.8	3.272	ITF5[a]	30.3	2.113	UKD1	1.0	1.356
CZ06[a]	193.7	6.507	FI13	6.8	1.234	ITF6[a]	97.7	3.520	UKD2	1.4	1.394
CZ07[a]	176.8	6.152	FI18	5.2	1.252	ITG1[a]	297.5	7.782	UKD3	7.9	1.555
CZ08[a]	167.3	5.989	FI19	6.2	1.240	ITG2	33.3	2.054	UKD4	4.2	1.451
DE11	1.0	1.486	FI1A	7.0	1.200	LT00[a]	396.5	10.233	UKD5	4.8	1.474
DE12	0.9	1.460	FI20	0.1	1.126	LU00	1.2	1.199	UKE1	1.6	1.398
DE13	1.0	1.458	FR10	3.8	1.227	LV00[a]	278.9	7.445	UKE2	0.6	1.369
DE14	0.6	1.473	FR21	9.1	1.370	MT00	47.1	1.907	UKE3	2.2	1.418
DE21	4.2	1.591	FR22	11.2	1.403	NL11	1.2	1.464	UKE4	4.7	1.472
DE22	2.2	1.596	FR23	14.4	1.454	NL12	1.7	1.469	UKF1	0.7	1.386
DE23	2.1	1.592	FR24	5.6	1.254	NL13	1.3	1.479	UKF2	0.7	1.396
DE24	2.0	1.571	FR25	7.3	1.294	NL21	2.8	1.529	UKF3	0.5	1.382
DE25	2.6	1.569	FR26	10.9	1.390	NL22	4.0	1.536	UKG1	1.8	1.415
DE26	1.8	1.526	FR30	38.5	2.025	NL23	1.4	1.478	UKG2	4.1	1.468
DE27	3.5	1.557	FR41	16.8	1.555	NL31	0.9	1.469	UKG3	9.8	1.622
DE30	11.5	1.876	FR42	3.6	1.283	NL32	1.9	1.462	UKH1	2.8	1.454
DE41	29.6	2.252	FR43	4.9	1.290	NL33	3.3	1.492	UKH2	1.0	1.416
DE42	7.2	1.724	FR51	14.0	1.404	NL34	0.3	1.414	UKH3	2.7	1.465
DE50	1.0	1.496	FR52	18.9	1.482	NL41	2.9	1.491	UKI1	3.0	1.473
DE60	0.2	1.506	FR53	14.4	1.422	NL42	1.9	1.485	UKI2	4.0	1.502
DE71	2.7	1.523	FR61	21.7	1.555	PL11[a]	335.4	9.783	UKJ1	0.2	1.394
DE72	0.8	1.485	FR62	25.7	1.627	PL12	344.7	9.832	UKJ2	0.6	1.413
DE73	1.0	1.504	FR63	5.1	1.246	PL21[a]	447.6	12.453	UKJ3	0.6	1.402
DE80	50.4	2.705	FR71	19.8	1.556	PL22[a]	526.3	14.553	UKJ4	0.7	1.430
DE91	7.0	1.658	FR72	6.3	1.280	PL31[a]	351.4	9.849	UKK1	1.7	1.420
DE92	8.6	1.679	FR81	28.9	1.711	PL32[a]	352.5	9.955	UKK2	1.4	1.405
DE93	13.9	1.808	FR82	16.6	1.476	PL33[a]	189.0	6.273	UKK3[a]	16.3	1.737
DE94	6.9	1.595	FR83	2.6	1.166	PL34[a]	188.4	6.046	UKK4	2.9	1.425
DEA1	8.7	1.636	GR11[a]	77.9	3.148	PL41[a]	408.2	11.563	UKL1[a]	44.6	2.418
DEA2	4.8	1.541	GR12[a]	219.4	6.325	PL42[a]	221.1	6.947	UKL2	3.7	1.449
DEA3	3.1	1.508	GR13	14.9	1.770	PL43[a]	139.0	5.059	UKM2	4.6	1.419
DEA4	2.1	1.507	GR14[a]	80.2	3.210	PL51[a]	323.7	9.698	UKM3	15.2	1.667
DEA5	6.9	1.602	GR21[a]	47.2	2.464	PL52[a]	142.9	5.331	UKM5	0.8	1.310
DEB1	1.2	1.462	GR22	23.2	1.892	PL61[a]	283.7	8.456	UKM6	2.8	1.317
DEB2	0.5	1.438	GR23[a]	93.3	3.449	PL62[a]	219.8	6.780	UKN0	11.1	1.535
DEB3	1.7	1.481	GR24	24.8	1.956	PL63[a]	281.9	8.233			

Notes: Aggregate Cohesion Policy expenditure on INF for the entire 2014–20 period (€, millions); Tcost, estimated reduction in transportation costs (weighted across all regions) (%).

[a] Less developed regions.

Source: Authors' estimates based on EUROPEAN COMMISSION (2014) data.

in Fig. 6. They show that the impact of the ECP is heterogeneous across EU regions. In particular, regions in the new EU member states and southern EU would benefit substantially from the ECP investment in RTDI (left panel) and transport INF (right panel). In both scenarios, the policy-induced GDP growth effects vary between 0.01% and 2.75% above the baseline, though the pattern is different across the two scenarios.

The results also show that the maximum estimated increase in productivity (as reported in Fig. 3) is larger than the maximum simulated GDP increase (as reported in Fig. 6). In Fig. 3 there are only two regions with productivity increase above 4% (PL31 and PL32), and there are only three regions with productivity increase between 3% and 4% above the baseline (PL34, PL35 and PL62). In 12 other regions the productivity

increases between 2% and 3%; and in 26 regions between 1% and 2% above the baseline. In the vast majority of regions (224), the estimated productivity increase is between 0% and 1%. In contrast, the simulated GDP increase is more homogenous across regions (Fig. 6). These results are interesting because they show how, through the inter-regional linkages, the positive growth effects of the ECP in the less developed regions diffuse to regions that were not (or were less) directly affected by the policy support. Knowledge spillovers seem to play a particularly important role in determining the spatial distribution of the R&D impacts.

Fig. 7 compares the ECP investments and GDP impacts of these investments in the less developed regions with those in the more developed regions. In all four diagrams, the *x*-axis measures the development

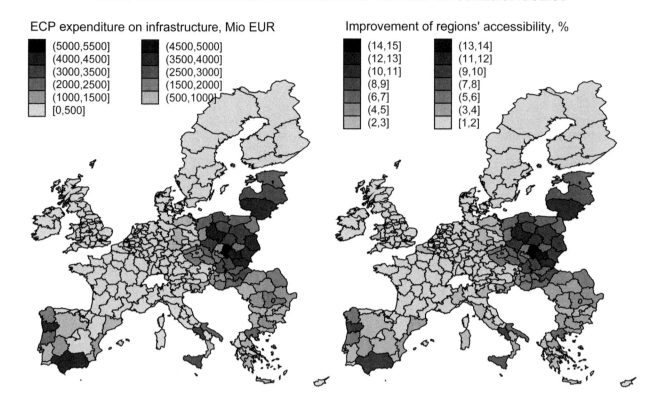

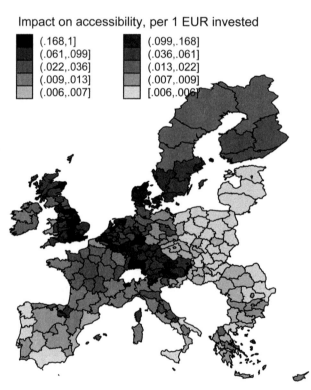

Fig. 5. Infrastructure (INF) scenario construction (exogenous policy input into simulations): (left) European Cohesion Policy's (ECP) expenditure on transport infrastructure in 2014–20 (€, millions); (right) estimated improvement in regions' accessibility due to the ECP's investments in transport infrastructure in 2014–20 (changes in per cent); and (bottom) estimated marginal improvement in regions' accessibility due to the ECP's investments in transport infrastructure in 2014–20 per €1 of investment. The middle panel represents the policy shock used as input in model simulations; the left and right panels are reported only for background information Source: Authors' estimations based on EUROPEAN COMMISSION *(2014) DG REGIO data*

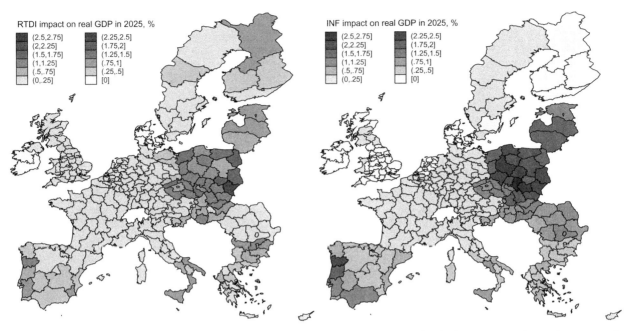

Fig. 6. Simulation results: (left) Research, Technological Development and Innovation (RTDI) impact on real gross domestic product (GDP) in 2025; and (right) Infrastructure (INF) impact on real GDP in 2025. Percentage changes are from the baseline
Source: Authors' simulations with the RHOMOLO model

level of regions (log GDP per capita): less developed regions are on the left, and more developed regions are on the right. The y-axis measures the share of ECP in the regions' GDP: the left panels capture the share of the ECP investment in regions' GDP (RTDI top, INF bottom); the right panels capture the change in real GDP due to ECP investments (RTDI top, INF bottom). In other words, horizontally Fig. 7 compares policy input with policy output, whereas vertically Fig. 7 compares RTDI scenario with INF scenario. If the relationship between policy input and output were linear, then the size of the squares/circles and their location on the vertical axis would be identical between the left and the right panels.

This, however, does not seem to be the case. The vertical position of the plots in Fig. 7 suggests that, on average, the more developed regions (circles on the right) receive a lower share of ECP investment in RTDI and INF in terms of their GDP than the less developed regions (squares on the left). The relative size of the squares/circles (which is proportional to the size of the investment in millions of euros) shows that the less developed regions receive not only a higher share in terms of GDP, but also higher amounts in euros for their investments in RTDI and INF (squares on the left are considerably larger than circles on the right).

The annual ECP investments in RTDI range from 0% to around 1% of the regions' GDP (top-left panel). The return of ECP investment in RTDI ranges from 0% to around 0.25% (top-right panel). The relative size of the squares/circles and their location on the vertical axis shows that the impact of the ECP investment

in RTDI is non-linear in the level of regions' development. In the case of the INF scenario, the annual ECP investment ranges from 0% and 5% (bottom-left panel), showing a significant variation between EU regions. The bottom-right panel in Fig. 5 depicts the impact of INF investment on GDP. In contrast to the RTDI scenario, there seems to be an inverse 'U'-shaped relationship between the returns from INF investment and the level of regions' development. In the short run, this can be explained by the necessary absorptive capacity, which regions must possess in order to use the ECP investments efficiently. As the absorptive capacity increases with the level of the regions' development, the more developed regions can use the ECP funds more efficiently.[17]

In terms of the multiplier effects (compare the right panels with the left panels in Fig. 7), the results are exactly as those in the QUEST model because, for the purpose of the present study, RHOMOLO was calibrated with QUEST. For the whole EU, the RTDI policies have an investment multiplier of 0.21. The investment multiplier of transport infrastructure policies is somewhat lower at 0.15. However, as described above, there is a substantial variation among regions. In some less developed regions, where the absorptive capacity is sufficient, the investment multiplier is higher than 0.50, implying that every invested euro in transport infrastructure increases GDP in the supported regions by at least €0.50 in the medium run (2025). In addition, given that the supply-side effects accumulate over time, the long-run gains to welfare are substantially higher, even when discounted over time, as in the QUEST model.

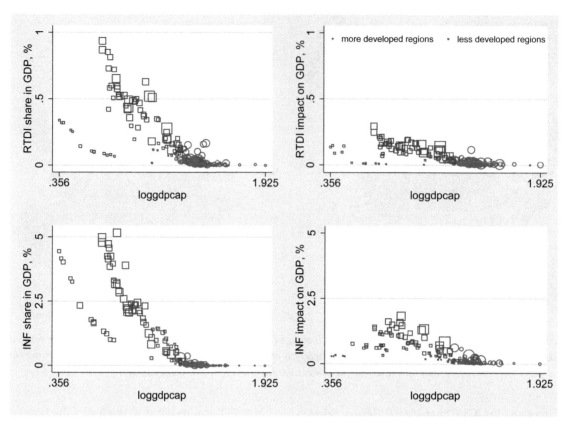

Fig. 7. Simulation results: (left) policy input – Research, Technological Development and Innovation (RTDI), top; Infrastructure (INF), bottom – into the European Union regions; and (right) policy effect (RTDI top, INF bottom) in the European Union regions. The size of the squares/circles represents millions of euros (policy input, left; policy impact, right)
Source: Authors' simulations with the RHOMOLO model

Sensitivity and decomposition analysis

What drives these differences in the impacts between EU regions? First, as shown in Figs 3 and 5, policy interventions and, hence, scenario inputs in RHOMOLO are differential across EU regions. Regions located in the Eastern and Southern parts of the EU are both the largest recipients of the ECP funds and the largest beneficiaries in terms of GDP growth.

Second, regions themselves are heterogeneous. For example: the relative importance of transport costs in the traded goods value differs significantly between regions; regions with higher initial transport costs benefit relatively more than other regions. The structure of the regional economies also matters: 'non-treated' regions with a higher share of tradable goods (e.g. in manufacturing) benefit relatively more than regions with a lower share of tradeables (e.g. in services). Geography plays a role as well: the remote regions in RHOMOLO benefit less from border-crossing transport cost reductions than central regions.

Third, the endogenous channels of adjustment are multiple and the net effects are non-linear in the level of policy shock. In general equilibrium models, such as RHOMOLO and QUEST, a policy shock, such as an increase in TFP or a reduction of transport costs, triggers changes in relative prices/costs. For example, the output price in one sector changes relative to the output price of another sector; the input price of one factor (e.g. labour) may change relative to the price of another factor (e.g. capital); the output or input price in one region may change relative to the output or input price in another region. Depending on which prices/costs change, relative to the prices/costs of competitors, the adjustments take place through different channels: the sectoral channel of adjustment; adjustments through factor supply and demand; the spatial channel of adjustment, etc.

This section presents decomposition and sensitivity analysis results for a selected set of variables related to the spatial channel of adjustment. In RHOMOLO the spatial channel of adjustment works, for example, through the relocation of firms (and production factors) between regions, and is determined by two first-order effects: (1) the market access effect (increase in firm output; decrease in average costs), and (2) the price index effect (decrease in the cost of living; decrease in the cost of intermediate goods); and one second-order effect: (3) the market crowding effect (competition on input markets, competition on output markets). To decompose the aggregate effects, the above simulations (combined RTDI and INF) were run twice: first, all variables in RHOMOLO are

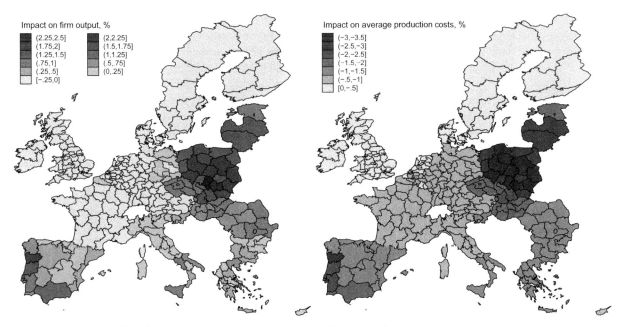

Fig. 8. Market access effect: (left) policy impact on firm output; and (right) policy impact on average production costs. Percentage changes are from the baseline
Source: Authors' simulations with the RHOMOLO model

endogenous (as above); and second, the selected variables are fixed exogenously at their baseline value. The differences between the two sets of model runs are plotted in Figs 8-9.

On the output side, the market access effect is related to an increase in firm output (left panel in Fig. 8). In RHOMOLO increasing firm productivity or reducing transport costs makes goods less expensive. A lower price of goods allows households (and firms) to buy

more goods, which implies higher demand, higher output and hence higher profits for firms. The left panel in Fig. 8 confirms that firm output is increasing in all regions, particularly in the less developed regions. Larger increases in firm output in the less developed regions explain part of the higher GDP growth in these regions.

On the cost side, the market access effect is related to a decrease in average costs (right panel in Fig. 8). In

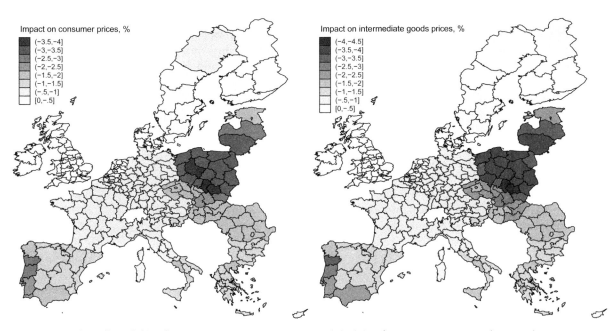

Fig. 9. Price index effect: (left) policy impact on consumer prices; and (right) policy impact on intermediate goods prices. Percentage changes are from the baseline
Source: Authors' simulations with the RHOMOLO model

RHOMOLO, due to fixed production costs, higher output reduces the average production costs, and hence increases firm profitability. The right panel in Fig. 8 confirms that the average production costs decrease in all regions, particularly in the less developed regions. Larger decreases in production costs in the less developed regions explain part of the higher GDP growth in these regions.

For consumers, the price index effect implies changes in the cost of living (left panel in Fig. 7). In RHOMOLO lower transport costs reduce the price of traded goods, which implies that goods are sold at a lower price. The left panel in Fig. 7 confirms that the consumer price index decreases in all regions, particularly in the less developed regions. Larger decreases in the cost of living in the less developed regions explain part of the higher GDP growth in these regions.

For producers, the price index effect implies changes in the cost of intermediate goods (right panel in Fig. 9). In RHOMOLO lower transport costs reduce the price of imported goods, which implies that intermediate goods are bought at a lower price. The right panel in Fig. 9 confirms that the price index of intermediate inputs for producers of final demand goods decreases. Larger decrease in the cost of intermediate goods in the less developed regions explains part of the higher GDP growth in these regions.

Finally, the market crowding effect on input markets captures the fact that agglomeration of firms increases competition on local input markets, as a result of which firm profits decrease. In RHOMOLO more firms compete for a smaller pool of labour. The market crowding effect on output markets captures the fact that the agglomeration of firms increases competition on output markets, as a result of which profits decrease. More firms compete for a smaller share in the exports market.[18]

The decomposition analysis of the simulation results suggests that the key ingredients of the new economic geography theory: (1) the market access effect (increase in firm output; decrease in average costs); (2) the price index effect (decrease in the cost of living; decrease in cost of intermediate goods); and (3) the market crowding effect (competition on input markets, competition on output markets) are crucial for identifying the geographical distribution of the gains from economic integration. Hence, the role of spatial CGE models, such as RHOMOLO, is particularly important when the means for structural adjustment are limited, and should be targeted at places where they can be expected to contribute most to prevent a further widening of economic disparities and prospects.

Limitations and future work

Several key assumptions need a closer examination when interpreting results of the presented simulations using the RHOMOLO model. First, it is assumed that all ECP policies are implemented according to the ex-ante time profile foreseen by the EUROPEAN COMMISSION (2014). In reality, however, there may be delays in policy implementation, and these delays may also vary significantly between member states. The absorptive capacity of regions and the funds available for co-financing the ECP are the two most cited reasons for delays in the implementation of the ECP funds (BRANDSMA et al., 2013). The implications of this assumption for the RHOMOLO simulations is that, in reality, the medium- and long-run results would be delayed compared with the results presented above.

Second, the financing of the ECP through contributions to the EU budget is not explicitly modelled in the present study. In reality, however, as any other category of public expenditures, the ECP investments have to be financed through taxes. The increase in taxes for the purpose of financing the ECP investments partially offsets the positive growth impacts displayed by the simulation results. It is likely that the effect of financing reduces the positive impact in the member states that make the largest contributions to the EU budget. In order to address this issue, the RHOMOLO model is calibrated to the macro-dynamics of the QUEST model, which accounts for all the taxes in a fully dynamic forward looking general equilibrium framework.

Another limitation of the recursively dynamic approach is in generating results over time. The main dynamics in RHOMOLO are the long-term effects of human, knowledge and physical capital accumulation, which continue after the funding has ended. While inter-temporal optimization and forward-looking expectations are at the basis of the decisions underlying the theoretical underpinning of dynamic stochastic general equilibrium (DSGE) models, such as QUEST, they are still not among the main features that are well captured in recursively dynamic models yet (BROECKER and KORZHENEVYCH, 2013). In order to address this issue, the present study aligns RHOMOLO simulations with the fully dynamic QUEST model. The results show that Cohesion Policy support to the R&D investment would put the less developed regions as a group on a continuous track of closing the technology gap with more advanced regions.

CONCLUSIONS

Regional development in the EU and regions of the member states shows an uneven geographic pattern which shifts with time. ECP provides the means for partially offsetting the adverse effects of economic integration and for assisting the less developed regions. In negotiating the allocation of funds, and even in selecting the categories of investment to be supported, the member states attempt to maximize the benefits of belonging to the single market. Politically, it is almost inevitable that the negotiations will focus on the expected direct effects and financial benefits and on the desired shifts in demand. From the EU point of view, however, the interest is much more on assessing how much in the long-term the EU economy as a whole benefits from the advantages of the single market and on making sure that, while further opening the market, the development potential and innovation capacity of all regions is fully exploited, leaving no regions behind. For the purpose of being able to calculate and show the indirect and long-term effects of EU funding as well as the effects of EU policies at the regional level, this paper presents a spatial general equilibrium model in which the economies of all NUTS-2 regions are linked through international trade, factor mobility and spatial knowledge spillovers.

Two simulation exercises with the RHOMOLO model highlight what is at stake. The first assumes that the support to research and innovation from the Structural and Cohesion Funds will allow the less developed regions to increase TFP and reduce their distance to the technology frontier. This is based on micro-econometric evidence of the effect of R&D on TFP and empirical evidence that domestic R&D will make it easier to absorb the knowledge from elsewhere and so help the catching up of lagging regions. The model allows for differences between sectors, and for shifts in the sectoral composition of production in the regions, which typically depend on the extent to which the gains in productivity are translated into competitive advantages.

In the second exercise, the reduction in transport costs resulting from the investments in infrastructure financed with contributions from the Structural and Cohesion Funds are carefully assigned to the regions and to all bilateral connections between them. Even though the largest part of the funding in the category of infrastructure is directed towards the member states that joined the EU in the past decade, it can be shown that the investments have positive effects on the more central regions as well, precisely because they benefit from improved connections with so many of the regions to which the funds are allocated. This reinforces the point that although with the enhanced mobility of capital and firms it may be difficult to simulate where the demand and shares of profits will end up, it is in principle possible to find a redistribution of the benefits of greater economic integration that leaves all regions better off.

The results of the decomposition and sensitivity analysis suggest that without spatial linkages and knowledge spillovers, there would be little effect on the non-supported (less supported) regions in the long-term. The results also suggest that given the free mobility of capital within the single EU market, it is difficult to pin down where the demand resulting from the availability and use of EU funding will end up, despite the

attempts to do so in the decomposition and sensitivity analysis. This does not take away the fact that shifts in demand play a major role in the agglomeration process. As a conclusion, from a policy point of view, it should be stressed that the availability of Structural and Cohesion Funds enables individual regions to develop their capacity for improving both productivity and the standard of living. The closer the investments are directed at remedying the structural impediments and removing the bottlenecks to regional development, the greater will be the potential for reaping the benefits of economic integration. The strategic choices of the member states and regions are increasingly scrutinized and the model presented in this paper may help to cope with the interactions and show which scenarios of public investment support would be most beneficial for the EU economy.

Acknowledgements − The authors acknowledge the helpful comments from and valuable contributions made by Stefan Boeters, Steven Brakman, Johannes Broecker, Leen Hordijk, Artem Korzhenevych, Hans Lofgren, Philippe Monfort, Mark Thissen, Charles van Marrewijk, Renger Herman van Nieuwkoop, Damiaan Persyn, Attila Varga; the participants at the European Economic Association and Econometric Society conferences in Glasgow, Oslo, Malaga and Gothenburg; as well as the participants at the seminars and workshops of the European Commission. The authors would like to thank two anonymous reviewers as well as editor of the special issue for their suggestions and comments. The authors are solely responsible for the content of the paper. The views expressed are purely those of the authors and may not in any circumstances be regarded as stating an official position of the European Commission.

Disclosure statement − No potential conflict of interest was reported by the authors.

NOTES

1. The same applies to Croatia, which joined in 2013.
2. RHOMOLO = Regional HOlistic MOdeLO.
3. See BRANDSMA et al. (2015) for a formal description of the latest version of the RHOMOLO model.
4. Labour mobility is introduced through a labour market module which extends this core version of the model with a more sophisticated specification of the labour market. This is described by BRANDSMA et al. (2014).
5. In the model the regional unemployment rates also enter the migration problem of workers.
6. The authors refer to the 2013 version of RHOMOLO, which was used for simulations presented in this paper. In the next updates of the base year RHOMOLO will be extended to include also Croatia.
7. Currently undergoing extension of the innovation module in RHOMOLO with additional features beyond R&D includes two elements. First, European Commission-based regional patent statistics and citations offer valuable information on technological proximity

across regions in Europe. Second, the inclusion of the micro-estimated data from the Community Innovation Survey is used to identify a broader set of regional innovation features – closely related to the policy domains identified in the current taxonomy of Cohesion Policy investments.

8. This is true for all five broad categories, but in particular for interventions categorized under RTDI. Some of the 123 expenditure lines can be associated with improving the public research infrastructure; some others with augmenting the regional knowledge stock as such or with creating incentives for private firms to invest more in R&D. A more precise delineation within the RTDI category would not be of much help either, because the stages of research, development, diffusion and use are known to be highly interdependent.

9. The split between the support to RTDI and human capital development is not very clear-cut. There are also overlaps with aid to the private sector provided under Cohesion Policy, a residual category which is as large as the RTDI part itself, and with the separate category of technical assistance.

10. This simplification means that the link between publicly funded research and the productivity effects of Cohesion Policy interventions is not fully explored in the simulations. In particular, the contribution of the structural and investment funds to increasing the absorption and innovation capacity at the regional level would deserve greater attention in future evaluations of Cohesion Policy.

11. See, for example, DI COMITE and KANCS (2015) for a discussion of alternative approaches for implementing and modelling R&D policies.

12. Firm-level studies have estimated the size of productivity elasticity associated with R&D investment ranging from 0.01 to 0.32, and the rate of return to R&D investment between 8.0% and 170.0% (see MAIRESSE and SASSENOU, 1991; GRILICHES, 2000; and MAIRESSE and MOHNEN, 2001, for surveys).

13. For further details and assumptions of the RTDI scenario construction, see DI COMITE and KANCS (2015).

14. For the purpose of simulations presented in the paper, all infrastructure expenditures are aggregated into one category and consequently modelled uniformly as transport infrastructure improvements. In reality, not all ECP expenditures are designed and implemented to improve transport infrastructure, but the dividing lines are difficult to maintain when looking at the actual expenditures across NUTS-2 regions. By far the largest part of the ECP infrastructure expenditures overall, however, is allocated to transport infrastructure (78.1%) (EUROPEAN COMMISSION, 2014).

15. For further details and assumptions of transport infrastructure scenario construction, see KANCS (2013).

16. All simulation results reported in this paper were produced using the 2013 version of the RHOMOLO model. See BRANDSMA et al. (2015) for a formal description of the latest version of the RHOMOLO model.

17. Absorptive capacity is not modelled explicitly in RHOMOLO, however there is a maximum of policy support that can be absorbed per year (0.5% of GDP). In addition, market imperfections, e.g. in labour and capital mobility, may lead to decreasing returns to public investment in the short run.

18. Due to dimensionality issues, this effect is not shown graphically.

REFERENCES

BRANDSMA A., KANCS D. and CIAIAN P. (2013) The role of additionality in the EU cohesion policies: an example of firm-level investment support, *European Planning Studies* **21**, 838–853. doi:10.1080/09654313.2012.722928

BRANDSMA A., KANCS D., MONFORT P. and RILLAERS A. (2015) RHOMOLO: a dynamic spatial general equilibrium model for assessing the impact of Cohesion Policy, *Papers in Regional Science* **94**. doi:10.1111/pirs.12162

BRANDSMA A., KANCS D. and PERSYN D. (2014) Modelling migration and regional labour markets: an application of the new economic geography model RHOMOLO, *Journal of Economic Integration* **29**, 249–271. doi:10.11130/jei.2014.29.2.372

BROECKER J., KANCS D., SCHUERMANN C. and WEGENER M. (2001) *Methodology for the Assessment of Spatial Economic Impacts of Transport Projects and Policies. Integrated Appraisal of Spatial Economic and Network Effects of Transport Investments and Policies*. Final Report. European Commission, DG for Energy and Transport.

BROECKER J. and KORZHENEVYCH A. (2013) Forward looking dynamics in spatial CGE modelling, *Economic Modelling* **31**, 389–400. doi:10.1016/j.econmod.2012.11.031

DI COMITE F. and KANCS D. (2014) *Modelling of Agglomeration and Dispersion in RHOMOLO*. IPTS Working Papers No. JRC81349. European Commission, DG Joint Research Centre.

DI COMITE F. and KANCS D. (2015) *Macro-Economic Models for R&D and Innovation Policies: A Comparison of QUEST, RHOMOLO, GEM-E3 and NEMESIS*. IPTS Working Papers No. JRC94323. European Commission, DG Joint Research Centre.

DI COMITE F., KANCS D. and TORFS W. (2015) *Macroeconomic Modelling of R&D and Innovation Policies: An Application of RHOMOLO and QUEST*. IPTS Working Papers No. JRC89558. European Commission, DG Joint Research Centre.

DIXIT A. and STIGLITZ J. (1977) Monopolistic competition and optimum product diversity, *American Economic Review* **67**, 297–308.

EUROPEAN COMMISSION (2009) *Traffic Flow: Scenario, Traffic Forecast and Analysis of Traffic on the TEN-T, Taking into Consideration the External Dimension of the Union*. TENconnect: Final Report. European Commission, DG for Mobility and Transport.

EUROPEAN COMMISSION (2011a) *Identifying and Aggregating Elasticities for Spill-over Effects due to Linkages and Externalities in the Main Sectors of Investment Co-financed by the EU Cohesion Policy*. Spill-over Elasticities: Final Report. European Commission, DG for Regional and Urban Policy.

EUROPEAN COMMISSION (2011b) *Supplementary Model Calculations Supporting TEN-T Network Planning and Impact Assessment*. TENconnect 2: Final Report. European Commission, DG for Mobility and Transport.

EUROPEAN COMMISSION (2014) *Investment for Jobs and Growth*. Report on Economic, Social and Territorial Cohesion 6. European Commission, DG Regional and Urban Policy.

FRANCOIS J., MANCHIN M. and PELKMANS-BALAOING A. (2009) Regional integration in Asia: the role of infrastructure, in FRANCOIS J. F., WIGNARAJA G. and RANA P. (Eds) *Pan-Asian Integration*, pp. 439–486. Palgrave Macmillan, Basingstoke.

GRILICHES Z. (2000) *R&D, Education and Productivity: A Retrospective*. Harvard University Press, Cambridge, MA.

KANCS D. (2013) *Model-Based Support to EU Policymaking: Experience of the RHOMOLO Model*. Financing and Assessing Large Infrastructure Scale Projects STOA. European Parliament, Science and Technology Options Assessment.

KANCS D. and SILIVERSTOVS B. (Forthcoming 2015) R&D and non-linear productivity growth, *Research Policy* **44**.

KRUGMAN P. (1991) Increasing returns and economic geography, *Journal of Political Economy* **99**, 483–499. doi:10.1086/261763

MAIRESSE J. and MOHNEN P. (2001) *To Be Or Not To Be Innovative: An Exercise in Measurement*. NBER Working Papers No. 8644. National Bureau of Economic Research (NBER), Cambridge, MA.

MAIRESSE J. and SASSENOU M. (1991) R&D and productivity: a survey of econometric studies at the firm level, *Science, Technology Industry Review* **8**, 9–43.

MARTIN P. and ROGERS C. (1995) Industrial location and public infrastructure, *Journal of International Economics* **39**, 335–351. doi:10.1016/0022-1996(95)01376-6

McMORROW K. and ROGER W. (2009) *R&D Capital and Economic Growth: The Empirical Evidence*. EIB Papers No. 2009/04. European Investment Bank (EIB), Economics Department.

OKAGAWA A. and BAN K. (2008) *Estimation of Substitution Elasticities for CGE Models*. Discussion Papers in Economics and Business No. 2008/16. Osaka University, Graduate School of Economics and Osaka School of International Public Policy.

PERSYN D., TORFS W. and KANCS D. (2014) Modelling regional labour market dynamics: participation, employment and migration decisions in a spatial CGE model for the EU, *Investigaciones Regionales* **29**, 77–90.

POTTERS L., CONTE A., KANCS D. and THISSEN M. (2013) *Data Needs for Regional Modelling*. IPTS Working Papers No. JRC80845. European Commission, DG Joint Research Centre.

THISSEN M., DI COMITE F., KANCS D. and POTTERS L. (2014) *Modelling Inter-Regional Trade Flows: Data and Methodological Issues in RHOMOLO*. REGIO Working Papers No. 02/2014. European Commission, DG for Regional and Urban Policy.

THISSEN M., DIODATO D. and VAN OORT F. G. (2013) *Integrated Regional Europe: European Regional Trade Flows in 2000*. PBL Netherlands Environmental Assessment Agency, The Hague.

VARGA A. (Forthcoming 2015) Place-based, spatially blind or both? Challenges in estimating the impacts of modern development policies: the case of the GMR policy impact modeling approach, *International Regional Science Review* **38**.

VARGA J. and IN'T VELD J. (2010) *The Potential Impact of EU Cohesion Policy Spending in the 2007–13 Programming Period: A Model-Based Analysis*. European Economy Economic Papers No. 422, European Commission, DG for Economic and Monetary Affairs.

VENABLES A. (1996) Equilibrium locations of vertically linked industries, *International Economic Review* **37**, 341–359. doi:10.2307/2527327

Index

Tables are shown by a reference in **bold** and figures are shown in *italics*.

9780367191399